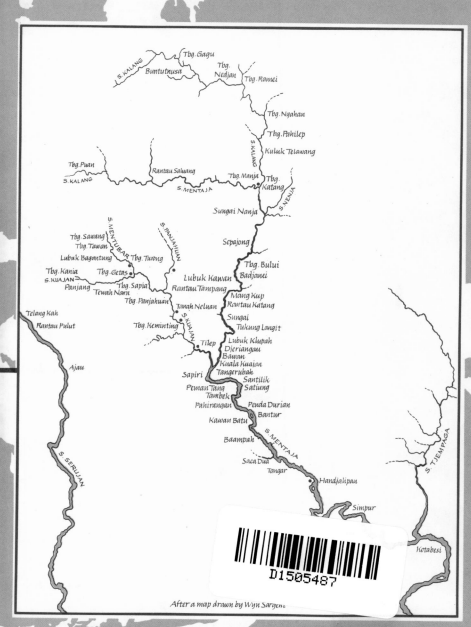

ISLANDS

PACIFIC OCEAN

MINDANAO

Davao

S. KALANG
Buntutnusa
Tbg. Gagu
Tbg. Nedjan
Tbg. Ramei

Tbg. Ngahan

Tbg. Pahilep
Kuluk Telawang

S. KALANG

Tbg. Puan
S. KALANG
Rantau Saluang
S. MENTAJA
Tbg. Manja
Tbg. Katang
S. NENJA
S. KALANG

Sungai Nanja

Sepajong

S. MENTUBAR
Tbg. Sawang
Tbg. Tawan
Lubuk Bagantung
Tbg. Turong
S. PANJAHUAN
Tbg. Bului
Badjanei

Tbg. Kania
S. KUAJAN
Tbg. Getas
Panjang
Tbg. Sapia
Tewah Naru
Lubuk Kawan
Rantau Tampang
Mang Kup
Rantau Katang

Tbg. Panjahuan
Tanah Neluan
S. KUAJAN
Sungai
Tukung Langit

Telang Kah
Rantau Pulut
Tbg. Keminting
Tilep
Lubuk Klupah
Djeriangau
Bawan
Kuala Kuajan
Tangerubah
Santilik
Satiung

Ajau
Sapiri
Peman Tang
Tambek
Pahirangan
Penda Durian
Bantur
Kawan Batu

Baampah
S. MENTAJA
S. TJEMPAGA

Saca Dua
Tangar
Handjalipau

Simpur

S. SERUJAN

Kotabesi

D1505487

After a map drawn by Wyn Sargent

FLORES

S   I   A

TIMOR

TIMOR SEA

0   Miles   200

My Life with the Headhunters

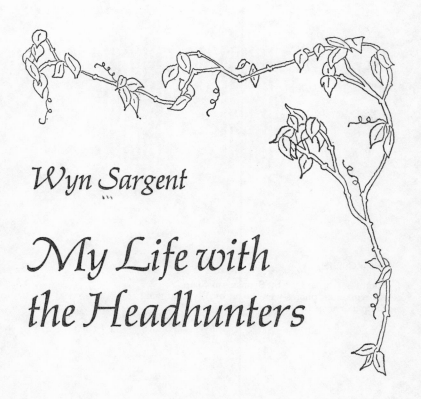

Wyn Sargent

My Life with the Headhunters

Doubleday & Company, Inc., Garden City, New York, 1974

Photo Credits:

Photos 1, 12, and 14 by Sjamsuarni Sjam
All remaining photos were taken by Wyn Sargent
Endpaper map by Maxine Reams

ISBN: 0-385-08974-0
Library of Congress Catalog Card Number 73–10545
Copyright © 1974 by Wyn Sargent
All rights reserved
Printed in the United States of America

To Jmy and Panggul.
They inspired the dream in the first place.

Contents

8 *Contents*

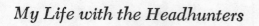

My Life with the Headhunters

Chapter One

A Proposition

"Well gee, Mom! Why can't we hunt for the headhunters? I've never seen real headhunters in my whole life!" said Jmy, my twelve-year-old son.

I had never seen headhunters either, but I could think of no reason to hunt for them now.

But I was to find a reason. And very soon.

The summer of 1968 was just beginning, and from all indications it was going to be a long one. Indonesia would see to that.

"Indonesia" was the label used to describe a corner of the world that had been sprinkled with over three thousand islands to link the fabled South Pacific to the exotic Indian Ocean. And they were beautiful islands. Some were splashed with emerald jungles, many spiked with soaring volcanoes, and a few of them were mere dots above the foam. But each island was independent of the other, without a common cultural or political heritage of any kind. They did not share history, religion, or even language, and the country was just too big, too scattered, and too hot to make journalism and photography fast, easy work.

The necessity of using an interpreter slowed down the

works too, although Sjamsuarni Sjam was one of the best in the country.

Sjam had been raised on snakes and nails in Atjeh, Sumatra. The town was infamously known as the hotbed of some kind of revolutionary movement for centuries, and, as Sjam's geographical parent, it had made her a heller. Before her tenth birthday she could chew tobacco and drink hard liquor and still do the work of ten men without grumbling. By the time she graduated from the University of Djakarta, she was pertinacious and hot-bellied for travel. Nitour, Inc., a tour agency, had given her the opportunity.

When I met Sjam she was far from being a sweet, innocent thing. She was thirty-five years old, knew the numbers of her country, and could keep a fair score. I liked her from the moment we met.

We were on the island of Borneo, ten miles west of Bandjarmasin, when the entire headhunting business began, but none of us knew it was beginning at the time. It was early afternoon and the sun was just low enough to cause even the tiny pebbles to throw giant shadows on the ground. We had finished an interview with Noormijati, Indonesia's first female glider pilot, on an airstrip that was unkempt, unrepaired, filled with chuckholes, and strewn with papers, broken glass, wire, and all kinds of debris left by people who had no use for any of it.

Standing ankle deep in the trash, a little apart from the gathered crowd, was a young boy, perhaps nineteen or twenty years old, dressed in a flashy yellow jump suit. Tucks had been sewn into the suit to tighten it enough to show off his narrow hips and good leg muscles. Canted to one side of his head was a brown straw hat. The side brim had been pressed up, and it was held in place with a large safety pin, safari fashion. Beneath the hat was a face filled with mischief and eyes that flitted about as restlessly as caged moths. There was a little straw protruding from his sensual mouth, and when he smiled at us, the straw turned up and a cockiness that came from too many conquests of one kind or another moved into his eyes. He was restless with energy, and, to get rid of it, he snapped his fingers at his sides with little reports that were sharp and resounding even from where we stood.

I would have done well if I had remembered that boy and his safari hat and fled at our next encounter.

Although we had rented the best car in town, it was one without brakes. Urged by Sjam's signal to collect us, the old wreck began to roll out onto the airstrip, and when it arrived within a few feet of us, the chauffeur leaped from the car and pushed his feet against the gravel to halt the auto's forward motion. Both the car and the driver suffered from severe tire punishing. One from the rocky roads, and the other from overeating.

We settled ourselves on a back seat so low that nothing could be seen through the windows and in between coil springs that stuck through the plastic cover. Little wads of gray cotton and black horsehair poked through holes left by the springs and spread over the seat and floor, and sometimes the cotton puffs jumped up into the air when a breeze passed through the open windows.

The old jalopy bumped and rattled down the dirt road that led to Bandjarmasin, going about ten miles per hour, all the while stuttering in little jerks as it went.

When we arrived at the Ki Damang Guest House, the driver picked out a likely embankment to slow the car down on, and then, while we were still moving, he bounced through the door and tossed a brick behind one of the front tires. We jolted to a dead stop. The coil springs had heated themselves to an unbelievable temperature, and we were joyful to be able to stand up and place some distance between us and the springs.

The Ki Damang Guest House was the best accommodation in town. It was set back beyond an iron fence and was fronted with a copious, pretentious sign, "Five Rooms With Bath," which had been wired to the street gate. The interpretation of the sign revealed five bedrooms with one tiny, and nearly inaccessible, lavatory at the south end of the building.

Over the house grew a rust-colored bougainvillaea which had, years ago, joined forces with a neighboring white vine, and together they had climbed up the front of the house, covered the roof, and sent their festoons and leaves into the sky, while some of them fell down over the windows. The guesthouse looked like a huge bush.

It was six-thirty in the evening when we heard the heavy footsteps pounding on the outside porch. Then the footsteps stopped, but there was no knock. Sjam frowned a little, her eyes darkened. The doorknob squeaked, turned a slow revolution, and when the door came forward the hinges screeched rustily. The old door opened, banged itself against the inner wall, and in the frame stood the boy from the airstrip with his safari hat in his hand.

"*Selamat malam,*" he said, rocking back and forth on the balls of his feet and whipping his hat against his leg at the same time.

The little straw in his mouth had been replaced with a new one, and because he was smiling broadly, the straw had turned up. There was a foxy look on his face, very wise and knowing, as though he had a good thing to tell and had saved it all day for recounting and now desperately wanted to get on with it. He stiffened his legs, thrust one hand deep into his trouser pocket, and with the other hand whipped his hat faster and faster against his thigh.

He crossed the room and sat down on a bench next to Sjam, holding his hat with his hands between his knees. Sjam began the volley of Indonesian between them. As she spoke the boy studied her face with intent eyes, eyes that were hard and sharp with no cockiness in them. When it was his turn to speak, he twisted his neck around to study me for a moment and then his eyes moved over Jmy. His words came easily enough, straight spoken. Sometimes he jerked his hat up and down to emphasize a word.

At one time Sjam shook her head from side to side as

though to clear her mind and then leaned forward to understand better. The boy's eyes flitted over the room, alive with the excitement of whatever he was feeling. His voice rose to a feverish pitch, and then Sjam choked. She coughed to clear her throat and rubbed the corners of her mouth with her thumb and forefinger in concentration. Her fingers were still on her mouth when she muttered something to the boy, listened to his response, then laughter overcame her and she dropped her hand, choked again and her eyes rolled up until the whites could be seen.

The boy did not laugh. He bent his head to inspect the safety pin on his hat.

Sjam slapped her knees with her open palms, shook her head in disbelief, and then finally quieted down a bit and sighed deeply.

"Well," she said, "you'll never guess!"

At her words the boy bolted from the bench and onto a rattan stool next to Jmy. He sat down and jerked one leg over the other and began to bounce his foot up and down. He still held the hat in his hands, so he busied himself by creasing the brim with his thumbnail, and then he turned his head a little to study the inside of the crown.

Sjam was smiling queerly off the side of her face. She pulled at the lobe of her ear, trying to get a starting point, and then said, "Well, his name is Abdul Manif Chairul and he's a journalist from the *Riak Press* here in Bandjarmasin. He wants you to head an expedition to explore the Central Borneo jungles and hunt for a lost band of natives that are supposed to be living there!" She shook her head and rolled her eyes around again and then cupped her chin in her hand.

Abdul had taken the little straw out of his mouth and was pressing it into his hatband. There were four more straws lined up neatly side by side in the band. He looked up and his eyes were shining with excitement. They were also filled with a cockiness that was nearly insulting.

"Why me?"

"Well," said Sjam, "publicity, I think. You know, a woman with a small child, Americans, good photographic and recording equipment and all that. But wait until I tell you! That's *unexplored* territory he's talking about and those 'lost natives' are *headhunters!*"

"Headhunters!"

"Yeah!" Sjam laughed and rolled her eyes up again. "He thinks that if you can go in there and keep your head then maybe others will follow!"

Abdul stretched his legs straight out in front of him and balanced his hat on his knees. He leaned forward from the top of his stool when Sjam stopped talking, and turned his head to look at us. His relaxed face had tightened a little, but it had not lost its cockiness.

The proposition was preposterous, but I supposed it was flattering in a way.

"Tell him no, but thanks, anyway."

Jmy was filled with so much excitement that he finally exploded.

"Gee, Mom! Why can't we hunt for the headhunters?"

Although adventure had always lived on the doorsteps of both of our lives, Jmy had an edge, at that moment, on the courage that dwelled within.

Morning had punched itself through and the sun was now taking on richer, redder tones. The tones would spread a parching, dusty shine on Bandjarmasin to make the day of July 1 as warm as June 30. Indonesia was a land of just one temperature, hot.

And it was a land of just one food, rice. The houseboy from the guesthouse had advanced three great bowls of the unsalted, pasty grains to the breakfast table and the rice was still whispering with steam.

Sjam raised a coffee cup to her lips. Then she caught sight of Abdul sauntering into the room, her cup froze in mid-air for a moment before she returned it to the table. She closed her lips into a tight fine line and squinted her eyes at the boy.

"I wonder what he wants this time," she said, more to herself than to anyone else.

Abdul inspected our rice breakfast with interest, glanced at the coffeepot, and said, *"Pagi,"* morning. The crooks of his arms were freighted with books and papers, but his hands were free. He rolled a little gold ring around and around on his finger.

The blades in the small electric fan that hung from the ceiling spun noisily in their circular hole. Abdul stole a squinting look at the fan to fill in the time and fixed his eyes on Sjam and waited.

"Do you want some coffee?" she asked him.

Abdul grinned broadly and sat down at the table, placing his books in front of him. An excitement had stolen over him and it made his eyes directly merry.

Sjam passed him the coffeepot, which he declined with a wave of his hand. He began to talk. While he talked he generated energy and the excitement of it spilled out and poured over him so that all of him seemed to be in motion. His sharp dark eyes were constantly darting about over the three of us, the papers, the room, the table. It was tiring to look upon them. Sometimes he would shuffle through his books and papers, unlace the one he wanted, and then shove it under Sjam's nose as some kind of point for proof. Often he shook a paper a little to emphasize a point, and somehow it made the paper more important. His words were spat out with forcefulness and his voice rang with the naked honesty of them. When he finished talking, he smiled shyly, nearly modestly, and arched his eyebrows winningly as if he was begging to be taken into the corral of Sjam's affections.

As she listened to him, Sjam poked the fingertips of her right hand between the fingers of her left and she rubbed them gently back and forth and inspected his face with interest. Once she closed her eyes and nodded her head in agreement on some point, but soon she opened her eyes wide again and shook her head dizzily from side to side.

When the long ribbons of words were exhausted and the telling was over between the two of them, Sjam jerked her head in a motion toward Abdul and said, "Look what he's done!" And then she placed a neatly typed paper on the table in front of me.

". . . . . telegram: 'Nopol 471/VIII/rdg/perwk/ . . . Police Number 471 to the Governor of Central Kalimantan and Regent of Sampit . . . . to announce to you that a photo-journalist from the United States of America, Wyn Sargent, and her son, Jmy, together with interpreter, Sjamsuarni Sjam from Nitour, Inc., and one journalist, Abdul Manif Chairul, from South Kalimantan, have been granted priority to visit Central Kalimantan to research the culture, arts and traditions of the native people of Central Kalimantan . . .'"

"Wait! There's more!" Sjam said. Her face was filled with laughter, but there was no sound of it.

Some of the papers boasted large gold seals, and there were a few carbon copies that had been punched with an ink stamp. At the bottom of a single page of parchment a red ribbon had been pasted and its ends were cut to sharp points. It was from the Governor's Palace.

"Look at this one!" Sjam said, and her breath was com-'ing fast now. "It's an order for a police boat to take you to Sampit, wherever that is. It's signed by a Mr. Effendi Wiradinata, Commander in Chief of Police.

"My God, look! This paper authorizes a full military and police escort for the expedition!"

"Sjam, why did he do all this? I told him yesterday I wouldn't go!"

Abdul turned his dark eyes toward us. He pinched his lips together with his fingers, held them shut for a moment, and then he stood up heavily and walked across the room to a little bench against the wall and sat down. He put his elbows on his knees, clasped his hands together, and bowed his head. When he looked up he blew a stream of air into his clenched hands and bumped them softly against his mouth in rapid little taps. And then he sighed deeply.

"Miss Sargent," he began, "before, when the Dutch were here, I was only a being, maybe not even human, a nobody. We all were. But today, I am Indonesian! You know what that means? It means we belong to a country and for the first time in history our country belongs to us!

"I am brave of spirit and mind and it is my responsibility to build my country now. We must bridge our gaps of isolation and unify our differences and it is up to me and to my generation to do it. But Borneo can contribute to the development of Indonesia only if she is totally discovered. I want to begin that discovery. With your help I can get the financing to begin the exploration of Central Borneo."

"Well," I said, "if the majority of your generation feels the same way, then the future of Indonesia looks bright, Abdul. But I can't go into a headhunters' jungle with you. I have certain responsibilities to my son and to myself. Surely you can understand."

Abdul's eyes were clear now because the cockiness had deserted them. He nodded and reached up to pull a little straw from his hatband and stuck it into his mouth and then rolled the straw between his lips to one side of his mouth and smiled. His eyes sprinted over Sjam's face, then he stood and, without speaking, walked to the table to stack up his papers. When they were bundled beneath his arm, he straightened his shoulders to endure the momentary defeat he was feeling, nodded his head again, and strode to the door.

He did not appear brokenhearted.

The brightest spot in the Borneo communications system is the "World Wide News" broadcast each evening from a Bandjarmasin station. Although its source of information remains a mystery, the program is of the utmost importance to the Bandjar people. Farmers living on the outskirts of

town will leave their paddies unattended or their cows half
milked and trudge the long road to Bandjarmasin to hear
the "news."

The houseboy in the Ki Damang Guest House plugged
the whimsical wireless into an outlet of the old generator
in the living room and then set about adjusting the knobs
and antennas until a sputtering Bandjar voice filtered its
way through the static.

> ". . . Miss Wyn Sargent, wanita wartawan dari Amerika, dan
> anak laki laki ia . . . sputter, sputter . . . . . kepal polisi,
> Bandjarmasin ke Sampit, besok pagi pagi! Mereka . . . sput-
> ter . . . headhunters de Kalimantan Tengah . . ."

I bolted from my chair.

"Sjam! What did he say?"

"He said you are going to hunt the headhunters in Central Borneo! Leaving tomorrow, early. By special police
boat. With your son!"

Just then Abdul burst through the door. He held the little
straw in his mouth with smiling lips, his safari hat canted
bolder than usual on his head, and a cockiness had returned
to his eyes with alarming permanency. The morning newspapers were bunched up beneath his arm, tied with short
lengths of white string. They carried the story for those who
had missed the broadcast.

Before any of us could speak, a delicately feminine and
very young-looking man popped through the doorway,
passed in front of Abdul, and introduced himself as W. A. R.
Mathias, assistant to Governor Sylvanus. His hand jerked
out with his credentials and then in for a handshake, and
when he smiled his eyes turned up at the corners. He said
Governor Sylvanus was extremely happy about the expedition and had requested that I drop by the palace for a chat,
if I had time, before I left. When he stopped talking a soft,
sad look moved into his eyes and the little blue veins on his
temples pulsated heavily.

Effendi Wiradinata, the pockets of his police jacket drooping open from the overload of medals and ribbons, jumped through the door with quick little steps and stood behind the governor's assistant. He waited until it was his turn to speak and then he congratulated me on my courage. He stood on skinny legs, much too thin for his bulky body. His jaws were bulky too, and squared off by a chin that seemed forever jutted. He breathed heavily through nostrils plugged up with short black hairs, talking on and on about valor and courage and how grateful the Indonesian government was, and when he ran out of things to say, he pulled his knuckles until the military commander shuffled in beside him.

Commander Susarni's feet were heavy against the floor and they were tired. His face reflected that tiredness. It also reflected the weather of his worried disposition. The sweat poured off his body and brow and left large wet rings under his arms and on the back of his shirt. He pulled out a bandanna from his trouser pocket and rubbed it over his face and forehead and on back over his hair to the back of his neck. Then he puckered his eyebrows together until the bridge of his nose had thickened, and asked me if I thought *five* men would be sufficient for an escort. His words were nervous, jumpy, and worried like the rest of him.

The little room in the guesthouse had slowly been filling itself with people. Now it belched it was so full. Some of the people were spewed out into the driveway and onto the porch. The press had arrived and they dealt themselves between and through the people, jotting down names and dates with stubby pencils in little notebooks. One fellow held onto a small box camera, identifying him as the photographer. Everyone made much ado about getting out of his way whenever he wanted to take a picture. He had no flash equipment, and to produce a photograph from the available light in the room would have resulted in a photographic triumph. He laughingly greeted me as a "fellow photog" and withdrew in laughter because he rarely said a whole word in all the time he was there.

The small room was gray-fogged with the strong smoke from clove-filled cigarettes, and the men began to cough and hack until their throats were clear and some of them spat and others blew their noses. Someone shooed the people away from the windows, then the excited group began to breathe more easily and relaxed a little. A party was being organized in the kitchen. The men felt that if something had slipped their minds, they could remember it later and there would still be time to share it.

The conversation had just about dried up when outside, in the street, a band of musicians struck up the *Pantja Sila,* the national anthem of Indonesia. But when it was over the hum of voices within the room broke out again with forgotten things to say, remembered again.

I looked at the Indonesian crowd in a dazed bewilderment and found it difficult to grasp the reality of the situation. I was being drafted and I knew it, and although I was shocked, I was also intrigued. Today, in reflecting back on that moment, if some guardian protector had warned me that I was soon to feel fear, heartbreak, starvation, contract a variety of tropical diseases, search for and live with the headhunters and eventually become a headhunter myself, I might have booked passage on the first ship headed home. But I doubt it.

I knew I would go. Tom Sawyer had rolled the drums of my heart. The beat was irresistible.

At six o'clock in the morning of July 4, Abdul arrived at the guesthouse with his own brand of fireworks and bombarded us with explosive announcements.

"The police boat is here! Leave at nine this morning! Everything's settled!"

Well, we were ready. I'd felt a blond kid and a redhead would be conspicuous in a headhunters' jungle, so I had dyed Jmy's hair black, as well as my own, and we appeared strange to each other. Jmy looked like a Chinese coolie-kid and I resembled the Dragon Lady of the comic strip *Terry and the Pirates*. Well, at least we were in the right geographical theater.

Abdul corralled three *betjaks*, man-powered bicycles outfitted with three wheels and a carriage, and we settled the luggage and ourselves into the buggies and then set course for the harbor.

A jaunt over the dirt roads of Bandjarmasin in a betjak gives one a real test of courage and a firsthand view of the potpourri of sights and smells that make up the city. The tiny houses, built by untutored architects, line the riverbanks, seesawing on wobbly stilts, many without doors, windows, or even roofs. In front of the shacks the naked children splash about in muddy water about the same color as themselves, and nearby the fishermen spread huge circular nets across the dirty water and sometimes snare a child or two during the casting. There are many small boys squatted on the river's edge holding long bamboo poles that had been spiked with a sweet tree sap to trap and attract the dragonflies whirling about. When enough were caught, the boys would journey home and hand the flies over to their mothers to fry for supper.

The only social speck in Bandjarmasin is the market scene, and most of it is a water-borne business. The tawny-skinned merchants have converted their canoes into floating bakeries, butcher shops, and drugstores. They waft their way through the canals to sell their wares to the river shoppers. The brisk trading is infused with the lust and enthusiasm familiar to all Bandjars, who, after years of being cheated by the Dutch, have artfully learned to cheat each other.

The land shops are owned and operated by the Chinese, who overrun the city. The ragged coolies are the moneymakers and the moneylenders of Indonesia, and although Indonesia hates them, she cannot live without them. They make up the nation's economy as the bankers of Djakarta, the rice peddlers in Sumatra, the gamblers in Bali, and the smugglers in Borneo. Most of the Chinese are Communists and Indonesia fears them, but that is a theme that has run continuously through her tattered history for centuries.

When we reached the harbor we found it mix-mastered with every kind of boat and all of them were crush-squeezed together into a single smudge of color with a metallic glint. Behind the boats were the shacks that made up the waterfront's architecture, and above the shacks the great gnarled forest etched itself against a scorching sky.

"There she is!" shouted Abdul, pointing to a bulky mass that looked like a floating lumber room.

"That's one of our old war boats!" said Jmy. "A LCM or something and, boy, it sure looks beat up!"

POLISI blazed in bold white letters on the stern, and the letters gave the ship a sense of administration despite its lack of maintenance. The deck was covered with rust chips and studded with junk, splintered wooden crates, and broken chairs. A boxlike affair, not much better than a tobacco barn, sat on the stern. The bow looked like a dark closet with a tarpaulin thrown over it.

"There's the captain," whispered Abdul. "His name is Thaberany."

The captain had a pelt of black curly hair that spilled over the neck of his sweat shirt. The pelt hinted that his whole chest might look like a squirrel skin. He wore denim pants, ragged and frayed at the hems with little threads that jerked around his bare feet as he walked toward us. His face was badly wrinkled and burned raw red by the sun. The color ran high onto his forehead, where his black hair had finally stopped it. His salty, seedy face gave no distinct architecture of bone, but a sagging lower lip indicated some old grievance he carried around within his soul. He greeted us in stop-and-go English. "So, you are lady I take to head-hunters! Me, I am glad to meet. And this, your little boy? Please! The ship is yours. Sorry, I no speak English very large. We leave one hour. Excuse, please!"

Our police and military escort arrived at ten-fifteen. The little committee of five glum-looking men wore threadbare uniforms whose missing buttons had been replaced with safety pins. Steel helmets covered their heads, and 8-mm Madsen bayonet rifles had been slung over their shoulders. Across their chests were crisscrossed leather bands of ammunition. Each man held a mess kit made up of a stack of tin plates held together by a metal runner and topped off with a coffeepot.

At eleven o'clock the captain began to negotiate a little business of his own. He rounded up the Chinese stowaways and then hid them again under the tarpaulin cover and legalized their felonies by charging them a dollar a head.

We sat on the dock and waited for an hour to pass and then another and still another. At three-thirty a deafening blast from the ship's whistle announced our departure. We rose to cross over the wobbly, splintering plank to board the ship that was to complete the first leg of our journey into the headhunters' world.

The captain barked his "Cast off," maneuvered the old ship about, and then jigsawed his way through the boat-cluttered waters, heading south on the Barito River.

We scrambled topside on the narrow ladder near the fantail of the ship to the overhead of the pilothouse. For several hours the boat drifted by the shaggy palms that lined the water's edge. Behind the palms were volcanoes that jutted upwards into a buttermilk sky and became part of the perfect balance of water, mountain, and sky. The landscape changed suddenly and the glittering Java Sea spread dramatically before us, seemingly without boundaries of any kind. The horizon beckoned us to press forward.

The night had fallen over our shoulders like a greatcoat and then tucked itself in around us. It was midnight. The air was warm, the stars were white-bright, and some of them were so immense that one felt he should duck, especially for the low-hung ones.

It was three o'clock in the morning when I became aware of a problem that required quick attention. Unfortunately, nature has no special favor for one who has spent twelve hours at sea and where no restroom facilities have been provided. The Indonesian is better equipped than the Westerner to handle this problem, because most of his life is spent squatting either on a riverbank, at the market place, or high in a tree, and they develop an amazing sense of deep-kneed balance at a remarkably early age. I watched one of the Indonesian policemen perform this advanced state of attainment with an acrobatic antic off the side of the ship that earned both my respect and envy.

Early the next morning the policeman discovered the mysterious disappearance of his coffeepot.

Chapter Two

To Ride on the Shoulders of a Giant

It was impossible to sleep. We were listing heavily to port in a slantwise position that had added spice to the sport at the beginning of the trip, but now the fixed tilt left us exhausted from resisting the ship's efforts to boost us off our perch.

The tattered canvas that covered the hard corrugated deck of the pilothouse sent up a flapping racket.

The policemen and soldiers had bunched themselves together in a tight little circle. They sat cross-legged, smoking their clove-filled cigarettes in a serious mood. Each man was lost in his own little house of thought. None of them had volunteered for the duty to "protect and escort" and their assignment to the job had left them nearly resentful at the edge of going. They were pleasant enough when spoken to but they offered no adscititious conversation, and it was clear that no extended hand of friendship was in the deal.

Captain Thaberany was below in the pilothouse trying to hold the old ship together. He had told Sjam that he had made the journey to Sampit on several other occasions, but confessed he knew nothing about the territory north of it and certainly nothing about any people living there, if they, indeed, existed at all.

Abdul had squeezed himself under the tarpaulin that covered the Chinese, and spent several hours quizzing them on the possibility of "headhunters" living north of Sampit. The Chinese were delighted to have been asked a question of such huge import, but the upshot resulted in no information at all. They had their own business to worry about and most of it had to do with the smuggling of diamonds and drugs into Sampit and not getting caught in the act.

So far we had found no one who knew anything about the land or its people for which we were charted.

Well, maybe someone in Sampit would know.

There is no dawn in the tropics. When night is over, the morning rushes in like a shot without warning and fires the sky to a hot blue. The tangerine sun punches through the air with energy on its breath and with a heat capable of jolting anyone into an upright position on the spot.

Captain Thaberany had anchored the ship outside the delta of the Sampit River. It was low tide and the long brown sandbars jutted menacingly through the water when a wave passed over them and back again. Squirming around on those bars were brittle stars and strange red-colored fish. Sometimes a coral- and black-striped snake would wriggle by.

Around us the thick jungle bush had crept down to the water's edge in an unbroken line, and there was no hint of orchid or rising smoke or any other evidence of human life in it. It gave one the uneasy urge to want to poke around in the landscape or at least call out, "Anyone there?"

At two-thirty in the afternoon the waters began to come in and Captain Thaberany pushed the old LCM over the delta and into the narrow Sampit channel. It was a touchy job. He stood on the bow, spread his legs well apart for balance, and took up his binoculars to scan the river's surface for a telltale ripple, purl, or gurgle that would indicate something had moved in or out since his last voyage.

The rivers in Borneo are nightmares to navigate. Most

of them egress in a confusing network of deltas, sandbars, or shifting mudbanks which are ever changing. They baffle the pilot and endanger the vessel. Even when sailing the middle course of a river one could depend on a quick detour around a jutting inlet, islet, reef, rapid, or waterfall that had never been there before.

The hours dripped by and with them the miles after countless miles of vast and sullen jungle landscape. It was unhospitable-looking, void of human or hut, and the whole thing denoted sort of a lethargic, low note of some misfortune about it. When a lagoon came into view to relieve the scene, it was always dark and forbidding, and it made the nerves prickle with fear. There were no sandy beaches around the lagoons, only the jungle and the water and the close marriage between them.

A watery spume was scattering itself in the air and it dripped dampness over the jungle growth and then hung a rainbow in the sky that moved with the light, fading and forming again and again in different widths and colors in dazzling brilliance.

We passed the tiny fishing villages of Samuda, Tumbang Sungnaraken, Setinuk, and Serambut. The vast separations between the villages bore out the main determinant of the temperature in the tropics. The grave markers in their Moslem cemeteries stood as silent witnesses to the marginal existence and struggle of the people.

We finally arrived in Sampit at nine-thirty in the evening. The village was conditioned by its own native landscape and had become a part of it, low-hung and flat. It was not much of a "city," although a mosque, Christian church, and German Catholic mission had been built in the town and those creeping fingers predicted the area's probable future.

The inhabitants had migrated from Bandjarmasin and Samuda seeking new soil and peaceful surroundings. Having arrived in Sampit, they called it their home. A great gallery of them stood on the wharf as the LCM maneuvered into position for anchorage and the kerosene lanterns flickered over their brown faces and black eyes, giving them a rich mysteriousness.

A group of children had collected on a rickety dock, and when they were joined by another group their combined weight suddenly sent the bamboo and rattan poles crashing into the river. Some of the children disappeared into the water with the poles.

A whitewashed sign had been tacked to a wooden post and then stuck upright into the mud in the center of the village. The chipped, peeling black letters spelled, SAMPIT, KAB. KOTA WARINGIN TIMUR. Beneath the sign stood two government officials. Both of the men looked very stiff.

"The skinny one must be the *bupati* [regent]," Sjam said. "More brass."

The bupati was dressed in a military uniform that was loaded with brass fixtures of all kinds and with a gold braid that had been slung beneath his armpit. The braid anchored itself beneath an epaulet and accentuated his not quite stooped but very thin shoulders. He was a small man, nearly stubby, and he wore plain steel-rimmed glasses which partially hid some of the deep pock marks that covered his face. The pits ran out from his hairline and down the sides of his face, and in the flickering light the scars blushed blood-red. He did not appear to be a man who was interested in anything, one who thought of the future only when he was forced to do so.

Abdul moved his cigarette lighter over the bundle of papers he held in his hand to see them better. "The bupati's name is Rachmat," he said. "The second man to the regent is Karlimansha. Must be the one with him, there."

Karlimansha was a broad-built, nearly burly man whose chin had blossomed out and sunk onto his chest in rolls of fat. His great bulk had left his uniform popped open at some of the seams, with slicked places on the seat and on the inside of the thighs where the fat of one leg couldn't clear the fat on the other when he walked. He was hatless and the big duster of black hair on his head stood up in little spikes and in all directions. Although he stood a few feet to the rear of the bupati, he dominated the scene.

We said good-by to Captain Thaberany and went to meet the two government greeters.

"Ah, Miss Sargent," said the bupati in Bahasa Indonesian, "welcome to Sampit! I received word on the radio, no more than an hour ago, that you were coming here. Please forgive the crowding villagers. They have never seen an American before. Neither have I, as a matter of fact! Come, we will go to my house, where you are to stay."

The bupati turned to cross over the narrow plank and onto the riverbank, closely followed by the puffing Karlimansha, under whose weight the plank groaned and swayed.

On a dirt road paralleling the river the bupati arrived at and then leaned against a battered Willys jeep. As we approached he extended the palm of his hand and motioned us in. He slid under the cracked, warped steering wheel, touched a starter that brought life into the old wreck, and we clattered off down the road. The inner anatomy of whatever was under the hood clinked and clanked at every bump or chuckhole. Karlimansha trotted beside the jeep with one hand on the front fender, and the trotting made his tight-fitting trousers take on more abuse than usual.

We passed an intersection where the dirt road met another at an odd angle, and struggled onwards a few more feet until the old jalopy coughed severely and then died. It didn't matter anyhow. We had arrived at the bupati's stucco house.

The lantern lights stared through the squares of windows until the front door opened, and then the light escaped and bounced out over a front porch, a small yard, and a few palm trees. A piece of rotting rope hung from one of the palms, a remnant of a swing that had been placed there for a child. Beyond the yard was a fence of decaying palings that turned around the corner of the house and disappeared on its own accord.

Inside the L-shaped living room the plaster walls were unpainted and mildewed in places and powdery in others. Above the room hung a ceiling of brown water-stained cardboard held up by an occasional penny nail. The windows stood wide open because the dampness had swollen the sills and had left the nailheads sunk deep. The windows refused to close ever again.

The room was without much furniture. A roll-top desk occupied the small arm of the room, and on the side were several wicker chairs, a card table, and a porch swing that didn't rock anymore.

"The regent suggests that we sleep now," said Sjam, "and in the morning he will look into the possibilities of transporting us to the Mentaja River."

The bupati bowed stiffly, said good night, and left.

Behind the living room was a bedroom whose only furniture was a double bed and two canvas cots. Abdul and Sjam took the cots and Jmy and I piled onto the big bed. In no time at all we were asleep under the bupati's cardboard ceiling.

Outside the bedroom door, across a shabby patch of grass, were two little cubicles thought of as bathroom facilities.

One of the cubicles embodied a toilet bowl without a lid or cover of any kind and without chains to pull or levers to push. There was no hygienic tissue because the Indonesians regard it as unuseful to them. A cement box had been strapped to a nearby corner. When it rained in Sampit, the box filled up with water. A little tin cup floated about in the water, used by anyone who wanted to jolt the bowl into action by throwing water down its neck. I am not sure what the procedure was during the dry seasons of the year. But the whole arrangement was certainly an improvement on a coffeepot.

The sister cubbyhole housed a large water-filled cement

tank and another tin cup. The idea was to shower with cupfuls of water and then dress again without soaking one's jeans in the ankle-deep water on the floor. I was never able to master this routine.

A morning foot tour through Sampit proved to be one without many surprises. The greatest surprise was that the people had managed to exist at all. The regent had estimated 160,000 inhabitants living in the area, about 3,000 of them in Sampit, 30,000 outside of Sampit, and the balance "somewhere around in the jungle," maybe.

Most of the Sampit people worked directly with the earth to get their sustenance and transited from paddy to paddy. The nature of their work left them both illiterate and indifferent to history. What they knew or cared about the past came to them through their mothers or fathers. Most of the people understood that they were a part of a nation called Indonesia, which was bound by certain political injunctions, but that was the end of it. The word "America" was something mysterious, but the weather, the arrival of a boat, or the rice harvest had all kinds of joyful meanings for them.

A few of the people living in Sampit were educated. A very few. When they were they called themselves "craftsmen" and then turned out homemade objects which they sold in their front yards.

On the main dirt road of Sampit, facing the river, were the shops owned and operated by the Chinese who controlled the "import" business from Bandjarmasin. Their operations were set up in drugstores that sold hardware and in textile stores that sold thermos bottles and beneath the counters were all kinds of marvelous antibiotic drugs and diamonds and narcotics.

The Dutch had supposedly founded the village on the belief that a profit could be made from the surrounding natural and mineral wealth, a profit large enough to compensate for the miserable weather. There was never any large scale agricultural, mineral, or petroleum development begun, but the Dutch had put a dent in the lumbering business by building a small railroad into a part of the jungle land. The whole scheme died on the vine when the Dutch left the country, and today the railroad is hard to find, although parts of it show up occasionally in someone's front yard.

In 1966 the Djakarta government had sent the bupati to Sampit to lead the way to profit and to justify the existence of the village to the Indonesian nation. There were parts of Sampit that had been notably affected by the bupati's presence. Fly-specked calendars with black and white pictures of President Suharto had been pasted on the outside walls of some of the houses. There was a doctor's office on the main dirt road, and within its walls a government doctor from Djakarta moved about with his knives and needles. Fixed to the east side of the village was a tiny secondary school, and some of the younger children ran in and out of the school when they had time to attend the classes between paddy plantings. The bupati's proudest achievement was an inner-telephone network that was strung between the police station, the military barracks, and his own house, and although it didn't work, it had been at least installed.

A day on the equator is one that is lived in parts. The morning part is filled with all kinds of working activities and the afternoon is taken up with supper and a nap. "Office hours" begin again at five o'clock, and sometimes those hours are held on a street corner or someone's front porch and last until eight o'clock. But tonight an "official" meeting of the town's government leaders had been scheduled at the bupati's house for nine o'clock, sharp.

Sharply at nine, a great shuffling of feet rasped on the bupati's cement front porch, and then the feet fumbled through the open doors and into the L-shaped living room. A long library table had been placed in the center of the room, and the chairs scraped along on the tile floor to the table as the men pushed them forward and then seated themselves. When the cigars were passed, unwrapped, lit and puffed upon, the bupati closed the doors and called the meeting to order.

"Well, Miss Sargent, we thank you for your interest in the Mentaja and for your coming here to explore that area. These men have come here tonight to help you do just that."

The bupati introduced the military commander, Lieutenant Ajah and his assistant and his assistant's assistant. Edy Samsone, the police chief, introduced himself and his two assistants.

"Personally I see the venture not without daring," continued the bupati, "and your enthusiasm for the expedition has won admiration here in Sampit and among these men. None of our people have expressed an interest in undertaking such an effort. No one has researched the interior of the jungle land, so we are unable to tell you about the people there or the conditions that exist. I'm sorry."

"Yes, I understood that the area was unexplored and without information. I accepted the responsibility to research the Mentaja with the one reservation that I be allowed to direct the movements of the expedition."

"Yes, of course!" said the bupati. "Karlimansha and I have been here in Sampit about thirteen months, and we've tried to concentrate on the village of Sampit because of the commercial interests available here. There has been no reason for us to go into the interior for the good of our pockets right now.

"Anyhow, that jungle is a dark one! I've been as far north as Kotabesi, which is about two hours by motor canoe, and the possibility of carving anything out of that area is a remote one."

The regent slouched in his chair, crossed his left foot over his right, and took a sudden interest in the conditions of his fingernails. Sjam raised her eyebrows a little and squinted darkly at the gesture. The air in the room changed faces.

The bupati looked up from his nails, adjusted his glasses on the bridge of his nose with his forefinger, and said, "Would it be possible for you to draw maps and list the sources of any diamonds, gold, or any other mineral wealth you might find?"

"It is possible," I said.

The bupati sighed, nodded his head, and then smiled warmly.

"I'm giving you my houseboat. Not much of a boat, but it will sleep four people undercover. And you'll have a river captain, a cook, and we'll try to provide you with as much foodstuffs as possible."

"Is there a map of the Mentaja, perhaps an aerial map? And maybe a compass?" I asked.

The bupati threw his hand out, snapped his fingers at Karlimansha, and was passed a tissue-thin paper. Without unfolding it, he handed the paper to Sjam.

"The map shows the villages as far north as a place called Kuala Kuajan. It's a Dutch map, you can see the umlauts. I'm sorry to say that it's unlikely that there is a compass anywhere in Sampit. Oh, we are augmenting your escort!"

Edy Samsone groaned, slid down into his chair, and dropped his chin onto his chest. He covered his forehead with his right hand and without looking up said, "I'm sorry, none of the policemen want to go."

The military commander chimed in with the same complaint.

"We haven't got them either, sir. I just can't get anyone to volunteer!"

"What do you mean, 'volunteer'? Draft them!"

The bupati's voice was dry and grating. "Draft them! I want two more policemen and three more in the military command. Get 'em and give 'em guns! In the morning . . ."

Suddenly there was a knock at the door, and a brown-uniformed soldier pushed himself into the room.

"There's someone here to see you, Bupati."

"Not now!"

"Sir, he says it's very important!"

"Who is it?"

"I don't know."

"Well, what does he want?"

"He says it has something to do with Miss Sargent."

The regent frowned a little and the frown moved his glasses lower on the bridge of his nose.

"Let him in."

The soldier nodded, stepped backwards, and closed the door. Then the door swung slowly open again and in the frame stood a *headhunter*.

He was almost five feet tall. Barefoot. He stood with his legs well spread and his head held very high. His hair was black and curly, cut short, and looked like little coils of wire spinning around a face as black as coffee. At the hairline on his high forehead and around his temples were tiny drops of perspiration coursing over broad cheekbones that were well set apart. His black eyes were straight-lined, without squint at the corners, and they moved over each of us in the room, assessing and evaluating as they went. There were some straggly, unkempt chin whiskers sprouting beneath his full-lipped mouth and a mustache was trying to grow on his upper lip but without much success. His face was dominated by a flat nose that had the same width from the upper bridge to its point. It was not a beautiful face but it could be if he wanted it to be. Beautiful one moment, and not at all the next.

He was wearing new "white man's" clothes with threads hanging from the trousers. He seemed quite uncomfortable in them because they didn't fit well. He had wrapped a piece of rattan around his waist, through the belt loops, to hold his pants up. The cuffs almost covered his feet, but one could still see where the river fungus had destroyed his toenails and had left them bleeding.

When he finally spoke, the words were soft and cautious and his coffee cheeks deepened a little in color.

"I am Panggul. I come take Miss Sargent to my people in jungle. I take her. I bring her back!" His words were spoken in the Indonesian language, broken but understandable.

The regent leaned on his elbow on the arm of his chair and bent his head toward Karlimansha, who covered his mouth with his hand and whispered to the bupati, who had cocked his head to one side to hear better. When Karlimansha stopped talking, the regent nodded, raised his eyes to Panggul, and smiled.

"Karli says this man is a Dyak from one of the tribes in the interior. He could be a good guide for you and certainly he knows the Dyak dialects."

"What does 'Dyak' mean?"

Panggul understood the question. "Dyak," he said, "mean my people in jungle. Many tribes, many clans, but all people called Dyak. I am Iban clan from Dyak Iban tribe and also belong to another tribe, Katingan clan from Dyak Ngadju tribe."

"Karli thinks he has been in Sampit for about a year," said the regent. "He says the man sleeps in a canoe at night and roams the streets in the day."

"Why?"

Panggul lowered his head and closed his eyes and sighed deeply. A tiredness had suddenly left his shoulders sagging slightly. When he opened his eyes, there was a deep, habituated sadness there that I had not seen before and the sadness was exaggerated now because the man was weeping.

"I come here get help for my people. My people now crumble to dust in jungle. Way of living for Dyak destroyed, nothing left. Many have no clothes. Many have no homes. My people Great People. Today, they no remember their greatness. People have no food, no medicine, no hope. People need help to live, now."

Whatever the reasons for the present conditions of his people, Panggul was quarreling with history and its subsequent course of events. It was confusing to look upon his face. He appeared to be a strangely strong man and one who handled himself with an inner superior force, but it was a force that might prove deadening and probably it was one without pity. But he also looked like the kind of a man who could think about spring in the dead of winter.

"Karli," the bupati snapped, "get some clothes and shoes from the *militer* and record Panggul as the official 'Dyak guide-interpreter' for the expedition."

And then the regent leaned forward and whispered to the police chief, Samsone. Sjam heard the conversation between the two men and, without moving her lips, said, "Panggul is to represent you and the expedition but not the Kabupaten!" (bupati's office).

Jmy, for all his twelve years, could not keep up with the fast translations flying around the room and burst out, "What's happening?"

"That native, Panggul, is going to be our guide. He'll take us into the jungle, tomorrow," I said.

"Is he a real headhunter?"

"Well, I don't know, but he's friendly and he wants us to see his people."

That night I dreamt that I rode through the headhunters' jungle on the shoulders of a little giant.

Chapter Three

Sapiri, Jungle Gateway

Out of the first incredulity, I shut my eyes. A second, hard look materialized the phantasm into the houseboat the regent had offered our expedition.

Although it was the best vessel around, it did not pretend to look like a boat, and it reflected upon itself a lack of responsibility for ever having been one. A large box affair made of old lumber, and with the nail holes of its first use still showing through, was nailed down on the helm. The walls were badly discolored with brown watermarks and streaked with gray mildew. Behind the box, about midship, a small pilothouse roost, looking unraveled at its connections. A rusted fly screen covered the door and hung from one hinge.

"*Selamat pagi!*"

A hunch-backed Indonesian in dirty bib overalls which were out at the knees and seat and unbuttoned at the fly walked by, limping a little as he went. He held a hammer in one hand and a few short wooden bars in the other. Some penny nails hung out of his mouth at strange angles.

He crossed over the ironwood gangplank with exaggerated carefulness and stepped onto the houseboat and then disappeared into the wooden box. A moment later his sun-browned face punched itself through a tiny window in the side of the box, and he began to nail the wood bars over its opening.

"The bupati is taking no chances!" Sjam said.

We met the bupati in his Kabupaten office. "Again we welcome you to Sampit," he said formally, "and are grateful for the opportunity to offer you our assistance. Would you place your signature in the Registry?"

The cloth-covered ledger was well battered and the pages were curling and wrinkled, but more from the humidity than from use. The information was recorded: Wyn Sargent, American, photographer-writer; mission: exploration of the Mentaja, Kalimantan Tengah, Indonesia.

"Well," said the regent, "the boat's ready to go, but you'll have to wait for the tide to come in. There is rice on board and sugar and eggs, coffee and tea. Everyone here has chipped in a little and I've asked the soldiers to catch your fish along the way."

There was a stir outside the office and then a rattling of the door. A group of policemen and soldiers paraded into the Kabupaten, some of them looking bitter and the rest hurt. The men belonged to the drafted Sampit team, and they rounded out our escort to a comforting ten. None of them wanted to go, and a couple of them seemed as though they were campaigning an escape. Each man gave the bupati a final contemptuous snarl when he thought it was safe, and then entered his name, rank, and serial number in the Great Book and filed through the door of the Kabupaten.

We watched them drift their way down to the houseboat. Then we sat down to wait for another tide to come in.

It was two-thirty in the afternoon, after everyone had eaten and napped, when the captain decided the tide had come in.

Panggul met us at the gangplank wearing the clothes he

had on the night before, but strapped around his waist was a new and breath-taking ornament: an enormous knife hung from a rattan belt at his left side and a swatch of long black hair cascaded out of its handle.

We turned to say good-by to the bupati. There was a weariness in his eyes. "*Bon voyage,*" he said cheerfully, "we hope for a safe and successful journey."

We shook hands, smiled at each other, and agreed that everything would be all right, although neither one of us believed it very much.

To the Sampit people standing on the river's edge the fifteen people that made up the expedition's force must have represented a weird company. The ten soldiers and policemen were all nonnavigating individuals and hardly knew what to do with themselves aboard a "ship." When their feet touched the deck, they sat down quickly on whatever was handy, and tried to be inconspicuous. Abdul and Sjam, both of whom lived in their own little houses of cold isolation, appeared detached from the group, and our black native, Panggul, added further mystery to the picture with his human-hair-decorated knife. But the tall woman with the white skin, clad in men's jeans, and the little boy beside her left the spectators with shaking heads and clacking tongues.

The "first mate" catapulted himself off the gangplank and then whirled about to face an old Diesel engine that was wired to the starboard of the pilothouse. He shoved a rusty crank into the machine's center and twisted it around in an effort to bring life to the old motor. The engine shuddered and strained and finally caught. A blue smoke belched out and oil pellets were spewed over everyone standing on the dock.

The ship's bell, manufactured from a discarded bicycle tire rim, was hit with a lead bolt, and clanked out our official departure from Sampit.

The river captain ceremoniously bellowed a "cast off" and then returned to his pilothouse, shutting the screen door behind him. He perched himself on a high stool and with his toes on the great wheel encouraged the old house-boat into the harbor, northbound.

I think it was north. Neither of us had a compass.

We hunched our shoulders and stuffed ourselves into the crawlway that led to the main part of the wood box. The roof was so low that it scraped our backs and shoulder blades. Inside there were two planks that had been nailed to the wall to serve as bunks and nothing else. The mattresses were missing.

Termites had been working in the room with an unbeliev-able energy, scattering bits and pieces of debris every-where. There were bedbugs roaming the floor and a few crickets studded the low ceiling. When they became aware of our presence, the bedbugs scurried under the sides of the box and the crickets poked their heads out of the wood-work and assessed us with their beady black eyes.

We returned topside for a final look at Sampit. The little town was disappearing kaleidoscopically, leaving us feeling that something important had been left behind. Then the old houseboat struggled around a bend in the river and Sampit was gone.

The spirit of the jungle is sensed immediately. The air becomes suddenly heavier, the water muddier, and the landscape turns itself into a massive drama of towering, tangled trees. Large green-fingered ferns had tied them-selves to the trees and then dropped down onto the river and brushed the boat as we passed by. Bushes with great thorns, dangerous and threatening-looking, ground them-selves together with other tough jungle growths and then stretched forever upward to find their place in the sun. It was a strange wet wilderness of restless growing; one felt the life and death struggle between the tree and the vine.

Panggul was touring excitedly about the deck, checking into every corner and crack. He had the habit of thrusting his head forward when he wanted to see better or study something in particular, and now he strolled about, head stretched out with his hands locked together behind his back. He was proud of his position as Dyak guide-interpreter, and from time to time he gave it a touch of mettle by holding a little session of congress with himself on the order of things to come. He whispered to himself when he thought of something splendid, and then nodded when he agreed upon it.

Satisfied with the boat arrangement, he circled around the two drums of Diesel on the deck and came to squat down in front of us. It was a position that soon became very familiar and it never varied. He placed both of his feet flat on the ground so that his knees were level and pulled up tightly against his chest. Then he covered his knees with the undersides of his upper arms so that his hands hung down loosely from his wrists. He could hold this position seemingly forever.

He was grinning broadly and his dark eyes were half closed against the hot sunlight. "I very happy," he started off experimentally, "I very happy you see my people now."

He dropped his right hand to scratch between his dry toes. When he did the handle of the great knife swung forward and the hair swept over the deck in a little circle.

The movement raised Jmy's interest to its highest point and he broke over the edge of it and blurted out, "What's the hair on that knife?"

Panggul's eyes darted to mine and dug into them to search for something there that would allow him an honesty. Perhaps he received it, for he relaxed a little, unfastened his belt, and took the knife in his hands. The little cords of muscles jumped around his wrists as he pulled the hair between his fingers.

"Hair from head of enemy," he said simply. "Is Dyak knife. Is called *mandau.*"

"Do people hunt heads where we're going?" Jmy ventured.

Panggul's eyelids dropped. Then he slowly lifted them to gaze out over the river and his eyes were brooding darkly and they were squinted. A tightness crept over his face.

"Headhunting against law now," he said.

It was a happy answer if it was not inspected too closely.

The afternoon sun grew soft, dimmed itself a little more, and then suddenly went out all at once. With night emerged a new horror, one that came on a thousand wings, beating and thrashing about over our heads. Huge flocks of bats, eaglelike *elangs,* careened by in a frenzied effort to find roosts for the night, and behind them the long-necked *anggangs* with their grotesquely warped bodies. We fled below.

The little box proved to be cramped quarters for the fifteen of us but there was a certain comfort and warmth that came from the heat and smell of life. A fragile kerosene lamp had been nailed to the wall and the men flickered in and out of its tiny yellow flame in their passing.

But it was impossible to sleep on the boat. There was a stark conspiracy going on between the insects, the lamp, and the lack of privacy. The light threw itself through the barred window and small insects rode the beams into the room, and the moths, larger than butterflies, bumped their bodies softly against the bars.

The Indonesians never sleep without a light somewhere nearby. They do not like the dark. They also have weak bladders and there is a continual procession of moving bodies being steered about by the glow of a light all night.

Once you enter the jungle, you may depend on never spending a private moment, which presents certain problems. There were no restroom facilities on the houseboat, and if you could not cope with it, then you scarcely knew what to do with yourself in such an emergency. But a sarong, a coffeepot, and a coughing fit solve some of it.

Morning found us in the home of the animals that Noah forgot. Bands of wine-colored orangutans romped through the trees, swinging their bulky bodies from limb to limb and making little earthquakes of their own when they dropped to the ground. They were a playful lot, mostly harmless, but sometimes a group would race to the river's edge and badger our boat with their shrieking challenges to combat and fire stones and dirt clods at us.

From time to time a crocodile would raise its sleepy head and look across at our boat as it rumbled by and then let itself sink again and leave the rippling circles widening in the water.

Giant pythons festooned themselves in the trees, looking like the limbs they were wound around, and on a rare occasion their soft gray-white eggs could be seen cupped in a mudhole on the riverbank.

The rare tropical birds of the area, those that could be named only by the people who lived there, wheeled through the hot air, stretching their long necks and flapping their huge wings, most of them too bizarre to be considered beautiful.

Inches above the river the butterflies, larger than birds, pirouetted around each other in tight little quadrilles as the river snakes slipped under them in the water. Most of the river reptiles in this area were not poisonous, but the lizards that inhabited the marshes were rancorously deadly. They grew to such an enormous size that they were called dragons by the natives. One of them swam by the houseboat and stuck itself onto the end of Panggul's waiting mandau. He removed the poison sacks from its neck with exaggerated caution and boiled the lizard for lunch. It was delicious.

In the late afternoon we were treated to our first tropical rainstorm. To believe what a rain can do to a jungle, one must see it for himself. In a matter of a few seconds the trees are spread apart, the vines rip themselves from the trees and crash earthwards and the land is laid wide open by the plummeting force of the water. The great sheet of silver rain is terrifying and the noise of it is deafening.

Suddenly it's over and the hot sun bursts out, the trees shake their dripping leaves and spring upwards again, and the air becomes parched so quickly that it can dry up your laundry as stiff as a board in five minutes.

It was the night of the third day out. Panggul had been squatted on the helm of the boat for a long time, his hands dangling loosely from their wrists over his knees when suddenly he stood up and yelled.

"Sapiri! This Dyak village. We stop!"

The old engine gave a clunk and stuttered to a stop. We drifted a moment, listening to the current as it licked the sides of the boat tugging us downstream a bit until we hit something soft. Panggul leaped over the side of the boat and disappeared, leaving us wondering what to do.

The mudbanks rose fifteen feet straight up on both sides of the houseboat, and the village of Sapiri clung like a piece of river fungus to the top of the closest bank. It was camouflaged by the jungle, cemented into the jungle, and the only telling that it was there was to see one tiny roof top jab its point through the growth.

Panggul abruptly appeared where the jungle parted a little and he cupped his hands around his mouth and yelled. "They have funeral tonight. You all invited!" And then he disappeared again.

This bit of news spirited the escort into becoming worried men. They worried themselves with their minds and they worried each other with their eyes and then they worried everyone with their clothes. They changed into full uniform, pulled on their paratrooper boots, cursed at the laces, and then slapped helmets on their heads. All of them had fixed sharp bayonets at the ends of their rifles.

One of the soldiers forced a piece of brown cardboard against the barred window to cover the opening, and then sentried himself behind it. He peeked out through the sides whenever he thought he heard something.

This soldier and one other agreed to accompany us into

the village in civilian dress if they were permitted to hide pistols under their shirts. The remaining eight flatly refused to go.

We sat down to wait further news from Panggul. As we waited the air filled with the edge of some cutting fear, a fear of an unknown and unfamiliar thing, and we began to feel a little miserable. Hours dragged by. Abdul stuck his head in once and caught the feeling from the room and went out again.

The men sat on their hams on the floor, and some of them played with the ends of their fingernails and tried not to look at each other. Some of them smoked and the others just stared ahead without seeing, pouting with worried eyes, eyes that were glazed over with fear. I could hear the pounding of the man's heart sitting next to me, and Sjam's breathing had suddenly become hard and irregular.

A little panic was building itself up. We had just about resigned ourselves to the very worst, when a terrifying noise broke out of Sapiri, splitting the jungle air wide open. The noises sounded like natives howling and sometimes yipping until the cries turned into the shrilling screams of wild beasts. Then there was a thudding sound on the ground made from the pounding of bare feet. More cries came, wailing cries, and still more stampeding bare feet ran over the mud-packed earth, and all the while the sounds were coming closer to the houseboat.

The men looked at each other with wide eyes, bewildered and puzzled and a few jumped to their feet, grabbing their guns as they rose. A clenched fist shot through the window of the houseboat and the cardboard popped and collapsed. The wooden bars were sent to splinter in all directions.

Panggul's face poked itself against what was left of the wood window frame. His cheeks were bright red as though raw and the rims of his eyes were shot with blood streaks. There was a shiny, milky liquid on his mouth, and a few drops of it coursed their way over his chin and onto his already wet shirt. His eyelids drooped nearly half shut over his wide-set eyes, and he had great difficulty keeping his face centered in the window. He put his hands against the houseboat to steady himself and squeezed his eyes together apologetically. "Please to forgive. I drunk with *tuak*." He addressed no one in particular. Tuak proved to be a remarkable beverage. But I was to learn that later.

When the screams finally subsided a little, Sjam whispered to Panggul that only two soldiers would be going with us into the village, and she asked if there were any dangers. Panggul's huge eyes filled with the tears that come from a stinging, personal hurt. "No danger," he said. "Dyak only honor dead in first ceremony. They happy you here. Very special honor for Dyak."

We left our jewelry on the boat. It was possible that rings, identification bracelets, wrist watches would confuse a primitive people. Abdul left his glasses on the plank bunk. Tiny chunks of glass hanging on one's face might undo them entirely.

It was dark outside. The warm green smell of the nearness of the jungle assaulted our nostrils with its heaviness as we stepped barefoot off the houseboat onto a tree trunk. It was a Dyak ladder, a tree cleaned of its branches standing upright in the river. There were tiny nitches into which one was to put his foot: they had not been cut for a 9½B shoe size. Sjam pushed and Panggul pulled and raised me, surely if not swiftly, to the top of the ladder, where we climbed off into the jungle and stood in darkness until Abdul arrived over the edge with his flashlight.

There was no one in sight.

Mosquitoes roared by, their songs much louder than usual, and other night insects bumped into us with their soft bodies. The moon unveiled itself from a cloud and threw a dusky glow upon the ground, and crawling weeds were everywhere. Abdul turned off his flashlight and the sound from the switch was deafening.

Suddenly, there was a rustling in the trees behind me, and a tiny brown face began to percolate itself through the darkness; it withdrew and was swallowed up in the night before it could really be seen.

There was a skittering movement on the right, and again we had a fleeting glimpse of a blurred and indefinite face.

We hovered together in a bunch, but Panggul stood with his back toward us, a few feet away, and was peering into the jungle growth. I turned to look at Panggul and saw behind him, above his shoulder, a pair of frightened black eyes piercing their way through the dark, quite near and very still. Above the eyes the coarse black hair had been hacked off so the owner could see better. The eyes were set deeply into a little brown face that was glistening and smooth. A full-lipped mouth hung slightly open under a flat, spreading nose. Something glinted brightly above his left shoulder, metal, a blade of some kind, perhaps a spear.

Beside it, another face filtered through the darkness, and another and still another until we were surrounded by twenty-five or thirty tiny brown-skinned men. All of them were cut from the same piece of brown human fabric with the same four-, four-and-a-half-foot height, and their eyes glittered with fear, and sometimes the whites showed around the dark pits. Their bodies were remarkably smooth and their faces hairless except for a few men with straggly, untrimmed chin whiskers. They looked as though they had stopped breathing. Their bodies were tied up with stiffness and rigidity. Some of them had dropped open their mouths. The young boys were naked, but the men had tied short sarongs around their waists and those men held spears and blowguns at their sides, the metal tips pointing skyward.

They had shown themselves. But they were unmoving and silent and awestruck. They stared at us with intent eyes, sometimes fierce eyes, but always with frightened eyes and with so much preoccupation that they had forgotten to be embarrassed about themselves.

One of the older men looked a little nervous with his blowgun, and Panggul said something softly in Dyak that jerked all of them to turn their eyes upon him. But their eyes traveled back again to study the six-foot white colossus that stood in their pathway. Then they turned their heads and puzzled one another with their eyes and some of them frowned deeply.

In a sudden burst of courage one little fellow began to creep secretly toward me. His feet moved over the ground without sound of any kind, his eyes raised, fear-filled, toward my eyes and mouth. When he was within ten feet, he stopped, spread his legs and placed his hands on his hips. His chest rose as he filled his lungs with a deep, sighing breath, and then he looked back at his friends and grinned a little in triumph. The Dyaks blinked in amazement at the heroic attack he was making.

Encouraged that no disaster had befallen him, he threw back his tiny shoulders and with gusty boldness advanced another step, and then another until he was standing in front of me. He dropped his head far back to look at my face, and I bent my head forward a little to see his. We stared, uneasily, at each other for a long time, and neither of us moved.

Slowly his head turned sidewise, and he lowered his eyes to study my arms. Without a warning of any kind, his right hand jerked out and he pinched the hair on my forearm between his index finger and thumb, and he pulled as hard as he could. I was uncomfortably reminded of the proclivity of these headhunters to collect human hair.

He was openly puzzled. He turned to look at his friends again, batting his eyes in astonishment. He shook his head from side to side and then turned around to face me. He seemed satisfied now that the hair on my arm would not turn loose, but he gave it a second pull anyway. He stooped a little to inspect my hand and blew a tremendous blast of air on my fingers. I could not suppress a chuckle. The noise of it sent the little Dyak scampering back into the circle of men yelling, "*Sang Hyang Ikui Bui*" as he ran. (Great White Fish God.)

So the Dyak natives of Sapiri were responsible for bestowing upon me the reputation of the Great White Fish, a reputation that I was to enjoy for some years to come. They had seen me rise from the river, and it made excellent sense to them to use me to substantiate the stories of their ancestors about the great white fish that had once inhabited the seas of their birthland. Eventually the Dyaks came to regard me as a real person of flesh and blood but never as a fellow human being. Somehow I was just too tall, too white, and too foreign-looking, and they wanted me to be the Big White Fish of their dreams, anyhow.

The little committee of Dyaks began to relax. And so did we. With uncurled curiosity the natives edged in closer and closer to investigate our group. Panggul had stirred too. He was pulling a dark Dyak toward us. Abruptly the man liberated himself from Panggul's grasp and began to come forward under his own power. As he came, he sniffed at the air.

"This, Chief Niga," said Panggul.

He was a very dark-skinned man with a great duster of black hair on his head, most of it standing straight up. His shoulders were sloping and from them hung thick, muscular arms that were heavy and strong from a work that required lifting or pushing. His hands, although small, were fat, and he held them stiffly at his sides with the palms inward. His face was the color of black coffee, and an unusual saddle of black freckles danced across his flat, flared nose. His full lips, badly punished by the tropical sun, were chapped and peeling. There were large holes in his earlobes where earrings had once been inserted, and little flaps of skin hung from his ears like slender loops of spaghetti. His eyes were filled with the reserve and dignity respectful to his position. A mandau with human hair in its handle hung at his waist, and beneath it a short sarong had been tied.

I bent down and smiled at the four-foot chief and offered my hand in a Western handshake. The Dyaks in the circle around us stood very still. Their eyes moved from the chief to me and back to the chief again. Chief Niga looked at my hand, frowned in thought a moment, and then he gently covered it with both of his hands and grinned.

With the help of two interpreters, Chief Niga and I exchanged what we believed were the appropriate politenesses and courtesies for such an occasion. The chief leaned forward as I spoke to intercept the words because he felt he should understand them. The natives watched my mouth, and when the words came out they tested them with their eyes, and when no more words came, they giggled and squealed with laughter at the funny English sounds.

When Chief Niga spoke the Dyak language, it was spoken without effort, without the expression of verbal punctuation, and without emphasis of any kind. It whirled from his lips in breathy tones that rose and fell slightly, rather than words, and the tones ran together like a never-ending chord of blurred sounds.

After the exchange was over, Chief Niga invited us into the shack where the funeral was to be held. He turned to shout a command to the Dyaks that sounded like *"awuiiii"* and sent all of us stumbling down a path to the village.

The path began at the river's edge, continued for a hundred yards, and disappeared into the jungle growth. The Dyaks had built their houses of poles and thatch on either side of the path. There were only five straggling huts in the village and all of them wobbled about high on the ends of their eight-foot stilts. I learned that the shacks had been built over the body of a man buried beneath one of the main poles.

The funeral parlor turned out to be the last house on the right of the path because it was in the best shape. A single log, slot-cut, rose eight feet straight up and I was boosted, again, through the front door.

The frame of the house was made of bamboo, and bark skin had been tied to it with lengths of rattan to make up the walls. The grass ceiling pitched ten feet above the eight-by-twelve floor in the middle of the room and rested at a five-foot level on the bark walls.

There was no furniture in the room. Something that looked like a scarecrow rose in a spectacular arrangement in the center of the shack. It was made from dried branches and leaves and then dressed up with seeds, roots, shells, and other odd articles. It was there to keep the evil spirits away.

Behind the scarecrow the dead man lay in a coffin shaped like a canoe because the Dyaks believe he can sail his way into heaven. An ill-fitted lid had been cemented with natural asphalt onto the sides of the canoe. It was a bum job. The room was filled with the sweet, mousy smell of decomposed flesh, and the stench left one heady and sick with nausea.

A tiny fire built directly upon the bamboo floor sputtered in a corner of the room, adding gray smoke to the air that had already been breathed in and out too many times by too many people.

The little shack swayed from side to side on its shaky stilts in violent protest to the onslaught of Dyaks that paraded through the door. Some of the men brought torches with them and stuck them upright into the bamboo floor. Behind the men came the women and children.

The light fell on the people and danced over their faces and eyes with yellow flickers. There were many old, old women, too many to count. They wore sarongs that had long ago rotted and were now falling to pieces. They were very old women, old with faces wrinkled up and dried out, and they looked like old prunes sitting in tiny skeleton bodies.

There were babies, too many to count. Babies that were gaunt. Tired little babies with hunger written in their eyes and on their stomachs. Some of them whimpered, afraid of the noise around them, and they were drawn to the chests of the old women who held them. Only a pitiful handful of women looked young enough to be mothers and, like their babies, they were gaunt-looking too, and hungry.

The middle generation was missing. It was as though they had not been invited at all.

Everyone sat somewhere, some on top of others, and

when they were comfortable the titular head of the village struggled through the crowd to stand in the center of the room. He held his arms outstretched until a silence fell upon the Dyaks. Chief Niga turned to bring out the only things he had to offer.

He squatted down in front of me and tied a small pink jade bead on my wrist with a short length of rattan. He explained that it would bring me all kinds of good luck. Inadvertently his fingers touched my hand as he knotted the rattan, and the unexpected tactual contact embarrassed him a little. He looked up and grinned broadly, leaving me momentarily unnerved. He was chewing betel nuts and the juice had blackened his teeth. I was unprepared for the sight at such close range.

Niga offered me a clay bowl with everything that it contained, not just part of it. It was my introduction to Dyak food and it hit me hard. A post-mortem of the bowl's contents proved it to be a pig's stomach boiled in coconut oil. Every Dyak meal henceforth became a torment for me and every subsequent hiccup a reminder of an ordeal recently finished or of one that was yet to come.

The chief moved over and squatted beside Panggul and began to explain the routine of the funeral ceremony, and while he talked, a black ant crawled over his bare foot and up onto his toes. Niga reached down and crushed the ant between his forefinger and thumb and then punched the ant into his mouth.

Panggul turned to translate the procedure in his broken Indonesian to Sjam. I was thinking about the black ant when Sjam delivered her translation to me. Working with two translators was a slow process and one that consumed a great deal of time. Often an answer took so long in arriving, I had forgotten what had been asked.

I understood that we were to see the first part of a funeral ceremony, a blood sacrificing ritual based on the Kaharinjang religion of the Dyak people. The high priest was delegated to run the show, and he was called the *belian*.

The belian was a sharply angular little Dyak with a villainously long, beaked nose, and he was enthroned on top of the dead man's casket. He sat there cross-legged, his eyes staring upward and his cheeks flushed. He breathed with exaggerated shallowness, understandably.

The people were quiet now and listening and waiting. The belian raised a crooked index finger, and it brought six grass-covered Dyak men into the room, wobbling under the weight of the enormous masks that covered their faces. The masks were beautifully painted with purple and green root dyes and were elaborately detailed in their carvings to depict a dragon, a crocodile, fish, genie, water buffalo, and an orangutan. The Dyaks believed that when these sacred Bukung Kahajang dancers perform they are sending whatever animals are represented to the deceased, and the act makes his slot in heaven more opulent.

A lecherous old Dyak with a mischievous face sprang up and hit a circular brass gong that hung from the ceiling by a strong rattan rope, and it put the dancers in motion. They jumped about with quick little steps and imitated the movements of whatever animal mask they wore. The Dyaks watched them with intent eyes and the children stood stiffly rigid and some of them dropped their mouths open a little.

The dance stopped when the performer believed he had projected his point and the Dyaks looked at each other and nodded and smiled. The children crept back closer to the old people, quiet again, listening and waiting.

A boom on the gong heralded the arrival of a second batch of dancers, the Bukung Kambak, and the four half-naked men shuffled uneasily toward the center of the room. To conceal their identity, the men wore masks that had been cut from gourds and decorated with charcoal and chalk stripes. They were understandably nervous. The dance they were to perform was meant to portray the spirit of the dead man, and if they missed a step in the routine and were recognized by the gods, they believed they would die too.

Each dancer held a *selekat,* a short length of green bamboo which was split down the center and which he rattled to accompany himself. The dance lasted only a few minutes, and there was nothing wild or uninhibited about it. The men moved with practiced and sedately intricate steps and they seemed tremendously relieved when it was over.

The belian coughed loudly to clear his throat and then spat off the side of the coffin, and because the action was overcharged, it turned every eye in the room toward him. With this attention, he began to chant an invitation to the gods to attend the funeral and to bring with them a good will for the people or, at least, a neutrality. The chant was not clearly spoken. There were tones that rose and swelled, and when the belian ran out of breath there were little pauses. At one time his voice cracked and broke and it drew a giggle from some of the children. When he began the chant again, it was higher and the rhythm had quickened.

It finally ended on a medium pitch, and its ending shot two breathless Dyak men through the front door. They were covered with blood. They stumbled through the crowd of people toward the coffin, breathing heavily from the overload of the parts of a dead wild pig in their arms. I supposed the animal had been the owner of the stomach I had eaten. One of the men held the pig's head in his right hand, and he hung it on the scarecrow as he passed by. The long ribbons of flesh cut from behind the ears hung nearly to the floor, and little dribbles of blood splattered softly from the ends. The brain had been jerked out of the head and, along with the other bloody parts, it was heaped high on the coffin. The belian moved not even the slightest as the entrails were draped across his legs. He sat in a pool of rising blood.

The Dyaks were fired by the sight of the blood and their eyes glittered brightly, almost hungrily. Several of the older men jumped to their feet and raced each other to the coffin and thrust their hands and arms up to the elbows into the bright red gore. They drilled their fingers into the bowels and then, with breathless enthusiasm, smeared blood over the faces and bodies of everyone in the room. Not even the tiny babies escaped the adventure.

For a Westerner, a blood sacrificing can be a terrifying experience and one that could nearly cause him to expire on the spot. But blood to the Dyak represents a way of satisfying like nothing else. It creates all kinds of magical unions between the known and the unknown, and it explains everything that the Dyak does not fully understand. The blood itself is loaded with magic and its powers are unlimited. At this funeral it was used as an appeasement to bloodthirsty gods that were roaming about the place and as a general cleansing agent for the souls of the living Dyaks. (My soul was politely overlooked on this occasion.)

Suddenly the whole shack was on fire. The flames scrambled up the bark walls and licked at the grass roof, roaring as it went. The fire sighed deeply over the room and its hot breath singed and burned everything, including the people. The Dyaks screamed and hollered and yelled and cheered and laughed and loved every minute of it. They leaped high into the air to avoid being seriously burned by the falling sparks. When they had had enough, they began to clap their hands and bodies over the blaze and spit at the flames to extinguish them before we were all burned up.

The room was left smoldering, but the scorch gave a certain enjoyable correction to the odor in the room because there is no embalming in Borneo. The dead man had been in his coffin for twenty days. But it left the shack shabbier than ever.

The Dyaks not only played with blood, they played with fire as well, and as a finale to the funeral, the fire would light the dead man's path to heaven, and if a few careless Dyaks were burned on the foot, well, that would amuse the grieving family.

Before we left Sapiri, Chief Niga explained that the deceased would be buried in his coffin tomorrow morning and someday there would be a "second ceremony" to raise his soul to the seventh heaven, a location rather ill-defined as "over there." This wonderful resurrection would be accomplished by offering many heads to the major god of their religion, Sang Hyang.

"Human heads?" I whispered to Sjam.

Chapter Four

Dyak Love Affair

Water dominates the lives of the Dyaks and, therefore, the river is the center of all things. It is used for transportation, washing, drinking, and for the disposal of human wastes.

But although water dominates their lives, there are times when there is not necessarily too much of it. In this misery lie the seeds of great distress, and then rain is the answer to fifteen thousand prayers. To drink unboiled river water is the short cut to serious trouble. One of our policemen was sick as a result of having done it. "He will return to Sampit with the houseboat, tomorrow," Sjam said. "Panggul says we must travel by canoe now."

We were sorry to see the old houseboat go. Dilapidated as it was, the clanging Diesel engine had stuttered out a warm touch of "civilization," and its departure would take with it our final communication with that world.

The captain agreed to meet us in Kuala Kuajan in four or five weeks, and meanwhile we would follow the Mentaja River as far north as possible to explore whatever villages were on its banks.

We packed our foodstuffs into two small dugouts, bade farewell to the captain, and in the early morning hours headed for a village Panggul called Bawan.

Panggul said that the village was about three hours north of Kuala Kuajan. No distance in this area was ever measured in kilometers or nautical miles. It was reckoned by hours, days, or nights. The Indonesian newcomers had brought a few wrist watches into some parts of the land, and to some extent the Dyaks had absorbed the meaning of "one hour." But when the Dyaks separated themselves from the newcomers, they found they didn't have any timepieces of their own, so they quickly forgot how long "one hour" really was. Even Panggul's "hour" was unreliable. It could have meant the whole time from a sunrise to its set.

It's not much fun to travel in a canoe on a jungle river. There are too many things around that are frightening. The dark trees on the riverbanks overhang the river and throw down shadows that are unfriendly. Sometimes a limb is seen, worn smooth in the middle where headhunters have sat on it, waiting for an animal or the enemy to pass by. This makes the air gloomy and threatening.

The river itself is not without its own dangers. It gargles up a chilling chorus of its own from the noise of snakes. There are so many snakes that the water is always dimpled somewhere with the passing of them. Most of them are poisonous and therefore inedible. They navigate through the warm waters like little submarines, with only their heads sticking up, twisting and turning around like tiny periscopes. It is difficult to believe that one becomes bored with their presence, but it happens.

The Mentaja River is a full-time river and the Dyaks love to talk about it. They love to talk about how men had drowned in the river when it flooded and how men had died when it had dried up in spots, and then death came from crashing against the rocks on the bottom. The Dyaks had learned to live with the river and they bragged about it. You can brag about anything, I suppose, if it's all you've got.

We were discovering that the Dyaks were a limited and unfortunately unresourceful people. They were tribes who had never invented an alphabet, had no concept of calendar time, had never built anything more monumental than shacks of poles and thatch, had never used the wheel or plow, depended entirely upon canoes for transportation, and had no more self-government than a chief who had, perhaps, earned his position by cutting off human heads.

When we arrived in Bawan, we discovered that the Dyaks could not be regarded as architects or carpenters. Their huts slumped at strange angles, and some of them looked as though they had been pushed off their stilts by a giant hand. If a tree fell on a house and mashed out the corner, then that corner was mashed forever. Nothing is ever repaired in a Dyak village.

Some of the Dyaks in Bawan had tried their hand at farming but without success in raising a crop of any kind. Therefore, Bawan was starving.

Ingan was chief of the village. When he saw Panggul he saluted him by touching his forehead to the ground. "Talking drums tell me you come," he said. "Please come to my house."

We crowded into the little shack that Ingan called his home, and before we could sit down there was a sudden splintering and shredding of bamboo and one of the policemen disappeared through the floor.

"*Tidak apa apa*," Ingan laughed. "We need new floor, anyhow. Now I make! This make time satisfactory. If no thing happen, if no joy or tragedy, then time is nothing. I have hole in floor. I make new floor. Two doings for time! Nothing to nothing make no time at all!"

It was our first touch with Dyak philosophy, a philosophy that unfailingly embraced the sunny side of every dark cloud. It had been given by one of the sunniest spirits that ever lived. The dark shack was lit up with the lightning Ingan lived within, and all of us felt the excitement in the air when Ingan invited us to his son's wedding. "We met bride's price. We very lucky. Brides not cheap! Now we have good old-fashioned Dyak wedding in Badjanei. My son,

Ukung, already prove he brave man for girl, Napiah. He do
Kenjah, Dyak war dance, and we paint charcoal tattoos on
calves of his legs. In old days, must get human head to
prove brave and then put tattoos on legs."

"How did Ingan get his tattoos?" I whispered to Sjam.

When Sjam asked the question, Panggul bristled and his
eyes slitted darkly. His reaction startled me. "Oh," laughed
Ingan. "Get tattoos many ways. Yes, many ways! Ingan
have tattoos because he very brave. Yes, very brave man!"

There was no more explanation than that, and one look at
Panggul's face was a good indication not to pursue it.

We spent the rest of the afternoon chatting with Ingan
and learning a little more about Dyak love affairs.

Less than a century ago, the Dyaks were married by parental appointment and often at the fragile age of ten. It was
not uncommon to find that brother was often married to
sister if the family tie was of the fiercest in nature.

Sometimes polygamy was practiced, and it is not unlawful
today. A man could have as many wives as he wanted and
could take care of, and it strengthened the tribe in number
and prestige. But sorry is the Dyak who, under today's
starvation level, has found himself strapped with more than
one wife, especially in villages like Bawan.

The marriage tribalism today remains nearly the same as
centuries ago. The bride's price is divided into three gifts.
The first is given before the marriage, an engagement offering (*punduntan*), and usually consists of a white rooster
and a piece of black material for the bride. There is a gift
given at the time of the wedding (*batu pisek*) of silver arm
and leg bracelets and sometimes silver earrings. The after-
wedding gift (*bantun kadja*) is meant for the bride's family
and consists of sarongs, black hens, and invariably a gourd
or two of tuak.

These gifts do not buy a girl. They are merely a compen-
sation to the bride's family for the loss of an able-bodied
worker. Somehow they make things right again.

After the wedding the girl leaves her family, gains a husband, and experiences a new independence. She does not become enslaved by her husband's every wish and command, as one might think. If he mistreats her, she can, and often does, leave him.

The bamboo floors in the Dyaks' shacks are filled with holes because the Dyaks love to chew betel nuts. The betel nut is a narcotic, as well as the *sirih* leaf it is wrapped in, and together they create an astonishing amount of red juice in the mouth. When it becomes more than the Dyak can handle, he spits the juice through the holes in the floor. If a hole is unhandy to him, he simply cuts another within his range. In no time at all a floor can resemble a sieve.

It was my first night to be spent sleeping inside a Dyak shack, and I found that it was no fun to sleep on top of a spittle hole. The hole weakens the floor and there is the danger of falling through to the ground, seven feet below. To this may be added the bruises one suffers from the ragged edges of the hole.

The visitor learns, after one night, to survey the floor of his host's house during the daylight hours and selects a good spot to do his sleeping.

When the sun sinks, life in the jungle stops, not from choice but from necessity. The windows are barred and peace comes in with the night.

There are no bedtime preparations in the jungle villages. There is no brushing of the teeth or changing into pajamas. You come as you are and it is as ready as you will ever be.

The Dyaks lie on the floor, if there is room, shoulder to shoulder, feet touching feet, heads against heads, and talk among themselves until the talk becomes weak and then finally falls off, leaving them asleep and many of them with their lips forming the next word, left unspoken.

Aside from the funerals, life in the Dyak villages can be dull. A wedding offered all kinds of joyous excitement and no one who knew anything about it would miss seeing it.

Therefore, every native in Bawan showed up with his canoe at seven o'clock in the morning, ready to accompany the groom to Badjanei. To reach Badjanei meant a two-day trip with a stopover in Mangkup. In Mangkup we received our first lesson in the history of Central Borneo.

You can tell the friendliness of a village by its entrance. If there is only a stingy little ladder rising from the river and buried in the trees at the top of the bank, you are not going to be welcome.

Such was the village of Mangkup.

The sun had already left its sunset in the skies and the colors were lifting themselves from the treetops when we arrived. Despite the unfriendly ladder, we were happy to be off the river. It had suddenly turned itself into a putrid sewer and was stinking with refuse.

Panggul stood in the helm of the canoe listening to the village rather than seeing it. His eyes were brooding darkly and his lips had tightened into a fine, thin line.

Mangkup was stolen property and Panggul felt its theft as a personal loss. The village had been taken from the Dyaks by the Sampit-Samuda invaders. As early as 1910 the newcomers began sneaking into the jungle like creeping and crawling insects, and when they came they stayed. They came from the south, a few at a time, rolling up the rivers in canoes, and they came quietly, harmlessly quiet. They spread themselves out into the jungle and through the jungle and they built shacks as they went.

The Dyaks watched them come, perplexed and bewildered. A few Dyaks became angry and resisted them. Then Dyak women disappeared and sometimes children and the Dyaks were afraid. They sat and waited and watched and tried to think. Who were these people? Where did they come from?

In Mangkup the newcomers had driven the Dyaks from cover, burned their land, and they built shacks of their own on the ashes.

The defeated Dyaks went to live in other Dyak villages, and a few settled new villages farther north.

Mangkup was a bitter reminder that the Dyak world was falling apart, and Panggul was sunk in the awfulness of the remembered defeat. "No stay here," he said. "I sleep in tree tonight."

So Panggul slept in the trees that night. And Sjam, Jmy, and I slept in the canoe under the palm fronds.

It was six feet long, weighed about five pounds, and it was stretched across my chest.

"Mom! It's a snake!" whispered Jmy.

"Don't move! It's looking around," Sjam said.

Suddenly the snake bolted and was gone.

Panggul stood looking into the canoe. "No worry! Snake only little python. Not squeeze much. See in tree? He have many brothers and sisters there."

I looked into the palm tree that had sheltered our canoe during the night. It was beset with crawling baby pythons. I closed my eyes. And fainted away.

We arrived in Badjanei in time for the sunset. A jungle sunset, sentenced to live its life in but a few seconds, is like a sharp blow to the shoulder blades. It takes your breath away. The pinks are never pinker, the reds never redder, and the hot, dazzling fires forced from the colors are blinding if stared at too long. And then it's over almost as quickly as it began and the moon floods out its light over the earth.

Tonight the moon was full blown, making the jungle appear unnaturally white and dusty in its glow. The trees and ground looked dry and dead. In the shadows there was no shading, only black, and the jungle grass was without color, only white.

The night's sycophantic things, those that felt safe and not hunted in the darkness, began to move around on the jungle floor. The few remaining predators in the land would be at work now, a wildcat maybe, sniffing about for a warm-blooded meal and all the time hidden beneath the shadow cover of night.

Idjam, chief of Badjanei, met us at the river's edge and bowed us all the way to his shack. In the corner lay a little girl, ten or eleven years old, naked and burning up with fever. One look at the child was to see death still breathing. "Sickness part of our living," Idjam said. "Is normal. Everyday somebody sick or die. We have *dukun* [witch doctor] but he live in next village. Not get here in time."

During the night the little girl died. In the early morning hours the Dyaks quietly removed her body from the shack. And then they went about their business, as usual.

"We have wedding today to scrape the stars!" Ingan yelled.

Morning had come and the whole village was enlivened and noisy with the excitement of the marriage event. The children made most of it, running everywhere in the village, in all directions, perpetually in motion. A few of the dirtiest children were caught and thrown into the river where they were scrubbed as clean as anyone could get them. Then they were made miserable by their mothers, who tried to keep them from getting dirty again.

The old folks didn't bother to bathe. It didn't matter whether they were clean or not. The Dyaks were used to seeing dirt on each other, and a spruced-up Dyak would be conspicuous among his friends.

At the south end of the village Ukung was making a "Key of Life," and he had put his heart into his work. The Key was molded from clay mixed with a little pinch of gold dust, and it looked like a big question mark when it was finished. Ukung would carry the four-foot Key on his back to Napiah's front door, and the Key would officially "open" the wedding ceremony.

Napiah stood in the doorway of her father's shack and waited for all this to happen. She was very young, perhaps thirteen years old, and she was beautiful. Her dark skin was as rich as apples and her eyes glittered with joy.

The morning sun threw its golden color on the ground as the Dyaks streamed from their shacks and grouped themselves together in the middle of the village. The women pushed their stiff, clean little children into the group and tried to keep them as quiet as they could.

Idjam appeared in the doorway of his shack and nodded at the little committee in the center path, a signal that put the group in motion. The people moved off toward the south end of the village to find Ukung and his Key.

The children, their eyes blinking against the sun's dazzle, crowded around the Key and fidgeted their fingers together and wondered what to do. Most of them did not know if they should say anything, so they kept still.

Ukung stood behind the Key looking at the children. He had dressed himself with such lavish dedication that his costume would have done credit to a masquerade ball. He wore a white sarong with a big knot at his waist that threw his mandau at a strange angle. He had tied a Tingang feather to his left ear and had crowned himself with *sui* flowers.

And to all this he had added his own artwork, charcoal lines drawn between his eyes, across his forehead, and under his cheeks; pictures of dragons and snakes on his arms and legs. Someone had drawn a portrait of Napiah on his back.

Timah, Ukung's best man and bodyguard, stooped to test the firmness of the Key with his fingers. The children thrust themselves in to be sure they weren't missing anything, and one of them accidentally stepped on the corner of the Key. A little piece broke off, but it didn't show very much so there was no great damage.

Timah helped Ukung mount the heavy Key on his back, and together they started off toward Napiah's house, leading the little procession of Dyaks behind them.

Ingan, his dark face flushed with excitement, rushed up

and said, "This ceremony called Balian. When we reach bamboo gate, Ukung must cut bamboo with mandau, and if not cut open in one stroke, then wedding off."

Napiah saw Ukung lower the Key in front of the gate and she disappeared inside, shutting the grass door behind her.

Jumbli stood in front of the door, his arms folded over his chest, to play out his role as Napiah's bodyguard.

Ukung unsheathed his mandau and stepped up to the gate. Without hesitation of any kind, he raised his knife and brought the blade crashing downwards so that the bamboo fell into two pieces at his feet.

"He's won! He can get married now!" said Jmy.

"No, not yet!" Ingan said. "Bodyguards must fight. And if Timah not win, then wedding off!"

Ukung nodded to Timah and slapped him on the back for good luck.

Timah bolted toward the shack to battle with Jumbli. He climbed the little ladder well enough, but when he reached the top, his foot abruptly slipped out from under him and he skidded across the little porch and collided into the waiting Jumbli. The impact plummeted the two boys from the porch and they fell to the ground in a tangle of arms and legs. The fall knocked the breath from both of them and they rolled about on the ground, their arms clasped around their middles, painfully struggling to breathe again. Timah regained his breath first and staggered to a standing position. It was an effort that crowned him as victor.

"Now, is that all? Can they get married now?" asked Jmy.

"No, not yet!" said Ingan. "Ukung must throw spear through house to kill evil spirits. Then, get married!"

Timah handed Ukung a *londju* (spear) that measured nearly eight feet in length. Ukung held the spear with its metal point upwards, walked the length of the little shack, and stood in front of the window. If the spear was meant to travel through the house, the window offered a good chance for it to arrive at a halfway point at least.

Ukung raised the spear, pointed his sharp end at the

shack, and tossed it through the window. There was a little thud from somewhere within the shack from the spear's having landed on the floor.

The door of the shack swung open and Napiah danced out and stood on the high porch. She was dressed in *lemba* tree bark, and there was so much of it that her figure had to be left to trust.

The couple stared shyly at one another, realizing that now they could get married.

It was over. The pursuit, the gifts, the trek to Badjanei, the trials and tests of the "old-fashioned wedding" were over and finished.

The "marriage ceremony" itself was nothing more than a simple formality. The couple washed one another in pig's blood to cleanse the other of evil spirits and evil thoughts, and then they left the shack to bathe together in the river.

The wedding "feast" was held in Idjam's shack, a feast that would last as long as there was food and drink. The Dyaks were experts at building a party from inadequate materials, and the memory of the Dyak food served at these fiestas made me gasp. We would be expected to eat whatever was served if we attended the party. The thought was without relish of any kind.

Panggul had scheduled the village of Tumbang Puan as our next destination, and it was excuse enough for us to depart. No one missed us very much. The Dyaks were too busy eating and drinking and talking and even Ingan's mouth was so full of food that he could only sputter and nod his head in good-by.

Chapter Five

Grani

It was a chocolate flood.

It began vanilla, clear and clean with the first few drops of rain, but within an hour it was a deep brown fudge.

The Mentaja River had rain-swollen itself to the point of foolishness. It had boiled into an unbelievable rage and that rage churned out multitudes of frothy cascades. The echo of that angry churning could be heard ten miles away.

The river tore at its own edges and toppled its banks into bobbing mud-bergs, and then it roared into the villages themselves and the thundering, menacing waters burst open and knocked down whatever they touched.

It was a destroyer, that river. It was more than a destroyer. It was a murderer. The wild pigs in the jungle that had nearly died of thirst the week before now went squealing down the river, drowning.

The Dyaks suspected rancor.

When the waters finally subsided and the river had sulked back into its escarpment, there was not a Dyak in Tumbang Puan who did not believe that I had staged the drama personally.

The Tumbang Dyaks were not a high-strung people. Usually they took life pretty much as it came. But rain, flood, and destruction boxed up in a single packet had tuned some of them too high, and they snapped like cut violin strings and went whirling into darkness.

One of the men who hit the bottom of the black pit was named Grani. Grani was an old, old man. He was one of the few white-haired Dyaks I had ever seen, and his head was covered with a great snowy duster of it. His body was badly bent, warped up, and misshapen with swollen and deformed joints. His ungraceful figure radiated a discontentment with himself and with others, too.

Grani was a man who lived within his own little house of gloomy disappointments, and he took them out on anyone who got in his way. Most of his gloom came from a single past grievance, but the disillusionment of it was still sharp. Grani could never get used to the idea that he had not been chosen to be the chief of Tumbang Puan.

"That old Grani," said Panggul. "He plenty crazy man!"

Grani hobbled up to a safe distance and then crouched himself on the ground and stared at our group. He was hurling and thrashing his hands about in the air above his head as though he was arguing with some devil. They were big hands, much too big for his short, crooked arms. His palms were hard and blackened in the crevices, like the paws on an animal.

He bracketed us with his eyes but never looked directly upon any of us. He seemed to be groping among the bits and pieces of his mind to identify or justify our presence in the village.

In front of Grani, lying on the ground, was a short stick. He leaned forward abruptly, picked up the stick, and then banged it on the ground. Then he boosted himself into a half-standing position, turned on his heel, and wobbled off into the undergrowth of the jungle.

We could hear him screaming maledictions at whatever evil spirits he thought were hiding there. The vines shook violently under the lashings he gave them with his stick.

When he had cut down as many devils as he could, he

hobbled out, the stick under the pit of his arm, a look of triumphant transport on his face.

Panggul whispered to Grani and sent him limping down the center path, where he disappeared into one of the shacks. Before he left, he had narrowed his eyes at me with a chilling look.

There was a sudden shrieking of an outraged chicken close by. It seemed a pity that the wild jungle "poultry" so hastily went to the block for whatever occasion was on hand, whether it was happy, mournful, or apologetic. The chickens undoubtedly took a very dim view of the Dyaks and their blood-demanding gods. This sacrifice was meant for Kambe Hai, the devil-god of the Mentaja. It was urgent if the river was to behave again.

The Dyaks had more gods, spirits, and ghosts than anything else, and all of them were alive. Nothing ever died in Borneo. It was a very crowded place.

"Is called *kajau!*" Panggul said. "Hunt for heads!"

We were sitting in one of the few houses left standing in the village. Although the floor boards were well buckled and warped, the house was dry.

Panggul had finally agreed to tell me why the Dyaks hunted heads and how they did it. He had used the Indonesian word for "headhunting" and his voice had suddenly gone rusty, almost as though from lack of use. His eyes were dulled as though he wasn't seeing with them anymore.

His next statement shocked me.

"When they outlaw headhunting, they take heroism from Dyak! They take purpose for life!"

He paused, wiped his eyes with the back of his hand, and sighed deeply. "All over, now," he said, and bitterness crept over his face.

I suspected that Panggul had hunted a few heads in his lifetime, and this linked him directly to the headhunters themselves. He and a few others were the remnants of all that immeasurable greatness that stemmed from headhunting in Borneo. His face reflected a weeping love for those years, now regretfully gone by.

There has never been a systematic accounting of any event in Borneo, but Panggul knew the history of headhunting through his own personal experience and through his relationship to the tribes living in the Mentaja area. Half a century ago, headhunting was regulated by tribunal law, and those laws legalized each tribe's headhunting requirements. According to the tribes' needs, the laws were established and upheld in the village of Rian Sembali (approximately fifteen miles west of Tumbang Ramei), where the undisputed champion of all headhunters, Rambang Sawit, lived and ruled the Mentaja headhunters' world in 1890.

Sawit was credited with over one thousand heads, which earned him the unmatched title of *tamanggung*, king. He excelled in other skills, too, for his house boasted forty wives and several hundred children.

The members of Sawit's tribune included many *radens*, who were Dyaks claiming a minimum of one hundred heads to their good reputation. These men were the leaders of the headhunters' band, and their laws were abundant and varied.

Headhunting in the days when Borneo meant all of the island and the Malayan-Indonesian boundaries had not yet been drawn, many of the Dyak tribes ran double harness and shared each other's laws. Panggul (Tribe Iban) and Ingan (Tribe Ngadju) observed the same headhunting rules for marriage and manhood. If a man wanted to gain his majority or get married, he had to bring home a head. The head, aptly named the Trophy of Victory, was to be lopped off in a single blow. Any human being was fair play and the bravest Dyak took the head of his next door neighbor! The decapitated body stayed where it was felled, food for the vultures, and the head was brought into the victor's village, where it was displayed by the Ibans but buried by the Ngadjus.

The most demanding headhunting requirement came from those laws that were rooted in the Dyaks' pagan Kaharinjang religion. All of these demands were incorporated into tribunal laws in Rian Sembali to make them "legal."

A promise made to a dying parent, for example, to provide him with a manservant in heaven was believed to be fulfilled by burying an enemy's head near the body when he died. The number of servants sent with the deceased depended entirely upon how many were promised to the parent prior to his death. Sometimes the heads numbered in the hundreds.

The nastiest of these Kaharinjang religious demands involved the catching of a man, skewering him alive on the end of a twenty-foot pole, and then burying him in the ground, head down, feet skyward. This effort was meant to give power to the Bird of Paradise, Tingang, perched on the far end of the pole, to fly the celebrated deceased's soul into the seventh heaven.

The sects in the Tumbang Puan area, especially the Duhois and Sabaungs, hunted heads as a demonstration of absolute bravery and then drank tuak from the human skulls they had freshly decapitated. It was the epitome of their intrepidity.

The headhunting of the Katingan and Kahajan sects was motivated by revenge. Both sects forever felt injured by the other, and that injury gave rise to a nonstop retaliation between the two.

Some tribes buried their heads and other tribes displayed them. The Ibans, a northern tribe, believed the skulls brought strength and prosperity to the house, and they lined their shelves with as many brain pans as possible. They fed the spirits that dwelled within the heads by stuffing bits of food through the nose, eyes, and mouth.

Headhunting gave to all tribes strength and heroism, and to many young boys it gave manhood and marriage, sometimes at the fragile age of ten years.

At the end of the headhunter's trail were the rewarding

tattoos, proof of successful headhunting. The radens boasted, in addition to blackened calves, a dragon-lizard design on their thighs. Their daughters' wrists and the legs were tattooed with stars and stripes to elevate their status to royalty.

One day, in the early 1900's, the King of Riam Sembali counted his empire's inhabitants and found that the collecting of heads had become dangerous to the survival of the Mentaja tribes. Rambang Sawit, a wise old man, called for a summit meeting with all the tribal chiefs in Central Borneo, where he meant to lay down the ground rules for their souvenir-taking future.

King Sawit moved off his throne in Riam Sembali and journeyed to Baras Lidah (near the present day Mangkup) to join the other great chiefs. The Ot Danum and Ngadju tribes were the strongest in number at the meeting but there were also Ibans, Apu Kajans and Klemantans.

The Ngadjus, whom Sawit represented, had been getting the worst of the deal. Their "missing persons" numbered in the thousands each year, and Sawit was in no bargaining position. Had he been, it is a historical guess that all headhunting would have ceased on the spot.

The tribes deliberated for several months, with minimum incidences, and finally drew up a treaty among themselves and signed it in blood. It was agreed that the tribes would no longer war upon each other and that they would not avenge, nor collect heads for reasons of bravery or manhood. Only the stringent Kaharinjang headhunting demands were left untouched.

By reducing their own headhunting requirements to a minimum, the tribes had dealt themselves out as being simple savages. It spoke rather well for these Wild Men of Borneo to have suddenly become a people aware, a people able to integrate a new view of life with certain forms of social organization and progress.

But many Dyaks, upon receiving the news, found it difficult to become law-abiding citizens overnight. They were products of their traditions and their ancestral roots ran deep and sometimes bloody. These Dyaks found it impossible to behave themselves and then, in a moment of embarrassment, attempt to say "excuse me" when it was too late.

During the Indonesian Revolution in 1945 the Dyaks had a field day for four continuous years. Many a dead person was sent his long-promised manservant and a few thousand souls were flown nonstop to paradise and all at the expense of the Dutch.

Years later, in 1959, the new Indonesian capital, Djakarta, caught wind of the pagan practice and outlawed headhunting through an official act of Parliament. The black words punched on the parchment called headhunting clearly "murder."

But Djakarta was miles away and the Dyak was safe in his jungle. It did not surprise this writer to learn that religious headhunting persisted in the villages of Telangkah, Ajau, and Rantau Pulut on the Serujan River in 1969. In 1970 two of my next door neighbors were missing from the village of Lubuk Kawan because Sungai Hanja, a village one day north by canoe, was celebrating a funeral at the time!

Cutting off a man's head was done with the mandau and, as the decrowning instrument, it was a good choice. The Dyaks also have eight-foot *sumpitans* that are capable of shooting deadly poisonous arrows with great accuracy. But the tiny headhunter stands four and a half feet tall at best, and he found that the sumpitan was rather unhandy and cumbersome while running through a tangled dense jungle. To poison a man prior to taking his head was in bad taste, anyway.

When the mandau emerged as the decapitating weapon, it became sacred. The headhunter believes that a magic power lives within the knife itself, and since he believes himself to be his own magician he can conjure up additional magic for his mandau whenever he feels it is necessary. Animals are sacrificed, the blood collected and the knives are worshiped in rituals that offer both rice and blood to the mandau spirits.

In the village of Tumbang Puan the mandaus have the short red hair from the armpits of orangutans worked into the snub-nosed handles. Some are covered with sheaths upon which circular imprints of Dutch coins reflect the number of heads the knife has to its credit, rather like the notches cut on guns during the Wild West days in the United States.

I saw a few mandaus in Central Borneo that had been made from Japanese bayonets, the Rising Sun sharply stamped near their handles. Although the Japanese did not invade Tumbang Puan during their occupation in World War II, it is a fair conjecture that the Dyaks of Tumbang Puan invaded the Japanese on the shorelines.

Before a Dyak set out to hunt for a head, there was a routine he went through to prepare himself for the kill. This preparation was called Kenjah, the Dyak war dance. Born of unknown parents, Kenjah is probably as old as the Dyak tribes themselves. For centuries its practice was a total secret, and if a native skilled in the art taught Kenjah to another tribe, he was sentenced as a traitor and put to death by his own tribesmen.

When the tribal chieftains met to make peace, they brought with them their weapons and war dances and Kenjah was put on exhibit. It was demonstrated by the Kajan Clan of the Ot Danum tribe of northern Central Borneo as their own handmade method of murder, although they had not invented it themselves.

The first tribe to borrow Kenjah was the Dyak Bahau, who lived at the northern end of the Mahakan River in West Borneo. Later it spread to Dyak Udh Tahawung on the Kahajan and Katingan rivers in Central Borneo. Today the entire island knows and practices the once secretive dance, but solely for the purposes of ceremonial ritual, supposedly.

Tusi was the chief of Tumbang Puan. He was a dark-faced Dyak with skin the color of black-red, as though exposed to the sun all day. His dark-pupiled eyes were pitted into the surrounding whites and were startling against his coloring. He had a few long black-red hairs growing from a mole on his left cheek.

There were forty-five Duhoi, Katingan, and Sabaung Dyaks under Tusi's sovereignty. Most of these Dyaks were the remnants of a tribal caravan that had made its way to Tumbang Puan, having been burned out by the Moslems in Tandjung Djeriangau some seventy years ago.

Tusi, along with these natives, was planning a presentation of Kenjah for the strange white visitor who had possibly brought Hell and High Water to his village. The demonstration was to begin at midnight, Dyak time.

Panggul led us over the center path to an upper level of the village where the flood waters had already come and gone. The Dyaks were sitting cross-legged on the muddy jungle floor when we arrived.

There were clouds in the sky, about the color of gray rats, and the moon was hiding behind them. The clouds sailed around and reflected great moving shadows on the ground which made an eerie setting for the war dance.

Two rather startled and startling ten-year-old boys appeared on the sidelines. Their faces and bodies had been painted with charcoal (Dyak war paint), and they had stuck feathers and leaves in the headbands around their brows. Both of the boys wore short sarongs that had been caught up in a loincloth styling. Mandaus were strapped to their waists.

They bowed to the group and then waited. When a *karundeng* (flute) was blown, the Kenjah ritual began. The boys sprang apart, unsheathed their mandaus, and slid imperceptibly toward each other. Both boys were crouched on their haunches circling around and around the other in movements not unlike those of jungle monkeys.

Suddenly one boy jumped up and rushed forward with his mandau high above his head. When he was within a few feet of the other boy, he lowered the great knife and it whistled through the air as his opponent dropped to his knees to avoid the fatal contact.

It was a frightening close call. These boys were very young, flailing knives around as long as their own arms, and there was no defense against the constant chopping of the other except to duck in time.

Again and again the boys lunged and lurched at one another as they whipped and sliced their knives just inches above the other's head. The mandaus were shifted from right to left hand and handled as easily in one hand as the other.

In the last scrimmage one of the boys sent his knife over the other's head and whisked off his feathers and headband. Fury leaped into the eyes of the offended child, and he charged into his opponent with such viciousness that a feeling of grave uneasiness descended over the crowd.

A gong sounded and the Kenjah was over. The boys replaced their mandaus in the sheaths and stepped apart. But in the smoldering eyes of the featherless boy burned the desire to continue this headhunter's preparation for murder to its completion.

Tusi's son was dead. He died from malaria sometime during the night, and in the morning the village was as lifeless as the boy. Sorrow hovered on the doorstep of every shack.

Tusi's pain was heightened because he did not have time to properly prepare his son's body for burial. Chief came before father and there was just too much work to be done in the village. The boy's body was laid in a shallow water-cut ditch and mud piled over it. It would have to do for now.

"We go to house of Unda," Panggul said. "He still have house and he wait for you. He show you all Dyak weapons."

We walked through the mud toward the grass shack Unda called home. The jungle was rapidly fermenting now and it smelled of rot and decay. The Dyaks were moving the mud away from their houses. The dankness of the mud must have been stifling to the nostrils. Some of the men were bowed by the burden of awful heat and others by the burden of hard labor.

Most of the Dyaks had accepted the floor damage as a demonstrated animosity from their gods, and they were bearing it out with work and silence. But there were a few men who were still jittery about my being in the village.

Unda's shack stood at a slight tilt. The flood waters had unstuck two walls and carried them off somewhere, but the floor had managed to hang onto its poles. There was dried, caked blood on the doorstep from a recent sacrifice.

"Unda like you," whispered Panggul. "He not think you make water come to village."

Unda was a handsome Dyak. He was tiny and thin but his cheeks were fat and round and as bright as apples. He was grinning like a child who trusted everybody when he met us in the doorway and bowed us into his shack flushed with gaiety.

On the floor were arranged all kinds of weapons that Unda had brought out, not only from his own household but from the household of others. It was the most complete collection I was ever to see in Borneo.

The most important weapon to the Dyak is the mandau, and there were many of them. There were also *parangs,* knives similar in shape and size and sometimes referred to as the "working mandau" because it is with this knife that the Dyak does his labor.

The second most important weapon is the eight-foot blowgun (sumpitan), with its *sangkoh* (spear) firmly fastened to the end. These ironwood blowguns were first used by the Ot Danum tribe, and in the old days they were roughly shaped with the parang and then put into the river's current to smooth themselves. A platform was built and the Dyak stood on the top and dropped a hot coal into the wood's center to make it hollow. Today the holes are made with ironstone.

The Dyaks shoot arrows, not darts, from the sumpitans.

They are eight to nine inches long, made from a slender sliver of bamboo, and are tipped with a cone-shaped balsa wood feather. In the hands of an expert these arrows can travel one hundred meters without deflection of any kind. Some of the arrows have sharp points at their ends, some are barbed, and some of them are tipped with deadly poison.

The Dyak tribes have at their disposal two different types of poison. Both of them come from trees. *Siren,* the deadlier of the two, is extracted from tree bark and then boiled to a concentrated potency. As the poison boils, it changes colors as well as strengths from red to black, to yellow, and finally to white. Panggul believed that the white poison was strong enough to kill a 120-pound man in about thirteen minutes.

Ipuh comes from the roots of the *tuba batang* tree and is combined with snake or scorpion venom to strengthen its influence. This poison is used in the hunting and killing of wild pigs, monkeys, and birds. When the prey is felled, the Dyak must cut out the poisoned area as quickly as possible to prevent its spreading and spoiling the meat.

The Dyaks also trap their animals. Although their methods are primitive, they are effective. The *dondang* is the most widely used trap by the tribes in Central Borneo. It is a sharp bamboo spear that has been dipped in poison and then stationed in the jungle with hopes that an animal, or a man, will walk into it.

Sometimes the Dyak digs deep pits (*tambuwungs*) around his village and installs dondangs, pointed upwards, in the bottoms of them. An unaware victim can fall into the pit and lose his life at the same time.

To capture those animals, or enemies, that travel through the trees, the Dyaks hang nooses (*djarats*) in the branches. Once the trap is sprung, the luckless adversary hangs by his feet, or neck, until the hunter arrives to free the prize or take it home.

Unda was holding a bamboo spear with a poisoned tip (*salenkap*) in his hand, explaining how they are placed to protect a village, when Jmy touched my elbow. "Mom, there's that man again!"

A great duster of white hair bobbed up and down at the side of the house at floor level. It bobbed in agreement with Grani's limp. At a high spot on the ground, Grani's head moved up and his eyes appeared beneath the white hair and darted into the room like angry sentries. When he saw Unda and the Dyak weapons in front of him, he smacked his forehead with the palm of his hand in disgust.

Grani climbed the ladder, his chest pumping like a bellows, stopped in the doorway to catch his breath, skirted the wall, and sat down next to Unda. He was followed into the room by three gruff and mean-looking Dyak men and a young boy with a badly deformed leg.

"He bring son with him. He crazy too!" Panggul said. "Other men helpers of Grani."

Unda turned to nod at Grani, picked up another knife, and continued his explanations.

"This *dohong* is dagger," he said, "used by belian. Has blade like snake. Cuts on both sides. Can use to kill enemy. This knife, *duhung,* is like parang but use to cut meat from animals. Most dangerous of all knives are *tengger* and *mudjat* because blades poisonous and can hide under sarong on body."

Unda paused a moment and during that pause a snarling noise filled the room. The sound had come from Grani.

Panggul listened and then he turned to Sjam. There was a frown on his face and his eyes had darkened.

"Grani want to know why Unda show Dyak secrets," he said quietly.

Grani raised his hands in the air, made them into tight fists and growled again, and this time the growl was edged with anger.

Panggul flinched.

A few minutes dripped by and no one spoke.

"Maybe we should leave now," I whispered to Sjam.

Panggul rubbed his eyes with the back of his hand.

"Grani say Unda give you Dyak secrets. He want you give secrets too," he said.

"You don't have to do anything," said Abdul.

Two of the gruff Dyaks moved around and sat on either side of Abdul, and they kept him still and unmoving with intimidating stares.

One of our soldiers was leaning against the doorframe. He pushed himself off the frame, sauntered into the center of the room, and sat down in front of Grani. He looked at Abdul and then he cupped his hand around the butt end of the pistol that was hidden inside of his shirt.

Grani was outraged that anyone would sit in front of him. He let out a thundering howl and then stomped his foot on the bamboo floor. He was still howling as he scooted himself out from behind the soldier and across the floor until he had arrived between Unda and the knives. There he squatted and replaced his howls with cries and finally with whimpers. He whimpered more to himself than to anyone else and his eyes were pinched up so tightly that the underlids were fiery red. He began beating the sides of his head with his fists.

The soldier stayed where he was but he watched the old man with intent, unmoving eyes and he seemed to be enjoying what he saw. A queer smiled played over his lips as he lifted his shirt and unsnapped the button on the leather holster and withdrew the pistol and laid it across his legs. The Dyaks had never seen a pistol and the gun meant nothing to them, but the sight of it alarmed those of us who knew of its dangers.

None of us, including Panggul, really knew what to do.

Jmy moved closer to me.

"Mom, what's going to happen?"

"Do you still have some bubble gum, Jmy?"

Jmy pulled out a crushed pink square of gum from the pocket of his trousers.

"Chew it and make a bubble and give a piece of it to the boy, Grani's son."

When an enormous pink globule billowed forth from Jmy's mouth, the Dyaks were bewildered and then flabbergasted. They stared at the bubble with puzzled eyes and leaned forward the better to see. When the bubble burst, the Dyaks laughed, clapped their hands together, and punched one another to be certain that the other had not missed seeing the event.

But Grani was warped up with disappointment. His eyes narrowed to more than half closed and there was a little light of madness glinting in them.

Grani's son tested the gum with his lips, tasted its sweetness and put it into his mouth. He bit down on the gum once and then spat the wad on the floor. He touched it with his big toe and then rolled the lump around the floor with his heel. He reached down, picked it up and pulled and stretched it with his fingers until a multitude of tiny, sticky threads had wrapped themselves around both of his hands. The boy tried to pull the gum off but things only worsened, and then a feeling of frustration overcame him and he began to cry.

Grani had watched his son without understanding of any kind. When he reached out to pound the child on his hand, a part of the gummy network loosened and transferred itself to the old man's fist. Grani's eyes widened as he raised his hand to his eyes to study the pink mass more closely. A clump of gum was stuck between his forefinger and thumb, and when he opened them it stretched in a single thread. He scraped his finger on his leg and he thrashed his head from side to side in disgust.

Grani turned and spouted a stream of mumbles at Panggul, who lowered his head and said, "He say this no magic. Only make trouble."

"Well, maybe this will help. Tell Grani I'll put his son's face on a piece of paper. Tell him he can carry the paper with him and look at the face whenever he likes. It will be a present."

Grani liked the idea and he nodded in furious agreement.

I took the Polaroid camera from its case and shot the picture with the last bit of film that I had.

Grani took the picture in his hands. He held it closely in front of his eyes, squinted, moved the photo away, and then he looked at his son and back to the picture again. When the irrelevancy of the photograph finally related to his son's face, he burst out laughing. The laughter rang childlike, but there was no angelic innocence in its tone. It was a shrilly cackle and one filled with insanity.

"Panggul, can we leave now?"

Panggul answered, but no one heard him. Grani was pounding the bamboo floor with his fist, and when he was finished he shook his fist at me and yelled at Panggul at the same time.

"He want more magic," Panggul said quietly.

"Sjam, that old man is sitting too close to those knives for comfort. We've got to get out of here!"

It may seem strange to the Westerner that a guest is not allowed to leave the presence of a Dyak unless he has permission. To get up and simply walk away from these natives would automatically cast all kinds of suspicions upon our group and those suspicions would follow us wherever we went, along with a few Dyaks at our heels, and all of them endeavoring to make those suspicions a reality. Unda had the power to grant our departure, but the man sat dumbly on the floor, trying to understand the sudden turn of events. A blank incomprehension had invaded his face and had left him useless.

There was an exchange of Indonesian, Dyak, and ideas and Sjam said, "Yes, Panggul thinks he can get us gracefully out of here in a few minutes."

Bubble gum had adhered itself to the Polaroid picture and Grani began to pick at the sticky strings. The photo pulled apart. He puckered his brows together and frowned darkly. He looked at the boy and at the picture again and suddenly he threw out his arm and smashed his fist into the child's cheek. The boy screamed and covered his face with his arms before Grani hit him another blow on the head.

And then I did something I was to regret the rest of my life. I switched my tape recorder to ON position as Grani struck his son again and again. Blows to the head, shoulders, body and smashing strikes to the face and all the time Grani screamed and screeched his disappointments over the torn photograph. He tore at the boy with his fingernails and left bleeding wounds on the child's arms and legs. When the boy tried to escape by crawling across the room, the three gruff Dyaks grabbed the child by his feet and brought him back again.

I rewound the tape and flipped the switch to PLAY and Grani's voice transmitted through the speaker.

Grani stopped beating the child and looked up. His eyes spirited irritably across the room, searching for the source of the parroting mimic. Then he saw the little black box.

The man was reduced to madness. His eyes became crazed, the saliva in his mouth thickened, and frothy bubbles began to erupt from the corners. "You take my soul!" he screamed. "You take my spirit away and put in black box!"

Well, now I'd done it!

Grani was surrounded by Dyak weapons, all of them lined up neatly in front of him. One of the Dyaks pushed a mandau closer to him with his foot, and Grani grasped it in his black hand and raised its blade high above his head. He lowered the knife, banged it on the floor and the sharp cutting edge splintered the bamboo. "This mandau cut many heads!" he bellowed. "This mandau now cut off head of you!"

Grani gulped air as he shuffled himself into a standing position. He lurched forward. The three Dyaks rushed to help him, stood on either side, and held their hands out to keep away anyone who might interfere with Grani.

Grani wound the mandau up in a clockwise motion,

sprang forward, and swung the knife at me. The blade passed over my head by mere inches.

Panggul and the two soldiers jumped to their feet at the same time. One of the soldiers struck his fist into the face of the Dyak nearest him and the blow flattened the man to the floor. The other soldier jabbed the barrel of his pistol into Grani's stomach. The old man screamed out with the pain from it.

The Dyak on the left caught Panggul with a smashing blow between the shoulders and Panggul fell heavily against Grani and both of them lay sprawled on the floor.

The gun fired and the noise of the explosion was deafening. The bullet had narrowly missed Grani's right leg. Panggul jerked himself up, stretched his hand over the soldier's wrist, and clamped down hard. With a flicking motion he bent the soldier's wrist and sent the gun clattering to the floor. He put his bare foot on top of it. The soldier backed off, grimaced, and held his right wrist with his left hand.

Panggul, one foot on the gun and the other foot holding Grani's shoulders to the floor, waved his hand in a signal for us to leave.

My legs felt stiff and immovable as we climbed down the log ladder onto the muddy ground. A dizziness with edges of pain touched my forehead.

When we reached the riverbank we heard footsteps behind us and we turned to see Panggul standing there panting from exhaustion.

"We must leave Tumbang Puan," he gasped. "I sorry."

Panggul said something to Sjam and then ran toward Chief Tusi's shack.

"Let's go," Sjam said. "Panggul said that two of our soldiers borrowed a canoe and went back down the river. They've got malaria."

We crept out into the river's muddy water and got into the canoe. Seconds later, Panggul came flying down the riverbank and we slid off into the current, heading downstream.

"Look!"

Grani and a committee of Dyaks stood on the riverbank, staring after us.

And then they plunged into the jungle in pursuit. All of them had mandaus in their hands.

Chapter Six

Spirit on the Rainbow

The hurried-up departure from Tumbang Puan found us helping the canoes along with paddles and prayers. We dashed through rocks and rapids until the river finally wound uphill and calmed itself down a bit. It was in this calm that we tied the two canoes together with rattan strappings and made plans to spend the night. The middle of the river was as safe as anyplace, if one was running from headhunters.

It was hot. It was a rare evening if the night was ever cooler than the day in the jungles of Central Borneo. The heat hangs around in the air because there are no soft breezes to send it on its way, and the torridity urges the vegetation to sprout the clock around. Borneo is very overgrown.

There is nothing beautiful about a jungle at nighttime, especially when one is out in the open in the middle of a river. The trees on the banks were the tallest we had seen and there was no kindness in any of them. The massive foliage laced itself between the trees like a woven wall and stood against the sky, dark and brooding. Great outcrops of enormous roots had burst through the mudbanks, and above them, on the ridge, were their elephantine trunks.

Directly in front of us was a group of large banyan trees

that appeared to be straddling the river. Panggul said that Njaring Pampahilep lived in those trees and it would do well to stay clear of them. Njaring Pampahilep was a devil-god and the Dyaks understood him, since they had invented him.

They had invented Djata, too, who was supposed to be the benevolent god of the river and in whose care Panggul had placed us for the time being. He had cut the third finger of his right hand with his mandau and dripped blood food into the river for Djata, which was more than any of the rest of us had to eat that night. We were hungry and our nerves and muscles throbbed from it, but not a person made mention. We were very good sports.

The stars banged their way through the treetops and then raced each other over the sky. They were so bright that their sharp points could be seen and some of them mirrored themselves in the river. A star could be picked up in hand in one scoop.

The beauty of the stars was overshadowed by the ugliness of everything else. Even the night insects scared the dickens out of us. Whatever they were, they came out to visit us and thumped their soft bluntness against our bodies and left us swatting at the air, hoping that they wouldn't sting us or be smashed against our skin.

There were little committees of mosquitoes that buzzed around us and a few bats windmilled by, always too close for cheerfulness, and with them the dismay one feels in their darting shadows left on the river and ground.

Beneath the star-studded water were all kinds of river snakes whipping around, enough of them to start a whole dynasty. Panggul said that the snakes lived submarginal lives in this area because there was no food for them. He thought that those snakes that had survived had managed to live on either faith or stupidity.

It was scary and no one slept. Except Jmy.

The sun jumped up into the sky at five o'clock in the morning and when it arrived it plunked down its hot gold upon the ground. The shine made the jungle growth bristle a little and pay attention to the coming of a new day.

We washed our faces in the river. The soldiers took turns watching each other shave with broken glass. Djata had stolen everything from the expedition that he could: razors, spoons, a wrist watch, two combs, Abdul's pocketknife, Sjam's shoes, and my toothbrush. I suppose that if one carries around a toothbrush in his shirt pocket, he deserves to lose it.

We shoved off right away. We were not held up by breakfast because there was no such thing in the jungle. *Makan,* "eat," would roll around about one o'clock and all of us looked forward to it. Today's rations would be thin, a few beans, maybe, and a little coffee.

Flying ants, as large as horseflies, had invaded the area, and the first thick cloud of the swarming insects flew up the river and into the canoes, head-on. They stung us with their bodies and left us scrambling to put our arms over our faces for protection. But Panggul threw out his hand and grabbed as many as he could hold in his fist and then smashed them into his mouth! *"Makan, makan!"* he yelled. "Very good for eat!"

The second onslaught of ants sailed into the canoes from the starboard. We squinted our eyes against their huge batting wings and then clapped them up as fast as we could and shoved the handfuls into our mouths.

If one is hungry, anything is likely to be good to eat, and the flying ants were delicious. Since then, however, I have been able to get along without them.

It was another night to be spent on the river, but we were so tired we didn't care.

Suddenly there was a penetrating scream that burst from the adjoining canoe and scared us all half to death.

Abdul flashed his light over the crouched figures until it fell upon one of the soldiers who was hysterically waving his hand in front of his face. The tears were streaming down his cheeks. "Something bit me!" he shrieked. He began to beat his hand against his knee, sobbing at the same time until the breath in him finally choked up.

Panggul leaped into the canoe and grabbed the man's hand in his own as Abdul stretched across the water to pinpoint his flashlight on the soldier's hand. Panggul slashed the ham under the soldier's thumb with his mandau and the blood ran thickly out over the knife and across Panggul's hands onto his pant legs.

"I saw it!" said one of the policemen. "It was a green snake, with red streaks around its eyes. Must have been four feet long!"

The soldier, his tears dried now, looked helpless and without expression.

"Is poisonous," said Panggul. "Is a little poisonous."

The soldier sobbed once more and then fainted away.

"He O.K.," said Panggul. "Just good scare for him." Panggul knotted a rattan cord around the man's wrist, gently wiped his sweaty forehead with the back of his hand, and then returned to our canoe.

The night closed down without further adventure, but we were all wide awake and watchful. Both canoes were filled with whispers about the dangers that floated around us and from time to time a whizzing zipped by and endorsed the rumors.

No one slept. Not even Jmy.

We were weak and lightheaded from the three days of river living, flying ants and a snake bite when we arrived at Rantau Saluang. The village seemed wondrous to us.

Rantau Saluang was sculptured into the jungle rather than from it. It lay beneath trees whose boughs and branches twined over the seven shack houses that made up the total architecture for the inhabitants. It was a shady village but not cool.

We walked crablike into the settlement because it was

the best our canoe-cramped legs would do, and surrendered ourselves to its people.

Panggul and the chief of the village babbled the dilemmas of the Dyak language until they thought that they had understood one another, and finally Panggul said that we could have coffee and then sleep. The twelve of us shuffled into the chief's shack and stretched, for the first time in three days, full length on the floor.

Ten hours later we were awakened by a chilling scream. "Tugal and Hanji get baby now!" Panggul said excitedly. "Maybe new Dyak boy for tribe!" Panggul shot out of the shack to arrange for us to visit the couple, and the chief brought out lunch. Fish and boiled tree trunk.

Sjam, Panggul, and I climbed up into the shack Tugal and Hanji called home. Hanji was a bandy-legged little fellow whose hair stood straight up in black spikes and he welcomed us with a low bow. Then he backed us into a corner of his shack and blockaded us with white *tjempaka* flowers.

"These flowers from deep in jungle," said Panggul. "When baby born, father take tjempaka and throw over room. This make evil spirits get out of house quick."

Tugal lay rigid on the floor in the corner of the hut, and the pain from childbirth had set her jaws like granite. The muscles on her face were flexed from agony.

"Dyak father bring own baby into world. Wife of belian come to tell father how to do," said Panggul.

A high jangling scream came from the corner of the room, but it failed to put Hanji or anyone else in motion.

Panggul, a man who could stand no pain in anyone, finally nodded at Sjam, got up, and went to the door of the shack and yelled at a passing Dyak.

Suddenly the belian's wife sprang through the doorway making a noise like an ungreased machine. She scratched her graying head on the left side and it set up an itching over her whole head. She began scratching it all over, taking her time. It made her look as though she were thinking very deeply. Her mouth was youthfully full-lipped and jovial and completely at odds with her excellent old age. "Sorry I late," she said to the numbed Hanji. "Uchin have her baby. Died. Pay attention, now."

The belian's wife squatted beside Tugal and with dirty hands and grit-filled fingernails stuffed boiled bark and a raw egg into the mother's mouth.

"Give strength for to born baby!" explained Panggul. "Should be rice but not have here."

The belian's wife shouted a few orders at Hanji which he obeyed without questions of any kind, and after a final gasp Hanji accepted the baby at the delivery. He cut the umbilical with his mandau, strode to the doorway with the newborn child in his arms and sent forth a crowing cock-a-doodle-doo over the village.

The belian's wife wrestled the baby from Hanji's arms, wiped it clean with the hem of her sarong and placed the child in his mother's arms. Tugal's eyes lighted with the pleasantness of motherhood.

"Now," said Panggul, "must take cord from baby and put in *tambuni.*"

The tambuni was an urn-shaped clay pot with a circular lid. The umbilical and placenta were placed inside, and Hanji dripped melted natural asphalt on the lid to seal it tightly closed.

The Dyak tribes took elaborate measures to hide the tambuni because the child's welfare depended upon its secrecy. If an enemy found the urn, he could cast a spell on it and the Dyaks believed that the result would be fatal to the baby.

No name would be given to the newborn child for a while. There had been a father's cackled crowing at the birth, but now the baby became an "it" and was not really worth mentioning anymore.

The child was given a hammock (*tujang*), a bunch of magic amulets, and a forty-day test period to prove itself. If the baby was taken from its hammock before the forty days had passed, the belian imposed a stiff *djipen* on the family, usually a white hen and an urn filled with jungle herbs. The belian would then pocket the hen but return the urn, now magic-casted, as a medicine for the disobedient mother.

The *djimat* (charms, fetishes, and amulets) was hung from the top of the tujang and was meant to bring good fortune to the baby. The charms were usually made by the mother and possessed occult powers. Some worked automatically, while others depended upon the will of the spirit that dwelled within it. The most popular charm was a bird woven from palm leaves and filled with cooked food and blood. It symbolized the mother's wish for her child to be free from captivity.

Other amulets included in the djimat collection were the long graceful leaves from the *sesarpat* tree to give the baby beauty of character and feature; the *njaru,* a black stone believed to be the result of thunder and which protected the child from the supposedly killing force; a short length of bamboo to give a co-operative life with all others in the tribe; a piece of black *kandahirang* wood for physical strength and the skull from the *gantang tandjaku* bird, one that was regarded by the Dyaks as superior in the jungle and in whose trust the soul of the baby was placed.

Above the djimat was a wiry covering of *duhi,* a thorny, bushlike bramble meant to catch any evil spirits that fell off the roof.

It took a great deal of magic to raise a child in Borneo. It was much less complicated back home. The only "magic amulet" Jmy had ever owned was a secondhand rabbit's foot he had won in a marble meet in the backyard.

The "god ceremony" was scheduled for midnight because the moon was full. The moon would not shine its light through the thick branches that covered the village, but it would be full, just the same. The belian had said so.

Many of the women of Rantau Saluang were busy getting

their "pregnancy wishes" together to co-ordinate them with the ceremony. The wishes were made from the leaves of five stately trees found in the area; *kadjundjung, pahaka, kaju tali, sawang,* and *sambelum.* The leaves were woven into tiny baskets and then hung from the ceiling. Some held food, betel nuts, or blood, and if they pleased the gods, the makers were guaranteed a quick pregnancy.

A committee of venerated women was preparing the ritual food for the gods. It was an incredibly complicated matter. The special serving plates from which the gods were to eat had to be dug up from the last ceremony, and no one remembered where they had been buried except the belian and he was asleep. It made the women jittery. All of the food should be simmered slowly and cooked to perfection before the sun had set and the plates *had* to be found.

At three o'clock in the afternoon, someone finally uncovered the three *piring manlawen* plates. The women were nearly beside themselves with relief.

The largest plate measured sixty centimeters across, was colored red, and required the most attention. A wild pig, one that had been roasted to last a full seven days, should have been placed upon it. There wasn't a pig in the whole village, and the women, somewhat chagrined, settled on a silver-scaled fish as a substitute. The fish was small but they pumped up the insides with betel nuts.

The second plate, small and yellow, was meant to hold a juicy fruit. Another misfortune. The women talked it over and finally decided that a coconut could be the "juicy fruit" despite its dried-up interior pulp, now brown and rattling.

On the third small white plate was poured a simulated porridge which the women hopefully felt would pass as "rice." It was river water and white gravel.

The final food preparation beat the sunset deadline by fractional seconds, and although the plates were not appetizing, they were, at least, ready.

It was nearly three years before this writer was able to piece together the components of the delicate fabric the

Dyaks called their religion. It was learned by gathering bits of information from the belians, the chiefs, and from the common native himself in the many villages of the Mentaja area, for no one person was totally aware of the vastly immense and complicated religious picture.

There were times when the Dyaks were reluctant to talk about their gods because those gods commanded their respect and their fears. At other times their information seemed contradictory. However, through it all, there emerged a religion they called Kaharinjang, and although infinite details may differ from tribe to tribe, or even from clan to clan, there was an over-all pattern that interlocked the basic religious print together.

From their historical beginning the Dyaks were products of surrounding environmental forces, some of them unpredictable and malign. The tribes often found themselves warred upon, their goods stolen and sometimes their women, and if they were not killed by the enemy, then they were attacked by animals, floods, lightning, or disease, all of which exposed them to further disasters. It made excellent sense to the Dyaks to conclude that these events were caused and controlled by some invisible powers or forces. The Dyaks, therefore, felt they needed something in which they could enlist a power to work favorably for them, rather than against them. The result was one of the largest and most complicated religions ever created.

Above all things was placed a Supreme Being, Sang Hyang, who was the Creator of the Universe and Ruler of Paradise, or the Seventh Heaven. He was an impartial god and rarely took an interest in the personal affairs of the Dyak people. He did not interfere in their events and was spoken to only by the gods of the other heavens.

Below the Prime Creator was a spiritual universe that embraced a great pantheon of gods, lesser gods, spirits, powers, and forces. Through these gods the Dyaks were able to solicit favors in time of great need and the enlistment was made through the Man of God, the belian.

Each god had a name, place of being, and was charged with a duty to perform. The gods lived in heavens numbering one to seven and were responsible for their order and maintenance as well as the selection of earthly humans allowed to enter the heavens after death. The lesser gods visited around from heaven to heaven to apprise themselves of what Dyak soul was currently in what heaven.

All of the gods had feelings and emotions. Some of them needed flattery, while others had to be appeased or avenged. The Dyaks, whose position in the religious structure was lowly and dubious, were constantly on the move preparing ritualistic ceremonies for these gods and most of them involved human sacrifices.

Following are the names of the Supreme Rulers, gods and lesser gods:

Supreme Rulers of Seven Heavens

First Heaven: Lewu Tatau Dia Rumpang Tulang
Second Heaven: Rundung Radja Dia Kamalesu Uhate
Third Heaven: Lewu Tatau Habaras Bulan
Fourth Heaven: Habusung Hintan
Fifth Heaven: Hakarangan Lamiang
Sixth Heaven: Lalang Kangkang Haramaung Ampit Puturg
Seventh Heaven: * Sang Hyang

* *Sang Hyang* had many names: Sangiang, Hathella Ranjing, Tambuli Rang, Sangiang Pu Umhung, Pahatara Ranjing Lawang Langit, Djata-Pahatare.

Lesser Gods of First, Second, Third Heavens

First Heaven: Rawing Tempun Telon
Second Heaven: Radja Dohong Bulau
Third Heaven: Mantir Luhing Bungai and
Radja Malawung Bulau

Benevolent Earthly Gods

Water: Djata (spirit form)
Earth: Naga (spirit form)
Animal: Gana (dragon)

Malevolent Earthly Devil-Gods

Forest: Njaring Pampahilep (spirit)
Water: Kambe Hai (spirit)
Earth: Djau (spirit)

Gods in Human Form

Sangumang
Sangkanak

It may be noted that there are no god helpers for Heavens Four, Five, and Six. The lesser god of the First Heaven, Rawing Tempun Telon, served as the assistant to those heavens and acted as go-between for the belian and all other gods. He was a very busy spirit.

Sang Hyang, as Supreme Being and Ruler of the Seventh Heaven, needed no help and reigned alone.

Within this spirit world lived benevolent and malevolent gods who spent their time on earth and could be spoken to directly by the Dyak people. These earthly gods were never allowed to pass into any of the heavens, but they were capable of carrying gossip to the doorstep of the heavenly gods; sometimes the traffic was unbelievable.

Some of the earthly gods had more prestige than others because they controlled those things most important to the Dyaks. Gana, the guardian-protector of hunters, was one of them. It was thought that Gana resembled a dragon, although no Dyak ever saw him, but he did exist, they swore, somewhere in the jungle. No Dyak would be without his seven *haruai* feathered headdress to alert Gana of his hunting plans and so beg for his protection.

The Kaharinjang religion cannot be considered animism in its purest sense, because the Dyaks do not worship nature. They respect and fear the phenomena found there, but they do not believe that the natural objects contain their own soul stuff. If a rock moved, it was because one of their gods had occupied it momentarily and was jumping around inside.

All of the spirits had personalities of their own and roamed the jungle at will. Djata, the benevolent water god, loved the river, but he could occasionally be found in a village mud puddle. Njaring Pampahilep, a spirit who openly favored the large banyan trees above all else, did, from time to time, take residency in other trees not so impressive. A Dyak took great care while walking through the jungle not to dislodge a boulder wherein Djau might be resting. If Djau was angered, he was capable of shaking the earth until the houses collapsed.

The jungle was filled with gods scampering about, and although it was crowded, this invisible spiritual universe answered the questions beyond the range of sight and experience in the Dyaks' world.

All of these spirits were clearly separated in the minds of the Dyaks from their own inner spirits. No ancestral chief's spirit ever returned to earth to occupy the body of a wild boar, nor was the soul of a war hero ever personified in fire. Those human spirits had other places to go. How they went and where they arrived are explained in Chapter Eleven.

It was a busy and complicated spiritual cosmos the Dyaks had invented for themselves and one that was loaded with problems. The man who held the delicate threads of the religious fabric together and made sense to all things was the belian.

The position of belian was given to the sons of tribal kings after they had completed the fifteen-day walk through the jungle from Tumbang Ramei to Bukit Raja, the center of the Kaharinjang religion. The aristocrats were accompanied on their treks by a female spirit named Kamelah, who owned the jungle pathway and reigned over it with her beauty. In Bukit Raja the belian candidates received holy water (*danum Kaharinjang*) from a mystery spring and met the two human form earth gods, Sangumang and Sangkanak. Since these gods were brothers, they were considered one and the same. After much meditation, the gods embodied themselves in the aristocrats.

If the belian lived a gray life in the daylight hours, he had only to wait for a midnight ceremony to put color in the air. He was an expert of the occult, the master of ceremonies at all religious rituals, and he stood unequaled in creating handmade glories. He loved it. Those glories measured the man in quality, and the more glories he could produce, the more marvelous he became. Some of his glories were on-the-spot wonders, and when that happened, one could see excitement light up in his mind, it was said, and then feel it growing over every spectator present.

Every Dyak in Rantau Saluang turned out for the "god ceremony" promptly at midnight. The program was held in a bald patch of jungle. Where the patch left off, the trees threw shadows on the ground in suggestive shapes.

There was a bit of light cheerfulness in the air as the Dyaks passed around the latest gossip to each other until the awesome belian stepped into the scene. Then that cheerfulness gave way to grave solemnity.

The belian looked like a man who had triumphed over sins he had never committed, and his luxurious costume, exhumed from its burial spot just minutes before the meeting, added to his pious position. The costume was not in bad shape, although bits of mud still clung to the red silk headband upon which was woven a picture of one of the symbols of life, the mandau. Over the belian's left ear an *anggang* feather canted slightly, a little worse for wear. A pig-bone necklace (*rantai babi*) and one of pure gold with a tiny bamboo pendant (*buluh perindu*) filled with sacred soil (*tanah malai,* symbol of leadership) hung around his neck.

He wore a knee-length butterfly silk *ontje-ontje* skirt which was tied with a hairy pigskin belt and buckled with two boar's canine teeth. The belt supported a grotesquely cadaverous, smiling human head. It was not shrunken. The Dyaks, unlike their Amazon counterparts, had never learned the art. But the hair from it grew long and black, and the skin, although prune-wrinkled and hole-punctured,

stretched over the bony frame and was remarkably well pre-
served.

"Head from enemy," Panggul said. "Maybe one hundred
years old."

"Do your people know the art of preserving heads?" I
asked.

"Belian know. But not know now, today. Secret lost many
years ago."

The belian's assistants arrived in single file, each with a
human head swinging from his belt. The purpose of display-
ing these heads was a visual demonstration to the gods of
the power and strength of this particular tribe.

All of the leaders wore mandaus and held sumpitans. The
belian held the sacred stick of pure rubber, a symbol of
spiritual power. On the third finger of his right hand was a
silver ring set with the black thunder stone, *njaru*.

The belian stepped into the center of the arena, folded his
hands behind his back, and began to rock on his heels. He
pondered the crowd for a moment, and then he pinched his
lower lip into a deep crease with his thumb and forefinger.
He frowned darkly until he felt he was ready to begin. Then
he stretched his arms to the heavens.

Softly he began to chant and his voice was low-keyed and
grave enough to give an impressive sincerity to the situation. And then, without transition, the belian's voice
pitched into higher octaves and his arms began to churn like
windmills.

"He tell gods we ready now," said Panggul, and a frown
of concentration settled over his eyes.

The belian wound up his chant higher and higher until it
became screeching and frenzied. It went on and on until
monotony moved in, and then the chant ceased to be a nov-
elty anymore. The symmetry of our eardrums was nearly
unbalanced as the belian began to hop first on one foot and
then the other in a dance meant to invite the gods to enter
his body. Abruptly the dance terminated almost before it
even became pleasurable.

"Spirits got in him now!" whispered Panggul.

The crowd was hushed. The Dyaks, never having had the opportunity to study or practice the art of oratory trickery and dramatics, were stunned and befuddled.

The belian, pleased with himself and the effect he had created, poured out another torrent of crying shrieks.

"My voice thunder, veiled in clouds," he boomed. "My voice, voice of gods!"

The Dyaks sat with faces as expressionless as stone. Their throats visibly began to tighten up and their feet moved restlessly. A few false starts were made before the people felt comfortable enough to talk. And then, one by one, the Dyaks asked advice on family affairs, marriage, and their futures. They were answered by the belian in a sort of creative poetry. One woman timidly asked for pregnancy, and upon hearing the warm, reassuring words from the belian her eyes lighted happily because she remembered the memory of childbirth.

But the belian could not retire on advice. He wanted a glory and one that would take place on the spot.

The belian narrowed his eyes as he cast them about over the audience. His face took on a crafty look. He squeezed his lips together and blew and then tapped the air with his thumb. His hands were placed on his hips and his lips moved slightly as he searched the crowd for the material he needed to make a glory.

Abruptly, his eyes came to rest upon a fragile-looking Dyak boy whose locks hung down to his bare shoulders. The child's face was unusually thin and had the shape of hills and valleys on it rather than features. The boy shrank under the belian's glare, terrified, and began to cry.

An older man, perhaps his father, poked the child to attention. He was embarrassed and humiliated over the child's behavior, for no Dyak would ever consciously anger a belian or a spirit. The old man pinched the boy on his shoulder and twisted his head up to face the belian, who had already crouched down on his knees in front of him.

The boy struggled to speak, his neck turned red, and he tried to build up layers of courage by mumbling heroic words to himself, but he could not withstand the overpowering attention he was getting. He began to whimper again.

Panggul, a man who could not stand to see pain in any child, yelled at the belian. The outburst placed Panggul in momentary disfavor with the spirits, gods, and belian, but elevated him a point in audacity and derring-do. He deserved a medal.

The belian, his eyes squinting sharply now, gritted his teeth in the boy's ear and the child nearly fainted away. He grabbed the child's hand and jerked him to his feet. A look of sternness crossed the belian's face as he dragged the sobbing boy over the bumpy ground into the center of the arena.

A deathly quiet surged itself over the people. Only the belian's panting breath was heard and above that the whispering noise his bare calves made as they rubbed together in walking. He stopped abruptly, looked around him, and his voice roared over the hushed crowd. "I command all spirits of Dyak people!"

His thoughts were coming slowly. As they formed he mumbled them under his breath. "I take spirit out of body of boy. I send to heaven. Spirit of boy see heaven. Then boy tell people heaven good for Dyak!"

The child's heart heaved painfully as the belian sat down cross-legged on the damp ground and cradled him in his arms. The boy rolled his eyes around in a hurting bewilderment. His head bunted itself softly against the belian's naked chest.

The belian began to gently rock the child back and forth in his arms. The human head tied to his waist tumbled to and fro on the ground with the movements. The belian's manner was gravely serious as he began his mesmerizing chant.

The belian's eyes appeared to have retreated into the back of his head, but they still glittered with craftiness. As he chanted, his mouth uncovered his coated tongue, swollen against his throat, and it fluttered like a huge white moth. Little balls of sweat rolled off the belian's temples and ran down his cheeks. From time to time he left off his chant to lick his dry lips with his tongue and then began again.

A dull sleepiness descended upon the people like a desolate fog. It engulfed the Dyaks into trancelike states and they became still and unmoving. Only the belian and his movements were sharp and purposeful.

The child sucked in his lower lip, let it go, and then, suddenly, his body became stiff. His eyes were shut and his mouth closed tightly. One hand clenched softly against the belian's naked chest.

The belian began to rock the boy back and forth in his arms, like a mother cradling her child. The movement scraped the human head about on the ground. The rhythmic swayings were sharp and purposeful. Sometimes he held onto a tone in his chant for a long time, and then he would lick his lips, sigh deeply, and begin his chant again.

It was long, tiringly long. Some of the Dyaks, without volition, bowed their heads and nearly went to sleep.

The child stirred in the belian's arms, stretched a little, and sucked in his lower lip. His body began to tremble abruptly and he clenched his hands together over his bare chest as though he felt a coldness sweep through him. His feet jerked and a shivering worked its way up his legs and into his body to his bare chest. Then his body relaxed weakly and became limp and finally lifeless.

The belian dropped the child to the ground. He stood. The belian looked over the crowd and then down at the boy. "Spirit of boy not in body. Spirit gone! Spirit ride on rainbow to heaven!"

The belian swept his arm over the spectators and pointed to a tiny opening in the trees where a rainbow had arched itself in the sky.

The Dyaks, their interest now raised to a high point and their mental apparatuses well muddled, sat speechless. They looked at the rainbow and at the belian and finally at the still body of the little boy, who lay crumpled at the feet of the Man of God.

The belian's breath came whistling now. "Now, I bring spirit back," he panted.

The belian puckered his brow into dark wrinkles. He reached down to pick up the child, held him by the armpits, and swung his lifeless form in the air. The Dyaks were afraid to look.

"Come, spirit, come!" the belian spat.

Nothing happened.

For a moment the belian forgot his image. A strange appalling fear and loneliness seemed to fall over his face. He hiked the boy up and placed his ear against the child's breast. He shook the child, gently at first and then violently, and the boy's head lolled loosely from side to side. "Spirit! Come back!" the belian screamed, and the words jerked a little.

The air had thickened itself with a thin mist and somewhere in the distance a clap of thunder could be heard.

As the rumble faded and fell away, the boy awoke and his face was charged with life. He brushed his eyes with the backs of his hands and looked about him. Cautiously, he freed himself from the belian's grasp and, once free, scampered half crawling, half running, into the waiting arms of the old man in the crowd. The "god ceremony" was over.

The costumes were carefully buried under the earth's crust where they were to remain until the next time, and the belian retired emblazoned to his bed. Every Dyak in Rantau Saluang was convinced that he had seen an instant miracle and one that had been performed on a rainbow. The import of that miracle was a huge lesson.

Sleep did not come easily for me that night. To have seen a rainbow at midnight was disconcerting. It confused one's composure.

I left it alone. Even today, I have found it better not to mention midnight rainbows in public.

Chapter Seven

A Safari Dwindles

Panggul had set our new course to Tumbang Ramei, a village on the Kalang River. He thought we could reach it within two days, but the great flood waters of the previous week had already flushed themselves away and the river was left shallow, rocky, and tough to travel.

It was our third day out, we had not eaten for the last twenty-four hours, and the grinding jungle living was beginning to show its effects on all of us. At each turn of the paddle the bones stuck out from the backs of the men, bones that had been padded with firm flesh a month ago. Abdul's plump cheeks had become sunken, shallow cups beneath his eyes, and the soldier seated next to him looked out through eyes that glittered with fever. My vision had dulled and I could no longer focus a camera.

All of us were suffering horribly from weather-punished skin, skin that burned and peeled and burned again before it could heal. Our gums bled, hair fell out, and we were covered with the ugly, weeping staph lesions that come from malnutrition and plagued our bodies with promised threats of infection. Jungle rot moved in under our armpits, and jungle fungus grew beneath our toenails and left them soft and yellow, like butter, and sometimes bleeding. From time to time a man would search his neighbor's face to reassure himself that he was better off than the other. It was pitiful and it was defeating.

The gnawings of hunger had cast us into a dimming, gray jungle world, leaving us lightheaded. When two of the men fainted, even Panggul's stout heart must have felt a momentary chill, because he replaced the smile on his lips with a tight grimace.

We bumped over the rocky river bottom, dragging on and on, and when the two canoes tumbled forward suddenly over a falling white rapid, the animation was exaggerated, but it seemed unreal because we couldn't feel the motion or emotion of it.

In the late afternoon we rounded a bend in the river and, imperceptibly, Tumbang Ramei stretched out in front of us. The joy we felt was instantly replaced with fear. There was a blank, white emptiness about the village and the air was freighted with silence.

Panggul stood up in the canoe and thrust his head far forward. He cocked his head to one side to hear better and then frowned deeply. A strange, wise look moved into Panggul's eyes. "Not good, here," he whispered, more to himself than to anybody else.

Suddenly, his nostrils flared wide and he threw his hand up to his nose. And then the jungle sighed deeply again, and the ghastly, grueling smell of death lowered itself over all of us and even the grasses bent beneath it.

"My God!" gasped Sjam.

There were two dead children lying on the riverbank at the entrance of the village. Their faces were black. The sun had twisted and warped their naked bodies and left the skin shriveled up like dead leaves stretched tight and shiny over sharply pointed bones. Their eyeballs were gone, eaten out by some monstrous thing, and in their place were two staring black wells of horror. Both of the faces grinned through withered lips at an agony they had experienced while living. Their hair had been hacked off and some of their fingernails were missing. They were Duhoi Dyaks, from a tribe that would make a funeral from the hair and nail clippings someday.

The bodies gave off a nauseous, stinking fume that filled our eyes with tears and choked off the breath in our lungs and left us with stomachs that wanted to vomit. One of the soldiers puked over the side of the canoe while another held his head. There was no substance in it, only water.

We buried our noses in the crooks of our arms, but the odor slid off the bank and rolled down over us like a large, heavy inescapable cowl.

Panggul licked his lips to draw saliva into his mouth and said, "Wait in boat." His tongue was thick and heavy when he said it. Little balls of sweat had formed at his hairline and they rolled down his face in little streams. He wiped his mouth and chin with the back of his hand and then cautiously slipped over the side of the canoe and into the water. He waded to the log ladder against the mudbank. When he reached it, he stood there a long time, looking up at the bony, decayed foot sticking over the bank above him. He would have to pass within inches of the dead children, and because he knew it, his face paled to a pasty yellowishness.

He pinched his lips together in a tight line against the pain of the odor, and then, trying not to look in the direction of the two children, he started up the ladder. At the top he staggered a little under the stench and began choking and gasping for breath. He shook his head from side to side as though to clear it, and then, abruptly, he plunged forward, bolted over the bank's edge, and disappeared into the village.

In the distance there was a faint scraping sound. A dark, ill-defined figure appeared and walked to a small mound of piled earth and squatted there for a moment and then jumped off into a nearby ditch. The scraping noises began again and with each scrape a little spurt of dirt flew up into the air. Grave digging. One more grave was being dug next to the fifteen tiny barrows already lined up, side by side.

Panggul reappeared at the top of the ladder, wavering slightly, his eyes as dim as though they were seeing nothing, lost and far away. The fingers of his right hand were wrapped tightly around three sumpitans and he leaned against them for support. Without his volition his eyes moved over the dead children and then he stumbled forward, slid down the ladder and back into the canoe.

"Many die," he said softly with tears in his eyes. "Sixteen now dead. Maybe cholera."

We moved out into the center of the river and looked back at the poor, sad-eyed village and sorrow settled into our hearts. But the saddest heart of all lay in Panggul's breast.

We were awakened by screams. Wild screams, screeching and violent screams, the screams of wild beasts. Directly above us, clumped together on a banyan tree limb overhanging the river, was a band of vicious orangutans.

When the current tugged at the canoe and carried us downstream a little, the apes swung onto closer limbs in pursuit and plummeted us with branches and sticks and all kinds of jungle debris.

"Sumpitan! Kill monkey!" Panggul whispered.

Jmy and I loaded arrows into the long guns and watched the monkeys race through the boughs, closer and closer to our canoe. The apes were the largest we had seen, and the long, loose hair that hung from their shoulders was colored a hot bright orange. When they snarled we could see their sharply pointed teeth and little strings of frosty saliva that stretched from the upper jaws to the lower. Their eyes were red and fierce. From their noses dripped long threads of yellow mucus. The apes had stringy, skinny paws that were puffed up with fat purple veins on the backs of them, and the veins stood out heavy and thick beneath the short hair.

"Get leader monkey," said Panggul, raising his sumpitan

to his lips and aiming at the squat, fat orangutan around
whom the others were gathering. Panggul puffed up his
cheeks, blew, and sent the arrow into the ape's right eye.
The monkey screamed in agony. As the monkey pitched
forward, Jmy's arrow pierced the animal's right scapula.
My arrow hit the beast in the derrière, which at the very
best was only a little painful.

The wounded ape wailed mournfully as he crashed downwards. His body thudded loudly on a lower limb and he
threw out his paws to catch himself. He tossed his head
back and howled and one of his eyes rolled up until only
the white showed, but the other eye, the lid shut, was held
fast by the arrow, unmoving. His great, hairy upper arms
flapped around his sides in a circular motion until one of
his paws fastened upon a little branch, and then he pulled
at it and howled again. Abruptly, his body began to twitch
and he jerked his head from side to side, but he made no
effort to put his paw to his tormenting and torturing eye or
to touch the firmly planted arrow. He sank down on the
limb, rubbed his belly against it, and began to crawl with
little shudders and jerks through the clusters of leaves on
the limb toward the trunk of the tree. As he groveled along
he left a little trail of blood and a thick white saliva on the
limb. He urinated and the wet covered the limb and splashed
off into the river. Whining and half crazed, the ape squirmed
his way toward the bank with all the strength he had left.

When their leader fell, the rest of the pack screamed
hysterically, scattered, and fled in panic through the arches
under the trees.

"Quick," yelled Panggul.

He bounced over the side of the canoe into the water
and the men scrambled after him. They dashed through
the shallow water to the river's edge and quickly scaled the
low embankment.

The injured orangutan had reached the bank and was
now slowly making his way over the jungle floor and into
the interior. We watched the chase and saw the tall grasses

waving and twisting under the movements of the men. Ahead, the swinging vines brushed by the ape as he crawled beneath the trees. And then one movement caught up with the other and there was a soft thud, a beast's whimper, and then the joyful cries of the men as they dragged the prize to the mudbank.

Panggul pulled his mandau from its sheath, tested the edge with his thumb and sniffed at the blade. He stooped to rub the knife briskly in the grass to clean it and then he rolled the monkey over onto its back. The animal's eyes were closed, one held shut by the arrow, the other by death.

As though practice had made him adept, Panggul raised his mandau and chopped off the head in a single blow and threw it to one side. He poked a hole in the skin at the neck with the tip of his knife, slit it the entire length and then, with one jerk, he slipped the skin off the body and onto the legs.

Panggul severed the paws, left them inside the fur pouch, and threw the whole thing on top of the head. The fur was crawling with gray, fat ticks, and they swarmed over the hair and onto the inside of the wet skin where the blood was blackening in long strings.

Panggul wiped his knife on the grass, cut the animal beneath the ribs, and shook the intestines out on top of the skin. Then he stuck his fingers into the ape's breast and dragged it down to the river to wash it.

One of the soldiers had made little supports from tree branches to hang our kettle and another came from the river with the water-filled pot and strung it in place. Together they built a fire beneath the supports and soon a languid coil of smoke arose. When Panggul returned, the flames were snapping and crackling around the pot and a little steam was beginning to pour out. Panggul cut the legs and the back into several pieces and threw them into the kettle.

And then we sat down to wait. All of us were starved.

We tried not to listen to the sound of the boiling meat as

it bumped around inside the pot. Sometimes a little of the water under the lid would boil over, and when it did, it sizzled fiercely on the flames and a splendid smell of meat would fill the air for a moment. It made the waiting harder than ever.

The men stirred restlessly and tried to think about something else. We busied ourselves with the burial of the head and skin and carved our initials on the tree trunks and then drew pictures on the ground with little sticks, and when we couldn't wait any longer, Panggul stuck his mandau into the boiling pot and stabbed the bubbling meat and served it into our desperate hands from the knife's point.

It was the first food to bless our stomachs in over thirty hours. The monkey was old and scraggly and the meat was tough and singularly oily, but we gorged ourselves to near unconsciousness. It was the cheeriest hour of our lives.

The soldier had lost his mind. At some time during the night the raging fever that lived within his brain had transformed the man from sane to mad.

He was a living man but there was no resemblance of it. When he talked, it was in whispers and you could hardly make out what he was saying. Once he said, "I'm hot! No, I'm cold!" as though these two opposites might balance themselves and make things right again, and then his body shook and trembled and he made pathetic little appealing gestures with his hands like some despairing, helpless creature. And then he didn't whisper or move anymore. The boy was dying by inches.

There were parching fevers written on the red, splotchy faces of the two policemen, and their eyes were glassy under it. And when the morning's great white sun began to burn like a hot ulcer in the sky, the two men fell away under the heat, like wilted flies. The trip was over for them too.

We were stunned by the sickness and disease that were so rapidly felling the members of the expedition, and we were scared too. The sick men were the forerunners of a promised calamity for those of us who continued, and we felt the limits of defeat. Except Jmy.

Jmy's natural yearning for adventure was one that nothing short of the real experience could satisfy, and as far as he was concerned, the safari had just begun and there was no reason for turning back. It made us feel foolish. Jmy tested his dreams. We were afraid to.

The one remaining soldier helped the sick men into the canoe, stationed himself aft to paddle, and we watched the little dugout slip out into the river and away through the rapids to whatever help it could find.

Panggul assured us we would find a village soon and so we continued northward. But it was a restless day, one that blackened and disheartened us.

At noon, Panggul and the men went into the interior of the jungle to search for food. We watched the limbs shake and fall as they hacked their way through the thick growth. After an hour had passed we could no longer see the falling vines or hear the chopping sounds made by their mandaus.

We had reached the northern section of the Mentaja, and there was not one square foot of arable land anywhere. There was just too much jungle to cope with, and even the primitive slash and burn method used by the natives would find them starving to death before the clearing of the land could come about.

In the southern half of the country the Dyaks had acquired, through their own methods, a few rice seeds, and with the planting of them their happiness and their lives had grown to depend upon the harvest of those seeds. Rice was so important to them that if a crop failed they were left broken and then they died.

The Dyaks were not farmers. They knew nothing of irrigation, crop rotation, insecticides, or cultivation. They simply put a seed in the ground and then they prayed for rain, and if it didn't come, the seed didn't sprout and there was no rice that year. If a rain came in herculean proportions, the crop flooded and the seeds were washed down the river and there was no rice that year. If it rained before the harvest, the rice mildewed and soured and there was no rice that year. And then death entered the little shacks and found the Dyaks with their empty stomachs and it wiped them out. Sometimes whole villages were left lifeless in a single year.

The hunger we felt in our stomachs was so sharp it was painful, and we desperately needed something, anything, to put into our mouths. When the men finally came crashing back through the tangled brush we saw their smiles and the sight of them lifted our hearts beyond belief.

One of the men had found a lizard, but it had been bolted on the spot. Panggul tenderly spread the rest of the curiosities on the bottom of the canoe, and we tried not to gasp when we saw them. There were a few chunks of rough bark, gray, gnarled roots with the dirt still clinging in the crevices, some bitter jungle grass, a handful of black ants that were trapped up in a large leaf, plus some shapeless wonders that had once been a kind of living thing but were now shrunken pieces of dried brown skin that rattled around inside if they were disturbed. But everything was edible, Panggul guaranteed it.

Sometimes one must divide his misery between dying in action or starving to death without lifting a finger. Either misery is discomforting but together they are a positive misfortune. So, we ate everything by swallowing quickly, without much preliminary chewing.

After seven days of river travel we reached Tumbang Hedjan, and our hearts gushed with joy at the sight of the village. It wore a shaggy coat of jungle vines. The Dyak Duhoi inhabitants hid beneath the coat as our tattered crew stumbled up the river ladder into the clearing.

The living force that held these natives together was a *dukun* (witch doctor). They had a chief, but he was incompetent. His family had reigned for years, but they had married each other so often that the present chief, Chief Mata, was left idiotic with incestuousness. No one in the village ever bothered him very much because even the slightest public notice threw him into desperate, convulsing fits. This condition the Dyaks ascribed to the animosity of their gods.

Chief Mata was also misshapen, rather left unfinished. His head was too large for his body and his hands were without fingers.

Although his role was only honorary, he was still the chief of the village, therefore the witch doctor grabbed his hand stump and dragged him forward to greet us, and all the while Mata pushed his feet against the ground, resisting the effort. When they arrived, both of the men were breathless.

The chief fluttered his club-hands about like huge baseball bats, and when they found the comforting hand of the witch doctor, they fastened themselves around it. He tried to fix his eyes on the ground in front of his feet, but the strain of attention was too much and abruptly he fled the scene in panic. At a safe distance away, he sat down on the ground, clasped his legs with his arms, and with his chin resting on his knees studied the little weeds that grew around him.

The witch doctor was very thin with a face more picturesque than handsome. His cheekbones were high and hard and his curly black hair spun in tight coils, like lettuce, around his face. His jaws were large and bony and there was a dark mole beside his upper lip. He scratched one hand with the fingernails of the other as he welcomed us on behalf of the shy chief, and while he talked a few of the Duhoi Dyaks stole from their hiding places to get a better look at us. They were a suspicious group, more than any of the other clans in the area, because they had suffered great losses from their many wars with enemy tribes and had been reduced to a pitiful handful.

The witch doctor's granite jaws began working up and

down from an attack of hiccups which he tried to control by pinching his nostrils together with a thumb and fore-finger. He finished the interview with a wave of his hand and backed off into his own shack, a few feet away.

We had arrived in the village in time for a celebration, and the afternoon rushed on with festivities. The natives were preparing for "Thanksgiving" because some of their dreams had finally come true and every shanty bubbled with the excitement of it. The news of the celebration arrived on the lips of a little child.

His name was Embang. He was the most beloved of all youngsters in Tumbang Hedjan, and the other children followed him about all day, hoping to reflect a little of the glow of his spirit. When Embang spoke, his voice was low and musical, and when he laughed, he sent out long ribbons of laughter that colored the air and overcame everyone nearby with giggles. Embang was without shyness of any kind as he sat down and gently pushed his hand into mine. When I felt his thin, bony fingers, it stirred my heart. Looking down at his hand, I was shocked to see that my own hand was beginning to resemble his.

In the afternoon I taught Embang a little nursery song about a cockatoo that had lost its teeth. He echoed the melody with no effort and then memorized the lyrics, although he could not understand the Indonesian words.

Embang watched with intent, interested eyes as I wrote the day's happenings in my journal. He asked to feel the paper and see the little marks on it and then he begged to "write" too.

He had never seen a ball-point pen. He held it in his hands and turned it over and over, rubbing the sides with his fingers and clicking the point in and out, all the time laughing and giggling. After a few tries he copied the printed letters that spelled his name and then he looked up with wide eyes.

"Is my name, ya? Embang! Embang! Embang!"

The sweet, dark music of his voice burst over the room,

and then he flew through the doorway of the shack and into the village to show everyone that his name was *written* on paper! He was beside himself with happiness.

It wasn't midnight yet but the Dyaks were so excited that they couldn't wait any longer, so the celebration began. The witch doctor agreed to run the show.

A witch doctor in Borneo is both a sorcerer and a sooth-sayer, and his powers to manipulate good and evil are un-limited. It was said of the witch doctor in Tumbang Hedjan that he could cast a spell on a woman's hair and fingernail clippings and she would become barren. Or he could point a bone at a man and cause death on the spot and then turn around and "heal" someone else standing nearby. If you displeased him, he would simply eat up your soul, but if you gained his favor, he would make your life prosperous for-ever. There was an absence of prosperous Dyaks in Tum-bang Hedjan because, it was said, the witch doctor was an exceedingly difficult man to please.

The Dyaks did not love him. They feared and respected him.

The witch doctor of Tumbang Hedjan was as well quali-fied as anyone to deal with the gods at the "Thanksgiving" ceremony. He fancied himself up in a shirt he had bor-rowed from our policeman and tied a ragged sarong around his waist to cover the black tattoo patches on his calves. The patches endorsed the people's fear of the man.

The celebration shack was decorated slightly and was a delightful change from the empty, cheerless Dyak houses which are sometimes trying on one's Western nature. The natives do not use furniture of any kind. There are no beds because it has never occurred to the Dyak to sleep any-where but on the ground or the floor, and he would con-sider a chair a ridiculous curiosity.

In the center of the shack rose an affair that looked like a cornstalk. Green jungle vines had been wrapped around the stalk, and the Dyaks had buried little clay plates in the tangles, which were loaded with bird skulls and the tiny, shrunken legs of grasshoppers as offerings. A newborn bird wobbled about in a coconut shell on top of the arrangement and it represented Djata, the benevolent river god. After the ceremony the little bird would be entombed, alive, in the river rapids. It was doubtful that the bird would live through the ritual ordeal, anyway.

The Dyaks aimed to ask Sang Hyang (Supreme Being) to attend the ceremony, and they had constructed a coconut palm throne for Him to sit in. They had thoughtfully hung a grass hammock beneath the palm heart where He could lie down and rest if He tired during the long evening.

There were a few chips of *gaharu* wood burning beneath the hammock. The smoke welcomed the good spirits in case they attended. Several wild tapioca roots had been thrown about on the floor to scare away the malevolent spirits.

A very old Dyak man, with white tufts of hair clumping down to his shoulders, marched into the shack and threw the head of a wildcat against the cornstalk, which nearly tipped over from the blow. The head was meant to be a blood sacrifice to appease the gods. Black threads of blood dripped from the neck onto the floor and then spread out, gathering dust.

The Dyaks came forward and placed their sumpitans and mandaus near the head of the cat to symbolize the laying down of weapons before the gods. It was a very cheerful place.

Everyone understood that the ceremony (Sang Hyang Bandar) was the time to pay the piper and not to ask for anything more, but several of the women couldn't resist placing a few personal pleas on the side. They secretly hung their pregnancy "wish baskets" from the ceiling and hoped that the witch doctor wouldn't notice them.

As planned, the witch doctor was the last person to arrive. He trotted into the room and seated himself too near the cornstalk and the tail of the borrowed shirt began to soak up a little of the wildcat's blood. "Sang Hyang in room now!" he said, and every eye raised itself to the coconut throne.

This began the ceremony. For the most part the witch doctor's powers were spontaneous and did not require elaborate cajoleries. He received the Dyaks, one by one, as they paid homage to Sang Hyang for answering their prayers. It was never clear what prayers had been answered or why the Dyaks were thankful, except, perhaps, that some of them were still alive.

Once in a while a native would ask the witch doctor for advice on some personal problem. The good doctor had advice on all subjects and it was ready for delivery for anyone who wanted it. Usually the advice was charged with common sense, but if it wasn't, it was nevertheless something the witch doctor believed with all his heart.

A child of seven or eight years asked the witch doctor why she was plagued with headaches. He placed a bird's egg on the girl's head, a type of Dyak X-ray machine, looked through the egg and into her brain to find the answer. When he thought he had it, he said, "Because someday, maybe, you have Sang Hyang's child. Clean yourself, be ready!" His answer nearly strangled the breath in her.

When the ceremony ended, it was still too early in the evening to go home, and it left the Dyaks feeling cheated. The witch doctor's sharp mind solved the problem by stretching the program into a double feature. He announced that he would ask Sang Hyang's spirit to enter his body since the Great God was in the room, anyhow. The Dyaks were thrilled.

The witch doctor sat cross-legged on the bamboo floor and closed his eyes in deep concentration. He began swaying to and fro, back and forth, chanting softly as he swayed. Suddenly, his legs began to tremble a little, and then they twitched, seemingly without his volition. His voice pitched higher and still higher and filled with a shrilling vibrato.

"Sang Hyang put spirit of woman in witch doctor!" whispered Panggul.

The witch doctor was singing sweetly now, his eyelids coyly fluttering. The impersonation performance was so convincing that the Dyaks were persuaded to flatter the female spirit within the witch doctor. They dusted his face with chalk powder, combed and arranged his hair, and praised his dress. The elderly Dyak with the white hair tufts stepped up and offered the witch doctor a betel nut, which modified the act a bit when he had to spit.

Then the witch doctor stood and began to move through the intricate steps of the *manasai*, a dance otherwise performed by women. The comical exhibition spread laughter over the crowd. It was an enjoyable show.

Suddenly a thin, haggard-looking Dyak man crashed through the doorway into the shack, his breath coming hard. Beneath his eyes were dark, blackish circles as though he had not slept for days, and his stomach looked as though he had not eaten for years. He held a tall bamboo cross in his right hand. The uppermost point of the cross was cut to a razor sharpness.

The Dyaks twisted their necks around to look at the young man, and when they saw the cross the laughter in the room was replaced by gasps and a few sobs.

"He hold *salagi*," said Panggul. "He in danger."

For centuries the Dyaks, who have no written language, have talked to each other by means of Totok Bakaka (Dyak communication), done with leaves, sticks, blood, and feathers. The salagi, bamboo cross, was part of it, used only in life and death circumstances.

Panggul slipped over to talk with the young man. When he returned he said, "He from Tumbang Ramei. Now dead twenty-two people. He ask witch doctor to help."

The witch doctor and I talked together until the morning sun appeared. We talked about the bad spirits in the water and how one could boil them to death, and about the bad spirits in uncooked food and in human filth, and how bad spirits jumped from one person's hand to another person's mouth when nobody was looking. The witch doctor understood these spirits very well since he controlled them. And he promised to kill every bad spirit in Tumbang Ramei.

We lost one of our policemen the following morning. Cholera. He was delirious with fever as the witch doctor lifted him into the canoe and set off for Tumbang Ramei.

The expedition that began with fifteen people had dwindled to seven hungry and scared individuals who had found themselves living like the Dyak headhunters with no food, no medicine, and no hope.

There is nothing in the world like a mighty jungle to display one's insignificance. We were whipped and we knew it.

Panggul had never given up, but when he saw the sick policeman off, he knew that if we wanted to live it meant returning to civilization. "Civilization" was a seven-day journey down the river to the village of Kuala Kuajan.

The day yawned wide open and the sun spread its hot shine on the earth as our Dyak friends in Tumbang Hedjan lined the riverbank to see us off.

When our canoe slipped into the frothy, seething world of white rapids, above the roar a tiny voice was heard singing a nursery song about a cockatoo that had lost its teeth. We looked back at the village. On the mudbank, below the shaggy vines, were written the giant letters that spelled EMBANG. And above the letters, a little child was waving.

Chapter Eight

Once upon a Hungry Day

When the blanket of gray clouds overhead split wide open, they sent down a blinding sheet of silver water. Panggul grabbed an empty coconut shell and tried to shovel out the collecting water in the bottom of the boat, but a short time proved the utter uselessness of his efforts.

The canoe spun in wide circles and smashed into rocks and roots and whatever else had put itself in the river road. None of us saw the *sawang* tree that had stretched its limb down over the river, but when the bough cracked into the soldier's face, we heard the gristle and bone of his nose crunch.

A reserve of inky black clouds marched in from the east and piled up with the overhead assemblage. The downpour worsened.

Puddles had formed on the jungle floor and from those puddles miniature lakes began to grow. The little lakes were whipped by the rain until they rose higher and higher and then they flooded. The spilling waters cut tiny rivulets and streams that channeled through the jungle gathering more water and becoming freshets. The rivulets and streams and freshets swept along the stones and roots in their paths and worked their way down to the river. They cascaded over the bank into the river and cut away the gravel around the roots of the bordering trees, and the trees bent over and were left defenseless.

Suddenly a vast toppling tree whitely silhouetted itself in front of us. With a roar the upper branches smashed down onto the river and the rapids tossed our canoe into the tree's grasp. The huge limbs held us in bondage and the tree began to circle in the current, bumping back and forth as it went. Our canoe rocked up and down over the river with the tree. We tried to free ourselves by pushing the limbs, but each time the tree returned with the current and we were helplessly trapped again. Then the small roots that tied the trunk to the bank let go, and the tree whipped around in a great arc and catapulted us into a pile of river rocks on the far bank and nearly tipped us over. And then the rain stopped.

The sun burst its hot breath on the jungle with such urgency that it left us bewildered. Its heat burned the air, and the sudden change made our eyes water.

We were drifting into a huge cavern of stones. A sense of safety had returned to us. The rocks rose in solid walls on both sides of the river and the jungle growth on the top of the rock wall glistened and waved itself crazily up and down in a turquoise haze.

That evening the sun looked like a drop of blood as it dripped over the horizon and was gone. The clouds formed into splinters and took on the sun's reflective glow, bleeding red with the brilliance of it.

The moon flowed into the sky from behind the crown of rocks above. The river had blackened itself to ebony. One by one the stars jabbed holes in the soft sky. It was another jungle night to be spent in the canoe.

Yesterday and all the other yesterdays had been churned up and ground away, and what had happened was so vague and distant that no one could remember it.

We had passed the village of Tumbang Ramei four days

ago and someone recalled that the two dead children had disappeared from the riverbank. We pressed on to the village of Ngahan, only to find it was one we could not enter. Large palm fronds flanked the entrance painted to depict death masks. They warned the outsider to pass into the village at his own risk. Panggul suggested that cholera had struck this village too, and it was probably true according to the death odor that hung about the place.

Tumbang Anci had been abandoned. The tall *pantars* (tomb monuments) rose skyward through the jungle trees and published the deaths in the village.

As we approached Tumbang Pahilep, disaster struck our expedition with a dry viciousness. The river was seeded with huge, jagged rocks, crouching like guardians at the entrance of the village. The river abruptly picked up speed and the energy of the current mix-mastered itself against the rocks and tossed and turned our canoe about with abandon.

The helm of the canoe dived into one of the rapids, turned itself around, and then thwacked into a jutting rock on the right embankment. The impact of the blow shifted the weight in the canoe and we were overturned and thrown into the foaming waters. The boat hit five of us broadside and carried us with the surging current. We were plummeted down a ten-foot waterfall into the furiously churning waters below.

Miles downstream we recovered the canoe and found ourselves wet and stone-bruised but without broken bones. An inventory sadly revealed one lost camera, innumerable rolls of exposed film, one of the cooking pots, and both paddles. It was an unspeakable, heartbreaking disappointment.

The men uprighted the canoe, and after we had settled ourselves in it, we looked back at that falling world of fiercely descending water that had been responsible for our latest desperate enterprise. Seeing how frightfully in earnest that waterfall was, I was terribly sorry I had gone over it.

Panggul said that Kambe Hai, the river devil, had wanted

to kill us. I felt that the jungle was trying to kill us too. The trees dropped their limbs over the river, and those limbs scratched and tore at our faces and bodies and left us lacerated and bleeding. Sometimes the trees harbored poisonous vines that buried their sharp thorns in our flesh and festered into half-dollar sized sores blistering into hideous infections.

Our canoe dragged along the dark, winding river looking for its own help. When it snagged itself on a rock, we waited like chips on a flood tide until the canoe was pushed off by the current and then we floated on down the river road again.

Hunger had followed us. The Dyaks in Tumbang Hedjan had given us a few tapioca roots to eat, but we had gobbled them up during the first few hours on the river.

In the evening of that day a small green fruit appeared in the river and bobbed its own course in the current. All of us grabbed at the fruit straightway and our desperate enthusiasm nearly capsized the canoe. We split the fruit seven ways. We ate the skin and the seeds and Panggul ate the stem.

On the morning of the second day we passed below some low, overhanging branches and a baby python dropped out of the tree and onto the shoulder of the policeman. The men grabbed the branches of the tree and steadied the canoe while Panggul shinned the trunk to raid the nest. The snakes were wiggling in all directions, and some of them dropped into the river, where we tried to catch them with our hands before they escaped. Panggul smashed the heads of six pythons with his fist and threw them into the canoe. He cut off their heads and pulled the skins off like stockings. Then we boiled them and ate them. Python meat is strangely pithy and spongy, but it tasted delicious because it was food.

It was hard to believe that it was only yesterday that the men had eaten their belts. Those that had them. The men had lost so much weight that when they removed their belts, their pants slipped down over their hips. Panggul promised to get them each a length of rattan to replace their belts as soon as he could. Wrapped around the waist once or twice, it would work just as well.

The men had softened the leather in the river, digging into it with their nails to encourage the leather to absorb the water and then, when they couldn't wait any longer, they popped the rawhide into their mouths and it was seemingly forever before they swallowed it.

In the evening the men looked over their shoes. They picked at the browned stitches on the soles with their fingernails and when they came loose, they yanked the leather off and soaked it in the water. Jmy and I ate a piece of one of the soles from the soldier's shoe. It had the flavor of old cardboard and was so tough that I couldn't break it down with my teeth. In final desperation, I swallowed the leather whole.

Except for leather belts and shoes we had had nothing to eat for two days. We were passing through an area where the sky was clean of birds, the river so low that no fish could live in it and the jungle so densely tangled that not even a snake could crawl through it.

All of us felt the blackening weakness that comes with hunger. That weakness canceled our judgment and our minds were left crippled with grayness. We had traveled too fast, too early, and, somehow, too late. We were shocked to find ourselves now starving to death.

The night wore away with the gnawings of hunger.

We sat huddled together in the canoe. Life had stopped.

All the things that made life meaningful had stopped. Ideas, little happenings, feelings, thoughts, remembrances had all stopped. Even the distaste for the ever-present heat and hunger had left us.

Starvation encourages the thoughts of cannibalism to become less chilling. Some of the men were thinking of eating each other.

And then, lethargy moved in and none of us had the spirit to go on and no longer the need to go on. We were dragged onward only by the knowledge that the canoe was moving beneath us.

Abdul's nerves had finally let go, and now his hands shook incessantly. He had a look of wondering on his face, as though he couldn't grasp the reality of the situation, and from this one sensed the near approach of madness about him.

He gripped the side of the canoe with his right hand in an effort to control the shaking that had abruptly mantled his body, and the skin over his knuckles burst open and the blood ran thickly off his fingers into the river. He muttered under his breath and raised his hand to his mouth and licked off the blood with his tongue.

Abdul had lost so much weight that his face was grotesquely cadaverous-looking and there was a thin, milky film covering his eyes. He vomited into the river and it looked like dark, clotted chunks of blood.

Abdul's lips were glazed with fever blisters. Whenever he licked his lips with his tongue, some of the ugly vesicles broke open and began to bleed again. He would hook the fingers of his shaking hand over his lower teeth to keep his painful lips separated.

The condition of the soldier was mournful. He looked like a broken bundle of sticks, muddy and blood-caked. He clawed continually with his skinny hand at the annoying hurt that lived within the broken bridge of his nose. The skin had been scraped off and the bone could be seen. The swelling from the break had closed his eyes.

His forehead appeared abnormally high because there were swollen cuts over his brow and the blood from them had matted his hair together at the temples.

Sometimes he fainted off into unconsciousness, and when he did his head would drop back against the policeman sitting behind him. Lately the fainting spells were more frequent and lasted longer.

During one of his unconscious moments, he sucked in his

underlip and bit it with his teeth. The lip splintered and blood percolated over his mouth and skipped down his chin in a little red line.

The sores on the policeman's temples had punched themselves out into the shape and color of red-yellow strawberries and looked like festering boils. The great pustules had developed from pellagra, and a few of them were paunched on his eyelids. They made his eyes look bulgy and myopic, and his eyelids, raw and red, could not stretch over them. One of the lumps, in the corner of his left eye, had already broken open and a thin, white butter dripped out and wet his cheeks.

The man was thin, frightfully thin, and little bags of skin, like loose flaps, hung down from his jaws. His lower lip sagged outward under its own weight, and sometimes his tongue rolled over the backs of his teeth, and then the teeth could be seen swiveling around and wiggling loosely in their red sockets.

Sjam lived within her own house of silence and looked out from it with grave calmness. She was a woman to whom hardships had proven incentives to fierce determinations. She had an idea that there was no heroism in starving to death, and if she were going to die, she would give it a touch of dignity and without hysterics of any kind.

A curious, twisted smile had visited her lips, and that smile revealed her as a person who could steal a victory by laughing at defeat.

Sjam had lost the rise and fall in her voice. When it came, the voice was no more than a whisper without pitch or stress. She held her head high and with her chin thrust forward, but there was an air of sickness and pain about her.

Her skin was yellowed and shriveled, and she seemed thick in the stomach as though there was a great swelling there, but her shirt fell loosely over the protuberance without showing its shape or size.

There was a large lump behind her ear, round and soft,

and her fingers explored it from time to time. She made no mention of the pain.

Only once did she cry out, and as much in panic as in pain because there was no escape from it anymore and there was no sanctuary to hide it in. She was leaning forward in the canoe when torture racked through the growth in her stomach. She groaned and clenched her teeth and her eyes rolled around in a hurting mist. A tight smile played over her lips and the false brightness of anxiety burned in her eyes.

You can measure a person by the way he handles pain and sickness, and a more valiant woman than Sjam never lived.

Panggul had unwittingly scratched his face was his fingernails and was left bleeding in his own beard. The wound was white and it glistened with purulence because it was infected and spreading. The skin under his eyes wizened and left tiny, dull gray pouches hanging like hammocks beneath his lids. His mouth was slack, grown loose from breathing through it, and the corners were black edged from sunburn.

Panggul suffered from a different kind of pain. His chin quivered as he tightened his lips over his mouth to stifle the sob that was trying to escape from his throat. He wiped his eyes with his fingers until they were dry, and then he clenched his hands into tight fists and laid them in his lap. He saw me staring at his hands and said, "I sorry. I very sorry," and he tried to smile a little.

The man was spartan. When he thought no one was looking at him, he wore a grim face, but when he met an oncoming stare, his face changed to bright cheerfulness. He felt guilty because he had brought us into the jungle and he was suffering the shame of its effects on us.

None of us blamed Panggul. It had been nearly two years since he had visited this Mentaja area, and the conditions had worsened beyond his imagination.

But the guilt was there and it lived in Panggul's heart

and marked him with a pathetic loneliness. He sighed deeply between his parted lips, sunk his chin toward his breast, and became silent.

Jmy was sick. Last night he had said, "I just got a stomach-ache," but the color of his face indicated much more. He had spent the night somewhere between pain and sleep. The aches scampered around in his stomach and through his bones, and in their vicious grip he fought the nausea and fever and chills that accompany influenza.

In the morning his eyes were streaked with the bright yellow arrows of hepatitis.

Jmy lay weakly in my arms and I could feel his body struggling against the pains and all the while he was telling me that he felt just fine. And then he said suddenly, "Gee, Mom! Your eyes are yellow!"

It was likely that I had hepatitis; everyone else in the expedition did. And from the aching bones and nausea that swept through me from time to time, I suspected that I had a touch of influenza, too.

My head began to throb. There were small blinding hammers that staccatoed rhythmically against my temples and behind my eyes. The small hammers gave way to sledge hammers and my head pulsed with pain from the pounding.

The thudding and throbbing aches were sent from my head to nibble at the back of my neck, and there they built themselves into greater pains that traveled on into the shoulders. My muscles were left rigid and tight with torment.

I didn't know what was happening to me, and dread began to gather in the corner of my mind. I tried to put a name to what I was feeling and to call it something that was familiar to me. And then, abruptly, the pain tossed out a cold shiver that left me shaking and trembling and the dread turned to panic. Malaria.

I could hear my own heart beating and scrape a little at each beat. Perspiration beaded itself on my forehead, and my clothing was soaked from it.

One moment I was freezing with cold and the next burning up with the heat. My heart raced faster and faster with the attack of the fevers. I clenched my teeth together so tightly that they loosened and then blood ran from the gums.

My stomach strained and tightened against the paroxysms until it finally gave up and the world grayed. I gripped the side of the canoe as a nausea dizzily twisted my stomach and I doubled over to retch.

The shaking seizures went on and on and they were still going on when the distorted phantoms born of a raging fever danced before my eyes. And then, death seemed strangely friendly and sleep a welcomed brother.

I fought for the safety of consciousness by clinging to thoughts about Jmy until my eyelids felt heavy, very heavy, and I closed my eyes. And there was nothing.

Chapter Nine

The Prescription

The Western doctors X-ray, test, cut, stitch, prescribe, and wait to see whether they have effected a cure or not. These techniques usually inspire hope in the heart of the patient and he expects to be doing very nicely soon.

But there is nothing reassuring about Dyak medicine. If one ever exposes himself to a witch doctor in Borneo and lives through it, then he need never again fear anything. Bones, seeds, roots, fungus, a little of this, a little of that, brew it, stew it, and a cure.

I will remember the witch doctor in the village of Kuluk Telawang for the rest of my life. And it is a certainty that I will never forget *The Prescription.*

Panggul squatted on his hams beside me, his dark eyes were brimming with gentle tenderness.

"We in Kuluk Telawang," he whispered. "We come last night. *Dukun* [witch doctor] make well for you, now."

Malaria is a horrendous and debilitating disease. My head still throbbed and the sweat tremors were chasing each other through my body, but after one look around the shack we were in, my curiosity woke up and took a fresh start. The scene was guaranteed to fire terror into the heart of a sick person and make him well again.

All kinds of junk were scrambled together on the floor and walls and ceiling, and everything was covered with dust and spider webs. There were shells, pods, dried leaves, and roots, and in little baskets there were sticks of some kind standing straight up like soldiers, and in clay pots pigs' ears floated about in black oil. In the four corners of the room were branches and long, gnarled roots and bones. Some of the bones had come from humans, femurs and tibias, and there were a couple of human skulls hanging from the wall by a rattan string that had been punched through a hole in the top of the skull and then looped down and came out of the mouth. There were antlers still embedded in the skulls of deers hanging from the ceiling that must have been centuries old. Other curiosities even Panggul could not identify, but it was certain that they were marked in the mind of the witch doctor.

The only pattern that emerged from the arrangement was that the "cheap" medicines, the roots, seeds, barks, and oils, were on the floor and the more "expensive" remedies, the bones, animal parts and teeth, were either stacked up in the corners or hung from the ceiling out of reach until a deal was made for them. To have accumulated this dizzy variety of so many "cures" must have been at a grave inconvenience to the collector.

The drama of a witch doctor is considerable, and although the cast is small, the action is vivid. The medicine men in Borneo come in every shade and color. Some of them are women. Witchcraft is a job handed down through the families, and if there are no sons, then the practices are carried on by the daughters.

The Dyaks are loyal to the witch doctor because they have nothing else, and they remain interested in him despite any failings they may have had with him because they are convinced that he is a man chosen by Sang Hyang.

The witch doctor is so necessary to village life that once he enters the profession he never thinks about retiring. The Dyaks pay him with food and sometimes with labor just to keep him happy and in the business. He is a master of the occult, both a soothsayer and sorcerer and sometimes, at the same time, his own chemist and laboratory technician. He can run a village on the side if the chief is an idiot, like Chief Mata in Tumbang Hedjan.

What might appear as nonsense or even as a dangerous practice to the Western physician is usually something that has evolved from the Dyaks' natural environment. The small community of amulets, fetishes, talismans, and charms that live within the witch doctor's little black bag are the most important tools of his trade.

The most desirable of all the magical objects in Borneo is the charm. I saw only one charm during the years I spent living with the Dyaks. It was a hard, round black seed, about the size of a shirt button, and the edges were as sharp as a razor. The seed had passed through the generations for so many centuries that its origin was cast in obscurity. It was owned by the witch doctor in Kuluk Telawang and there was nothing in the world that he could think of that was worth its trading.

The charm is the only object that has true automatic occult powers. A seed, stone, or shell, it is hidden in the house to expel the evil spirits and attract the good ones. The charm ensures an everlasting good fortune to its owner and to anyone else who comes in contact with it.

The fetish is the Dyaks' second choice of magical objects, but they are sometimes reluctant to take a chance because it does not work automatically and once in a while it goes in reverse. Inside the fetish lives a spirit of an irresponsible nature which is capable of protecting and aiding its owner, depending entirely upon the will of the spirit.

The *manik* (Dyak jade bead) could be considered a fetish, and it is worn on the body on some special occasion or for several days following that occasion. It cannot be worn every day because the spirit embodied within the fetish will become sluggish and any good it might do would backfire into a catastrophe, for sure.

A Dyak can wear an amulet around his neck all day long, and it protects him against the bad doing of evil spirits. If he doesn't have one of his own, then he can get one from the witch doctor. It can be a rock, a knot from a tree trunk, a tooth, or a gnarled root. It does not bring good luck and has no magic powers of its own, and therefore the Dyak combines the amulet with a talisman which brings him a formula for good fortune.

A talisman has extraordinary magical powers. It not only averts evil and brings good fortune, but it can also produce a miracle. But talismans are hard to come by because they are rare and expensive. Many Dyak babies become full grown adults before they are able to pay the witch doctor enough to have a *lamiang* (Dyak jade) strung around their necks or wrists to keep them in good health. A favorite talisman of the Dyak hunter is an animal tooth, worn around his neck, which is supposed to bring him all kinds of good shooting. Another favorite is a small wooden doll carried around by barren women in hopes that this talisman will cause pregnancy. The Dyaks, incidentally, are unaware of the connection between sexual intercourse and pregnancy.

The Dyaks are able, to a limited extent, to conjure up their own magic and shove spirits into "pregnancy wish" baskets or into a seed pod to hang around their necks, but there is just nothing more potent than a genuine crocodile's tooth procured at the witch doctor's shack and dispensed with a sophisticated touch of witchcraft professionalism.

Talismen, amulets, charms, and fetishes are hardly the raw materials of modern medicine, but even today they play important roles in the lives of the Dyak people. The Dyaks believe in their powers, and because they believe, it makes the magical objects work, and the fact that they work sometimes reinforces their beliefs.

The magical objects, which are believed medicinal, are used in conjunction with Dyak medicines; one would never be used without the other. The witch doctor usually starts with herbs because they are cheap and easy and he has a little bonanza of them at his disposal. He can use them singly or in combinations, and sometimes a moment of desperation will find him using all of them at once.

Herbs are used primarily to give strength to a body weakened by some illness: *pasok bumi* (leaves), *djamu* (brown dried weeds), *sesawang* (green leaf), and *banua* (shrubby weed) are some of them. If a person becomes too strong, and if the state is undesirable to its owner, then his body can be weakened by swallowing *kaju njilu*, a poisonous tree sap. An overdose would be fatal.

High temperatures are treated by eating *penawar sampai* roots that have been boiled in water and softened enough to chew. It is not uncommon for the witch doctor to bleed a feverish patient by cutting him on the stomach and shoulders with sharp bamboo knives.

If herbs prove ineffective, then there are other things the witch doctor can do, if his patient hasn't died in the interim.

Dyak medicine is based on the principle that the inexpensive cure will not be the effective cure. In the village of Kuluk Telawang the cheapest medicine in the witch doctor's shack was made from the dried petals of a red flower. The petals are boiled in water and drunk to ease coughs and colds. The most valuable item was something that looked like a bird's egg, white and round, and it proved to be a calculus that had been found in the stomach of a wild boar; its cure was said to be so remarkable that it would correct soft feet. The stone was to be swallowed whole by some lucky patient who was then confined to the shack until the doctor would retrieve the stone whenever it reappeared. Meanwhile, in keeping with its rarity, the stone had been stashed in a soft bark-skin pouch and was tied around the witch doctor's waist where he could keep an eye on it.

The remedies were numerous because the ailments were

many. Sometimes the witch doctor's cures involved shells and bones and blood, and if one didn't work, then he tried the other. For heart trouble the witch doctor asked the patient to swallow ground-up animal teeth: those of a wild pig were said to be the most effective. Deer horn soup was used to enrich the blood, and sometimes the Dyaks would suck on a transparent sliver cut from an antler for months at a time and it never wore out. Chicken grease and pig oil were combined as an ointment and to cure weak bones.

Blood was used to cure everything because it was magic. When a wild animal was caught, the Dyaks tried to doctor themselves by smearing blood over their bodies. Sometimes blood was used on a well person simply to help him sustain his good health.

The witch doctor was unfamiliar with "measles" or "chicken pox," but those red spots peculiar to children of a certain age could be cleared up with a soup made from dried snake skin that had been boiled in pig's blood and water.

Birds were important in Dyak medicine, and their raw hearts were swallowed to strengthen a weak brain and revive a poor memory. The livers of birds were wrapped around an infant's head to relieve night sweats, and if they didn't work, then the witch doctor covered the child's body with *mali mali* leaves soaked in bird's blood.

The most extravagant statement was the cure for old age, and it was one that was made impossible by the Kaharinjang religion. One is forbidden to exhume a body except for Teweh ceremonies. In this impossibility the witch doctor found safety. The cure consisted of the digging up of an ancestor's body, finding the spot opposite the corpse's mouth, and scraping off any fungus found in that place. The mold was to be boiled in water and drunk as soup.

The Dyaks do not consider death an inevitable state. As far as they are concerned a man was born to live forever, and if he died, it was because his defenses had been stolen by bad spirits and they had left him helpless. Age had nothing to do with death because the youngsters died as well as the older people.

The witch doctor in Kuluk Telawang was the oldest man in the village. So many years had passed by him that he had lost track of their number. He recalled that he had been born in Tangar, maybe one hundred years ago, and when his Katingan tribe moved north to Pahilep, he had gone with them. In Pahilep he had found love and taken up marriage with a local girl. The consequence was a mischievous daughter who irresponsibly ran away at the age of twelve with a rascal Dyak from Kuluk Telawang. The old man moped around Pahilep for years until he decided he couldn't stand living without being near the girl, and then he packed up his amulets and calculus and left his wife and Pahilep to live in Kuluk Telawang.

The Dyaks of Telawang had never had their own witch doctor before, and when the old man arrived, they were thrilled to have him. They built him a house, helped him unpack his magic bag, and started making office calls right away.

The floor of the shack swallowed its own dust when the great man humped into the room. He was wearing the smile of a fox, enough to scare a person into good health on the spot.

His eyes were small but as bright as a sparrow's and they were sunken into deep hammocks of wrinkled skin. His forehead was corrugated with wrinkles, some of which lapped on top of other wrinkles, and even the skin on his temples was shriveled up like the puckers on a prune. His nose was flat and lines cut down on both sides of it into his mouth and then ran around to his chin where they twisted out into radical circles. His lips had shrunken into a bowknot because he had no teeth, and their absence had collapsed the skin under his cheekbones into deep cups.

His pierced earlobes hung nearly to his shoulders and flapped about whenever he moved his head. His gray hair appeared to have never been cut, not once in his lifetime. He had tied it together with a piece of rattan that made his hair stick straight out like a stiff tail.

He wore a dirty sarong that had more holes in it than whole pieces and one of the holes gave a peep-view of the tattoos on his withered legs. There were jade maniks tied to both of his wrists and ankles, and a talisman of lamiang was cradled in the folds of shriveled flesh on his bare chest. Age and arthritis had badly gnarled his hands and left the knuckles horribly misshapen. The fingers veered off at a strange angle and the little space between his thumb and forefinger was held shut as though he was trying to grasp something that was slipping away from him.

At the age of over one hundred years, the witch doctor was not a brisk person. He shuffled himself over to where I was lying and he looked like he hurt all over. Each step was a struggle and looked as though it would be his last. Even when the witch doctor was standing as straight as possible, he was much closer to the floor than anybody else because his back was bent and his legs were bowed.

He dropped the few inches necessary to squat beside me, and the squat crowded his stomach up against his chest and his breath pushed out a vile odor. He leaned forward a little, bracketing and enclosing me with his eyes, and began to mumble some kind of chant beneath his breath. A squirt of betel nut juice drooled out of his toothless mouth and hit me on the chest.

Abruptly, unpredictably, the old man hurtled himself across my body and grabbed my waist with his gnarled hands and buried his head in my stomach. The shock that I felt was too deep for utterance.

The witch doctor took his time at everything and I thought he would never get up off my stomach. When he did finally straighten himself up, he pushed his forefingers on my eyes and pressed so hard that little specks of white lights danced under the lids.

He slowly rose to his half-standing position and every

tendon in his crooked legs creaked at the strain of so much movement. He turned to Panggul and squinted his bird eyes until the upper-lid skin nearly shut them, and solemnly announced that my condition was serious but not grave.

It is difficult, when lying on the floor, to maneuver oneself into a good position for defense, but I did the best I could by holding my hands across my middle.

Meanwhile, the witch doctor mentally drew up a little list of all the things he had to do to produce a cure. And, again, he took his time at it. He dropped back in the room, placed his knotted hands on his hips, and surveyed the junk around him with an appraising eye. He looked at the things hanging from the ceiling and the objects stacked up against the wall, and a visible excitement began to build itself up inside of him. Whatever he had in mind, it was certain he would have to go through the whole routine of it or he would injure the dignity of his witchcraft forever.

It took him nearly an hour to get things ready. At my feet he put two little wooden men holding raised mandaus. Their duty was to fend off the evil spirits if they dropped by while the doctor was busy with something else.

A large brass gong was suspended from the ceiling just above my head, and the witch doctor hit it with a stick every time he passed by. When the eardrums are exposed to the ringing of a brass gong, a splitting headache can become nothing more than a minor nuisance.

The witch doctor parceled out his leaves and roots and bones and seeds into a heap around me and to such a height I couldn't see over the top. He dropped to the floor, panting and throbbing from the exertion of the assemblage.

It was dusty inside there and difficult to breathe. When I could no longer calm the anxiety I felt for my escape, I peeked over the wall and took a breath of fresh air. The witch doctor was crouched up in the far corner of the room talking to a large mask he held in his hands. It had been carved from balsa wood, painted a deathly white. There were two little holes for eyes but no nose or mouth.

Panggul regarded the mask with a benevolent eye, nodding to himself and then to me in approval. He said that the witch doctor did not want to be blamed by the gods for anything that might go wrong, so he would cover his face with the mask to escape recognition.

I was worried and afraid but too weak to care. I collapsed into the bottom of the haystack and tried to make myself as small as possible.

Suddenly, there was a rattling noise and a long string of pig bones jumped over the top of the nest and the mask peered over the edge to see if I was still in there.

When it was gone, a drum appeared and the witch doctor squatted behind it. He began to beat out a rhythm meant to inform the gods what he was up to and to solicit their help at the same time. The drumhead was made from an orangutan skin and through two centuries of use a small hole had been worn in the center of it. Later this drum was given to me by the witch doctor as a souvenir of my visit to him.

When his gnarled fingers could take no more beating, the doctor stood and started performing the ritualistic steps that were meant to provoke self-hypnosis. The pace was painfully slow, clogged every inch of the way by the old man's age, and it was done more in the nature of groping than dancing. Some of the steps were scrambled together and without meaning. When a pattern finally came out of it, the doctor was left swaying dizzily to and fro until the motion defeated him and he plummeted heavily to the floor.

I sat up. The witch doctor was groveling on the floor, half crawling on all fours, his breath coming hard, and his whole body pulsating with emotion. He stopped, pivoted around on his seat, and then struggled to sit up. As he crossed his bowed legs, a globule of betel nut juice spewed out from under the mask and ran down his chest in a red river. The old man coughed, grasped the white chin of his mask, and raised it just enough to spit and then went back to being mesmerized again.

Abruptly he began scooting himself along on his derrière, pushing with his hands, until he had crossed the entire length of the floor. He lifted his mask again to see where he was, and then he picked up an object about the size of a small coconut. He tucked it beneath his arm, lowered his mask, and when he turned to scoot back, I lay down.

The object suddenly appeared in the air above me. It was the skull of an orangutan. The doctor held it upside down and shook it over my body. The bits of debris that filtered through the eyes and nose of the skull later proved to be crocodile dung.

The doctor slumped forward, unconscious. He collapsed one entire length of the nest when he fell.

It seemed an eternity before the old man came to, and when he did he was mumbling under his breath. Panggul held him as he removed the mask from his face. He gummed his betel nut, smiled a toothless grin at Panggul, and announced that he was ready to deliver the prescription that had been revealed to him during his trancelike state, a prescription guaranteed to cure my "serious condition."

I was digging my way out from under the sticks and bones when the delivery was made. "Panggul! What did he say?"

"He say to wrap leaf around unborn rat. You swallow whole. Everything O.K.!"

It is perplexing for the American to think of food in the simple terms of survival, but to the Dyak food is the central concern of life. In Borneo one is always hungry, even after a meal just finished, because there is not enough food in the land for the satisfaction of one's stomach.

The Kalang is partly at fault. It is a busy river and hurries by the villages with such speed that the fish have a hard time living in it. But in front of Kuluk Telawang the river pulls up and slows down a little in a natural eddy, and

1. Sjahsam and me on the morning after our brother-sister ritual.

2. Poles used in the Tewah ceremony.

3. *Sapundu*, a statue of
a dead person.

4. A witch doctor.

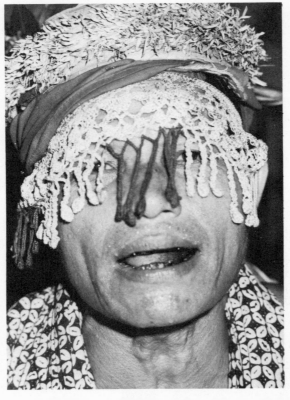

5. Typical house.

6. Jmy with a funeral dancer.

7. Jmy hauling a canoe on the Kalang River.

8. Child with a witch doctor's talisman.

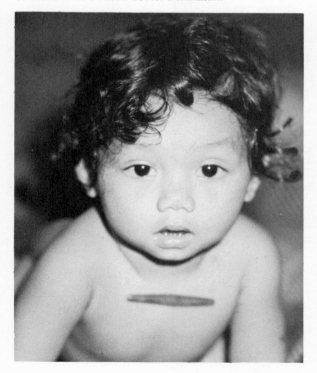

the water is just deep enough to house a scrawny little silver fish called *bracas*.

Nearby, in the jungle soil, a few rice seeds had managed to grab hold and had actually sprouted and given grain, and these few grains of rice with the bracas had kept the villagers of Telawang alive this year.

Acting on the noble impulse of sharing what little food they had, the denizens of Kuluk Telawang should be credited with having saved the lives of our starving expedition. Because of this sharing, many of the Dyaks went hungry for several days.

It is a universal unkindness to eat in plain view of those who do not have much food. Usually our group ate together, alone and out of sight, whether in the canoe, on the jungle floor, or in a corner of a Dyak shack. But today, it was to be different, as requested by the Dyaks of Telawang. They had offered up their bracas, and then they begged to watch us eat it in the hopes that the sight would somehow double their enjoyment of giving.

We had been cooped up in the witch doctor's dark shack for two days, unable to see one another and too sick to care, but now, outside under the bright sunlight, we found each other subjects of curiosity. The over-all picture of the group looked brighter. The soldier's nose was less swollen, and a great brown scab had closed the open skin wound. Jmy looked better although he was still jaundiced. A healthy coloring had returned to Abdul's cheeks, and with it a new determination sprang from his eyes. Sjam had stopped shaking and the policeman's pellagra pustules were drying up. We had survived, but everyone had his wounds.

The Dyaks collected themselves together in little bunches and stood at a respectable distance to watch. Some of them helped Panggul and the policeman gather sticks for a fire, and when it was ready, a burning ember was brought out from one of the shacks.

The Dyaks are careful to keep a fire going somewhere all

the time because, if they lose it, it must be started again with flints.

Panggul worked at a tired trot between the fire, the river, and the kettle. When the pot was full of water, he placed it directly upon the crackling flames and instantly the fire breathed up against it. When the water began bubbling furiously, an old Dyak man with tattoos on his calves hobbled up with the bracas and threw it into the pot. The fish was about ten inches long and could have been eaten by any one of us alone.

Some of the Dyaks edged in a little closer, thin from hunger and stoic from resisting it. They stretched their necks and whiffed at the air whenever the fish sent out its fragrance. Others whiffed at the scent of our strangeness.

In every village in the Mentaja we found a few Dyaks who were distrustful, and they were constantly on the watch for any sign of animosity from our group. In Telawang there were four of them, all older men, and they had backed away into the trees, ready to run on signal. They were not hostile. They were afraid.

The children stood about stiffly and stared with blank little faces. It was a hunger that had reached into their hearts and souls. Some of them watched the boiling pot, and when they heard the fish bump around inside, their eyes watered as well as their tiny pinched mouths. Other children turned their eyes away from the pot and studied their fingers or clasped their hands into fists and then blew on their knuckles and looked away into the treetops. And still others were squatted on the ground because hunger had overcome them and they couldn't stand up anymore. When the lid bounced up a little from the bubbling steam, and the aroma of bracas filled the air, their little noses wiggled and some of them ran their tongues over their lips. But there was no bitterness in any of them.

Panggul walked to the kettle and the children's eyes followed him. They glued their eyes on his hands as he lifted the bracas from the pot and put it on palm leaves on the ground. The children watched him throw a handful of rice into the kettle and then their eyes went back to the fish, loving it, caressing it.

Someone in the village had come by a set of metal plates. When they were brought out, Panggul placed the plates on the ground in front of us and served up the rice. When all the rice was out of the pot, there was still water in the bottom and he poured a little of it over the rice on each plate. Then he turned and cut the fish into seven parts with his mandau, leaving the bones inside for any one of us who wanted to eat them, too.

We were squatted on the ground, bent over our metal plates like animals, and began to eat nosily and wolfishly because we were expected to.

The Dyaks smiled and nodded at one another. The children watched each bite raised from the hand and carried to the mouth, and then looked into our eyes to see what emotion registered there. They were pleased that their fish had been found acceptable by our group.

The fish crackled under the men's grinding teeth because they had decided to chew up the spine, and when they swallowed, their throats flexed with exaggeration.

The oil from the fish had left a little grease ring around Sjam's mouth, and she licked at it with her tongue before she tossed another bite into her mouth. She worked her lips and tongue to separate the bones from the meat and then spat them into the fire, and some of the children saw it and sucked in their breaths and their eyes flashed with a fresh fever of hunger.

Panggul ate noisily but slowly. He chewed the same wad of rice over and over, not wanting to let it go until the last minute, and then his throat convulsed with the swallowing of it. When he was nearly finished, there was a piece of fish that lay untouched on his plate, and he scowled at the indecision of eating it himself or leaving it for the children. Finally he made up his mind, put his plate down on the ground in front of him, and got up and walked away. The little piece of fish was still on his plate.

We slept well that night.

Some days are meant to be great days, because of some joyous event capable of making that day worth remembering for the rest of one's life. The greatest days occur when nobody's looking. And life had planned this day to be great.

The morning came in yellow and hot. The sun sent down a golden glow and burned the grasses with its heat. It was time for the village to get up, but no one had stirred in the witch doctor's shack. The soldier lay sprawled on the floor next to the policeman, who had made himself a little nest out of the doctor's magical leaves, and Panggul was still asleep, curled up in the corner with his head resting on a root.

I pulled myself off the floor and struggled up to tiptoe to the door of the shack and look out over the day.

Standing in the middle path of the village was an old, old woman in a dirty sarong, holding a little boy by the hand. She was tiny, four feet maybe, and dried up with age, like a skeleton wrapped up in a cover of brown tissue paper. Her face was braided with wrinkles and streaked with dirt, and her black hair was matted together in little knots and snarls. Strings of skin roped her chin to her throat, and above her cheeks were heavy blue veins that ran into her temples. Her cheeks were sunken into deep coves beneath her eyes, and her mouth had shriveled into a tiny slit, running with red juice from a betel nut.

Although she was very old, she was still curious. She looked around everywhere and, from where I stood, she was apparently looking with nearly blind eyes. Her eyeballs were covered over with a little brown pigment, and a thick gray film lay on the irises.

She held her head high as though she was listening to the village talk to her and wanted to hear every word that it said. The boy was listening too. He was wearing a shirt and pants cut off at the knees. His short black hair sprouted from a head that was pathetically bony.

The woman relaxed her hold on the boy's hand long enough to scratch the palm of her right hand with the fingernails of her left, and the black tattooed bands of five-pointed stars on her wrists contrasted sharply in the morning sun. Her tattoos told on her. She was the daughter of a Dyak Iban chieftain.

She replaced the boy's hand in her own and cast a determined look in the direction of the witch doctor's shack. And then she opened her red-stained mouth as wide as she could and yelled: "Panggul!"

When Panggul heard his name, he rose straight up in one movement. He leaped into the doorway and looked down at the little woman in the middle path, and then he threw his head back and roared with laughter because the happiness he felt was one that laughing could symbolize.

The old woman squealed with delight when she saw Panggul, and pinched her eyes shut for fear of losing that delight. Little tears were squeezing themselves out through the shut lids, and when they found their way down her cheeks, she brushed at them with the back of her hand in annoyance.

Panggul hollered, "Is my mother and my son!" and jumped to the ground.

They raced to greet each other and loved the race because it was a part of an act that would bring them together. And when they met in the middle path, they screeched like peacocks. They hopped about excitedly in the dirt, their arms wrapped around each other in a happy madness, and their hopping and screeching brought every Dyak running from his shack to see what was happening.

When the people saw the trio, the older Dyaks smiled at each other and nodded knowingly, and the few young mothers of the village held their sons a little closer to their breasts. By watching the ecstastic moment, the Dyaks captured a little of it for themselves.

Without shame Panggul had blushed red with the passion he felt for his family. And then, suddenly, a shyness seized him and made him cry a little with strangling tears.

There was so much to say, so much to tell, but there was no beginning and no place to start, and it left them feeling about in the air for words.

Panggul had not seen his mother, Tewah, or his son, Nangi for two years. Tewah suddenly remembered this unforgivable record, and then all kinds of words came spilling out, singeing Panggul's chin whiskers. "Where have you been! Why don't you come home? Are you not interested in us anymore? You naughty boy, you don't love us! Look at your son! He is already a grown man!"

Panggul's spirit burned from the whipping she gave him, and he suffered a little from the smarting truth of it. Tewah grinned a forgiveness and her eyes crinkled up at the corners. Panggul's eyes laughed a little with pride and affection and took on a soft, shy look. He put his arm gently around his mother's shoulder and took his son by the hand, and together they slowly picked their way over the middle path and into the witch doctor's shack. Tewah could not see the path with her old eyes and had to feel it with her feet. When they climbed up the ladder and into the shack, the witch doctor greeted them warmly and enthroned Tewah upon an old root.

Tewah had arrived at the remarkable age of one hundred and seventeen, she thought. The Dyaks divide their year into fifty full moons, but if the moon didn't shine during one of their months, then that month didn't count. Everyone kept track of his own age, and hardly any two Dyaks ever agreed on anything that had to do with moons and months.

Tewah could not remember where she was born except that it was a place where great white fish swam in a great blue sea. It is probable her birthplace was near the China Sea, an area familiar to the Ibans.

Tewah was a member of a family blessed with so many children that their number escaped her. When one of her brothers surprised everyone by earning his Trophy of Victory with his next door neighbor's head, she married him at the age of ten. The pair set off for Hirin, a village north of the Mentaja, where they reared eight children including Panggul.

Panggul was born in Hirin, grew up in Hirin, and, as a Dyak Iban amid the Dyak Ngadjus, he married a Dyak Ngadju girl from Hirin. The girl died in childbirth when Nangi was born, and Panggul never recovered from the pain of it.

Nangi was now a sixteen-year-old "man," married and already the father of a baby girl. He had waited nearly two years for Panggul to return to Hirin, and when he was tired of waiting, he convinced Tewah they should set off to find his wandering father. They traveled south on the Tjempaga River and then walked the short-cut through the jungle to Kuala Kuajan, where the Dyaks in Pelanko told them that Panggul had taken a "big white fish" into the northern country. Both of them were mildly amused at a big canoe-boat they had seen in Kuala Kuajan because it made all kinds of noises whenever it wanted.

A little congress began to gather itself together as the Dyaks of Telawang moved in through the doorway of the shack, and the witch doctor pushed his herbs and branches back against the walls so that the people could sit down. The men squatted on their hams and bent their arms over their knees, and the women sat behind the men with their naked little children at their sides. A small fire burned in the center of the shack and sent out sputtering sounds from time to time, lighting the faces of the Dyaks.

Panggul hugged his knees and squatted beside Sjam so he could translate, and Nangi sat next to his father and leaned his head against Panggul's shoulder.

The chairman of the little congress was Tewah. The witch doctor had pulled her root into the middle of the room, and she sat down on it and thrust her legs straight out in front of her because her age wouldn't let them bend anymore. Her nearly blind eyes reflected the light of the fire and burned like black flames in her face.

The mood for the meeting was already set. Some great sorrow hung in the air that had no words. Tewah had hungered for someone to talk to about it all her life. Now, suddenly, life had heaped an unexpected audience upon her and she was going to make the most of it.

When she began her speech it was hard to make out what she was saying, and even Panggul had a difficult time of it. Then her voice became stronger, as though from practice, and the words were clear and meaningful. Tewah's message was one of love for her people and a demand that simple justice be given to them. "So, the Big White Fish has found that we are not unprincipled, vicious headhunters who are reigned by cannibal kings and living in a galaxy of native kingdoms!"

Panggul raised his head to look into the old eyes of his mother, and a pain and bewilderment moved over his face for a moment. And then he nodded and placed his forehead against his knees. When he looked up, his dark eyes were half closed and he stared into the fire, brooding.

"Oh no! We're not simple savages and never have been! It is true that our tribes are no longer as strong as they were once, but we are still a great people and proud of ourselves!

"Don't think we have always lived like this. When I was a little girl, my family followed the game and we hunted in jungles that were rich with fruits and wild grains and we fished in waters full of fish. We lived to enjoy a hundred years of good life. We didn't have houses because we didn't need them, and we didn't have to live in our own filth because the jungle was open and clean.

"When the newcomers invaded we ran from them until they encircled us and we couldn't go any farther. The newcomers wanted too many things for themselves. They still want them and they'll get them. Riches, possessions, positions, status, dainty delicacies that don't worry the Dyak. You know what we want? We want land to give us food!

"Now our people are dying. We bury our dead because they've starved to death or were sick without medicine. We've lost our middle generation and this is a concern that is frightening to all of us because by it we face tribal extinction and we know it.

"We must find someone who cares about the Dyak people, someone who will teach us how to live on this land. That's what we have to do!"

Tewah closed her lips tightly and her blind eyes were as fierce as a monkey's. She had run out of breath, but not out of dreams. At the age of one hundred and seventeen, she had maintained that remarkable gift of looking over the edge of a misery in the present and into a hope that lay somewhere in the distance of a tomorrow.

It would take three days by canoe to reach Kuala Kuajan. The natives of Telawang wanted to be sure we had a proper send-off, so they had been brewing tuak for several days.

I admired tuak on a few prior occasions and I was grateful for the hospitality that had gone into its making in Kuluk Telawang, but I was skeptical that it would improve one's condition if he was recovering from ill health.

A tribe that can produce good tuak is regarded as having achieved an accomplishment of the highest in nature and is given a reputation that is enjoyed for the lifetime of that tribe.

There is a special kind of coconut tree that grows in the Borneo jungles and produces a coconut able to give the milk that makes tuak possible. Although all coconuts looked the same to me, you may accept that the Dyaks know the difference.

When the milk is extracted, it is placed in the hot sun for about ten days, and during those days the heat performs all kinds of miracles and the milk transforms into something whitely foaming and often revolting both to the eye and to the taste.

The Dyaks calm the fermented liquid down with river water and add the juice squeezed from *sawang* leaves if they have it.

By now the drink is thick and still white, and if one blows on it, little wrinkles form up and pile on top of each other until that blowing stops.

When you drink tuak, you always drink alone because the Dyaks want to watch you and study your reactions. Not everyone drinks, because there is just not enough to go around to produce the effect desired, and it is better to have one person really drunk than many touched to only a mild silliness.

The Dyaks do not drink for fun; they drink to get drunk and it is not very often. If it happens once in every five years, then the impression must be registered strongly enough to give them something to talk about for those empty middle years.

It is impossible to hold tuak under the nose and breathe at the same time. If one is not overcome by the odor, then the tiny mosquitoes hatching out of it are sucked into the lungs through the nostrils.

And it is impossible to sip tuak because the Dyaks will not allow it. If there are no cups in the village, then you are given a coconut shell to drink from, and the Dyaks chant in unison, "*Oi, oi, oi, oi, oi,*" until every drop has been drained from the shell.

And then the shell is filled again and passed to someone else, who, out of politeness, never wipes the rim before he drinks.

Tuak has its own edge and it never loses it. The first shellful produces a little humming in the head right away, and from there on things get more serious.

There are three magic words, "*minum untuk saja,*" (drink for me) which can help a person get through an evening with dignity. They are said to the person sitting the closest.

Usually it is an older woman who has spent her whole life waiting for a sip to be passed her way, and when she receives it, she is usually disappointed.

At the farewell celebration, tuak had made Panggul a happy man, and he took that happiness and gave it to everyone in the room. He stumbled around in the shack, not because the tuak was deadening, but because it had made him forget he was walking. He sang songs as long as he could remember that he was singing and he sang them in a voice that was sweet and high and it sighed like a little breeze whispering through the trees.

And he was still singing when we set off for Kuala Kuajan the next morning.

Chapter Ten

The Initiation

It's never dull to talk about the weather in Borneo because of its great eccentricities. There are two or three rules to remember about that tropical climate. The first is that the rain is seasonal. It arrives in early October and departs in late March, a period called the "rainy season." There are no summers or winters, but there is a "dry season," and it comes along in April and lasts until September.

The second rule to remember is that the closer one gets to the equator, the wetter he can become.

The third rule is to forget the first two. Rain can arrive weeks early, weeks late, or not at all.

The current "dry season" had so far furnished us with two thunderstorms and a flood. The rain last night had sallied forth with unbelievable energy, and, to have been out in it and unthinkingly drawn a deep breath, one would probably have drowned.

The grass on the riverbank in Kuala Kuajan was still glistening with last night's raindrops, but Panggul was sitting on it anyway. There was a struggling expression on his face, as though he was trying to keep some kind of a secret to himself, one that was too slippery to hang onto much longer. He had decorated himself up a bit. An elegant anggang feather was stuck behind his ear, its horizontal white stripe blazing in the morning sunshine.

When Panggul saw us stirring about on the houseboat, he stood up, hurled his hands about in the air above his head excitedly, and motioned for us to join him. *"Pagi,"* morning, he said as we neared him.

He had wrapped a rattan headband around his brow to keep the feather in its place, and the band had pushed his black hair nearly halfway down his forehead, making his eyes appear darkly mischievous. There was an unusual sense of nervousness about him. He picked his mandau out of its sheath and abruptly began whipping it about through the grass in short little strokes, secretly staring at us.

The Dyaks are excellent at staring secretly. It is done with their eye corners. They can memorize every fragment of you, note the color of your eyes, count nearly every hair on your head, and offer a graphic and accurate accounting of your entire person to anyone interested, and all the while you thought they did not know you existed. It disarms a person once he discovers the sharpness of the Dyak eye.

Panggul dropped his glance and looked around for a dry spot in the grass where he could put his mandau, but there was none, so he held it in his lap.

Sjam and I were curious and we desperately wanted to help Panggul get on with whatever he had on his mind. But we had learned long ago that one never rushes a Dyak into anything, so we simply waited.

Panggul leaned forward and picked up a little stick to play with and then he bent it. The stick snapped and he threw the two pieces away, folded his hands together, and rubbed one thumb against the other. He sighed deeply, lowered his eyelids, and his long black lashes threw little spikelike shadows on his cheeks. Well, it appeared that he had given it up entirely.

He sucked in his lower lip and opened his mouth to make a beginning, but it was a false start. He ran dry in the middle of it. He threw up his hands, shook his head from side to side, laughed out loud, and suddenly the message blurted out. "My people are humble people. They not ask much of world. But tonight they ask make you Dyak woman. They want make you and Jmy member of Dyak Iban tribe. Iban belian come. He come with Dyaks from Nagarum. They make ceremony for you."

Panggul stretched his arms across the little patch of grass between us, holding his mandau in his hands. It signified the surrender of his tribe's weapons. "Wear mandau tonight. Now, go away from village. Come when sun behind tallest palm tree."

The relief that Panggul felt was so great that he could hardly wait to get away from us.

I looked at the mandau he had put in my hand. It was heavy, about three feet long, and lethal. The mandau gave a seriousness and profundity to the occasion. I wondered why these natives wanted to accept Jmy and me into their tribes. The forces of Dyak tradition run strong and deep. To include an outsider was unethical to them. It would cut into the Dyak's view of himself, his tribesmen, and his own environment.

Years later I learned that the Dyaks had simply wanted to leave a record of themselves on my life. Life to the Dyak is basically unreal and it remains unreal until he proves that he does, or did at one time, exist. The Dyaks believed that I would register their history and testify to their existence by becoming a member of their tribe and, in this case, a Dyak Iban woman.

Over the years I became a member of seven different tribes in the Mentaja area: Iban, Katingan, Kahajan, Sahiei, Sabaung, Duhoi, and Malahoi.

(Technically, the above are classified as clans or sects. Today, due to their limited numbers, the natives consider themselves as members of "tribes.")

In 1969 I became a member of the Dyak Mentaja through the efforts of the tribe's one remaining survivor. In 1970 the native died and the Mentaja sect became extinct, unless someone wants to count me.

It was flattering that the Dyaks believed that through my tribal membership they might gain an inch in their history.

While Panggul and his pals planned the festivities for the tribal initiation in Kuala Kuajan, Abdul, Sjam, Jmy, and I borrowed a canoe and paddled off toward Bawan.

Bawan was a favorite village of mine, although the Dyaks living there were in very bad shape. They had become a part of their own landscape of starvation, sickness, and disease in which everything was conditioned by everything else. They were great people because they did not ask for a handout from their prosperous Kuala Kuajan neighbors, but pathetic because they were dying from the pride of it.

The newcomers got fat on rice and fish while the Dyaks starved to death on tree bark and grass. The contrast between the sassy Kuala Kuajan people and the skinny Bawan natives was so shocking that it bruised one's conscience to see it.

Ideas about social humanism and tribal nationalism began to funnel their way into the back of my mind, and, although I didn't know it at the time, those ideas were the nucleus of a plan that would someday teach the Dyaks how to live self-sufficiently on their land. Later the plan materialized into an "impossible dream" and still later a dream come true.

When we arrived in Bawan, we were startled by the crippling silence that hung over the village. There was an odd sense of vacancy about the straggly huts on the bank. "Where is everybody?" Jmy whispered.

Somewhere in the village a baby cried a tiny cry.

"Over there!" Jmy pointed to the last shack on the path.

"Perhaps you'd better wait here," Sjam said. "I can send Abdul."

"No, we'll all go. Their welcome mat is out."

Dyak house ladders are carved from tree trunks and they are two-sided. They have both a smooth and a step side. A house will welcome or discourage a visitor with its ladder, depending on which side is faced outward.

We climbed into the house and peered into the dark one-room shack. Sitting in the middle of the room was Ingan. Beside him lay the body of a young man.

Ingan jumped up and came forward, wringing his hands, and, with a voice stretched tight, choked out, "My son! Ukung is dead!"

Ingan's eyes were staring past us, off into the river somewhere, filled with an expression of incomprehension that more pain should intrude upon his world already filled with pain. "Two days ago he fine. He happy with new bride, Napiah. Then fever come. He burn up."

Ukung's body lay on the floor, naked except for a gray-white cloth that had been wrapped around his hips. His face was blackening beneath his eyes and his flesh was thinning to transparency.

Ukung, strong, handsome, marvelous Ukung. Ukung, who had carried his Key of Life to his bride's door just weeks before, was dead.

No one in the shack wept. Each person closed himself off from the other and from the dead boy and wrapped himself up in his own little house of pain and sorrow.

Napiah squatted in the corner, dry-eyed, quietly drawing pictures on *djendjuang* tree leaves with part of a bamboo stylus. When the leaves were finished, they would hang over the door of the shack while the body was prepared for burial. As long as they were there, no one would be permitted to enter the shack.

A young Dyak trudged into the room holding a thick, spiny-rind and custardlike fruit, durian. He hung it over Ukung's body. The strong odor of the fruit would overtake the smell of the decomposing body, at least, for a while.

"The men are talking about what kind of coffin to make," Sjam said. "Poor people! They want to have a *kakurung* casket but they can't. They will probably settle on the *runi*."

The kakurung is a square box with an opening at one end. The body is doubled over with the head resting on the feet and then shoved into the box. The Dyaks believe that the feet can walk the soul, which lives in the head, straight into the Fourth Heaven. But Ukung was a full grown Dyak and a big boy and his body would require a very large piece of wood for this type of coffin. The manpower shortage and lack of food in the village would make the kakurung an impossibility. The men would cut enough wood for a *runi*, tie the sides together with rattan strappings, and hope that it would be good enough to get Ukung into the First Heaven on his own.

The most important thing to know about a Dyak funeral is the extensive tribalistic tradition that must accompany it. We had seen some of this tradition in Sapiri, a little more in other villages, and we were to see much more. Sometimes the embellishment that goes along with these affairs is confusing and difficult for the Westerner to understand, but the Bawan Katingan tribe lived by these ritualistic traditions. They are good for the natives because they are what this tribe does and what this tribe is.

We left the shack, stumbled down the ladder, and passed a bamboo stick that had been filled with water and placed at the entrance of the house. The message proclaimed a death. Anyone interested in knowing who had died was invited inside to see the body.

Abdul rushed up and said, "Look! An egg! I think Panggul sent it to the chief of this village. It means a guest from far away will be celebrated. You!"

"Then Panggul has invited the people of Bawan to the ceremony tonight."

"Yes! I will give it to the second chief and then we'd better be getting back. It's four o'clock and the sun is nearing the palms."

Sadly we turned our canoe around and headed back

downstream toward Kuala Kuajan as a gentle rain began to mist the hot air.

"Mom, look! There's a rainbow!"

Jmy pointed to the multicolored arch that sprang across the jungle sky.

"Stick your finger in your mouth, Jmy."

"Why?"

"It will erase your pointing at the rainbow. The Dyaks believe that if you point your finger at a rainbow, then you hate the angels!"

We drifted down the river and watched the sky begin to prepare itself for the incredible beauty of a jungle sunset that invariably adds a miraculous serenity to the strangeness of the land.

"Here they come!"

Paddling toward us, whooping and hollering with holiday energy, were seven Dyak men in a barkwood canoe. Most of them were costumed and war-painted.

The damong (religious teacher) stood in the helm of the canoe, quite puffed up with importance even though his role was not one of glorification. He had no magical powers of his own but he was a good master of ceremonies. He had woven *bebasal* roots into bracelets and had wrapped them around his wrists and ankles and had covered his naked chest with a *sangkarut* vest. The outfit was made from *tengang* tree bark and shaped like a *haruai* bird. It was a fancy costume but sadly missing its tail, which had been left behind in Tumbang Ngahan in all the excitement.

Mid-river, we joined the gang in their welcoming canoe and Panggul asked me to sit in front of the Rice God Messenger (Hambaruan Samenget Gangan). The man was frightening because his eyes were as black as soot and he had painted large charcoal circles around them.

Without warning of any kind, he abruptly took a deep breath, opened his mouth, and shrieked out the *mangandjak*, which was a shattering "*Lu-lu-lu-lu-lu-lu-lu eeeeeeeeeee-*

yyyyyeeeeeeoooooowwwwww" victory cry. It makes for a good send-off and certainly lifts the spirit of things, but it is an unforgettable experience if one is seated directly at the man's anterior.

The damong's assistant (Mantir Basara) had decorated his face and chest with charcoal drawings in spiraling designs, making him look wildly ferocious. The ferociousness was heightened somewhat by a long mane of black hair that hung over his eyes like that of a prairie horse.

The other Dyaks in the canoe, although not quite so colorful, were in party dress of one nature or another. They had all painted themselves to some extent, and a few of them had even found seeds and shells to tie around their necks. It was a highly decorated group.

"Good news!" Panggul said. "Dyak Katingan come from Pelanko. You be member two tribe! We should kill water buffalo! This very big ceremony. But no have buffalo. Iban belian ask people permission to kill water buffalo. This same thing. Almost. Make people very happy we ask. All O.K. with gods now."

The Dyaks hooted excitedly among themselves until we rounded the bend at the Kuajan River, and there Kuala Kuajan issued into view, wedged in its own jungle growth.

The village's most recent founders, the Indonesian Moslems, stood on the riverbank dressed in their finest outfits. Their lace overblouses and high-styled sarongs struck a dramatic contrast to the shabby, seminaked Katingan Dyaks who had walked up from Pelanko and who now clotted themselves together at the far end of the village. The newcomers' "we" group could be sharply distinguished from the Dyaks' "they" group from a mile away and not only from their dress. The major determinant of the "we" group was found in numbers and the distinction was mordant.

When the long canoe docked, we climbed the ladder and stepped into the village. The Pelanko Dyaks rushed to greet us. Panggul turned around and motioned for me to fasten the mandau around my waist. I fumbled about in the darkness, found the turtle-shell clasp, and after a few tries tied it on upside down.

The damong bounded forward, twittering as he came, welcoming us to the village, talking, and all the while smearing our faces with a rice powder that had been spiked with hot pepper.

There was a rustling to the right of us and a dark shadow advanced toward us, the belian. He was awesome.

The authority of this man was so great, it was said, that his word was taken on any subject without question. He was a big man, unusually big for Dyak. Every bit of him was well defined. There were strong lines running from his wide cheeks. The lines cut deeply through the flesh beneath his eyes, which had a coverlet of brown pigment over the whites. His buck teeth protruded from under his upper lip and he couldn't stretch his lips to cover them, although he tried. His hands were hard and his fingernails were as thick as shirt buttons. He wore a red headband that had been ornamented with a plume from the *tingang* bird. The feather was the extent of his ornamentation. Except for a scant grass loincloth he was naked.

He walked heavily toward us, shuffling his feet a little to emphasize his step. There was so much gravity in his manner that the crowd hushed itself into a profound quiet.

When the belian arrived within a few feet of us, he dipped his hand into the enormous seashell he was carrying, and began to sprinkle the ground with blood. As he sprinkled, he chanted the *mantera,* a prayer that was supposedly loaded with magic: *"Aku mahama beras dengan darah manuk, honiku beri tahu Njaring Pampahilep, Djata phoatara dan beri panudju paluut dan beri Gana tanah air di hi, supaja kami ni nada tjaruk ho, mada sakit mahorom dan air nada jaruh njanggau mejeri gawi kami ni seba kami hi manabang dkea tanga."*

"I sprinkle rice and blood to inform Njaring Pampahilep and Djata to inform others of this ceremony and ask them to give us happiness. I sprinkle blood for Gana to ask that the results of our works be not in vain."

He ran out of blood and chant at the same time and stooped to pick up a water buffalo horn that had been propped up against a rock. It was the largest horn I'd ever seen, perhaps three feet long. It had been elaborately decorated with human hair, thick and heavy, cascading to the tip of the horn and past it.

"It filled with tuak!" said Panggul. "All get drunk! Oh, gods very happy, now!"

It is believed that when tuak is *drunk* in a horn from an animal thought of as both sacred and brave, the drinkers, too, are thus symbolized.

The belian pushed the horn into action by drinking from it himself and sending the horn on its rounds. The natives lipped the rim with deep swallows, one after the other, not troubling themselves to wipe the vessel's rim between gulps. It was filled and refilled and when the horn had finally circulated around to me, the hair was quite wet and drippy and a thin film of spittle around on top.

"Mom," whispered Jmy, "are you going to drink it?"

I shut my eyes and lifted the horn to my lips, unhappily recalling a childhood warning, "Never suck out of someone else's straw!" at the same time.

But the Dyaks were right. After the first dizzy swallow, I felt quite brave.

Across the center path of the village the Dyaks had pulled a teakwood log and had decorated it with mandaus and haruai feathers. The belian stomped around behind the log and Panggul and the Dyaks went with him. Jmy and I were left standing alone on the opposite side.

The belian announced, "You cut this *pantan* [log] with mandau to the left, that all dangers and bad luck go. You cut this pantan to the right and bring peace to tribe. You cut this pantan through bottom so that sickness and disaster leave tribe."

It was a big order.

I unsheathed the mandau Panggul had given me, and managed to chop through the teak without damaging myself too much. This effort completed the preliminary Tahutan Pantai ceremony.

The belian reached over and took my hand and steered me toward a bird's egg that lay on the ground. He asked me to step on it. This little ritual was supposed to cast off any evil spirits that might be dwelling on my body or clothing. Compared to cutting through a wood log, breaking the egg was a breeze. I enjoyed the additional prestige of being a *good* person, having smashed the egg completely.

We paraded down the center path in single file into an assembly shack where everybody sat cross-legged on the dirt floor. No one cared very much where he sat, and many found themselves ensconced in betel nut spittle.

The ceremony began with music. It was music of the thinnest sorts because the Dyaks are sadly lacking in musical instruments. This is primarily due to the scarcity of materials and limited technology. But since they don't know this, the self-taught Dyak "musicians" strummed the *ketjapi* and *rabab*, which were squeeky wooden mandolin-type affairs with one or two strings.

But they disappeared quickly when the open-ended drums, *terbang* and *babung*, were brought into the room. The drums were hit with the hand and the noise they made sounded like their names. The terbang is the famous talking drum used by some of the clans for storytelling. The babung is larger and in the hands of an expert it can boom out a message for ten miles around.

Our ears were still ringing when the Dyaks performed their uniquely artistic legacy of dances. They started with the *manasai*, the traditional welcome dance, and the *selendang*, dance of celebration. Neither of these dances had a religious function, but they released the ecstatic feelings of happiness and friendship felt by the people.

The religious *suwantan* dance was enacted to honor returning warriors, although many years have passed since a warrior returned. The steps were extravagant and at times even frenzied. The dance was displayed at this celebration so that the younger generation could see it and perhaps remember it in case they ever needed it.

The *riam pandjang* depicted the passing over an imaginary waterfall, and although the dance was short, it was of special interest to me.

For a finale, I was asked to participate in the *bigal bigal*, a dance of friendship. It was necessary, for one reason or another, to reinforce each step with a substantial sip of tuak. There were many steps, all of them highly complicated, and by the time we finished the dance, we were all great pals.

At this point the belian announced that he would "secure" the village. He turned and marched outside, flailing his arms above his head as he went.

"What's he going to do?" asked Jmy.

"He see if any bad spirits come to village," said Panggul. "Or maybe enemy come. Belian must scare away!"

When the belian returned he was grinning broadly. The grin set free the rumor that all was well. The rumor darted around the room with amazing speed, and in no time the belian felt the flattery of his own importance.

Now the great man stepped up with a large, tuak-filled urn (*balang* or *tadjau*) and stationed it in the center of the dirt arena. (The clay in these urns is mixed with gold dust, and the Dyaks believe that they are made with the help of the Sixth Heaven god. The sculptured dragons that poke through the brown pebbled glaze echo a Chinese influence, but the Dyaks swear that the Chinese imitated them. A native earns his social rank in a village by the number of urns found in his shack. If they are filled with tuak, then he is considered a very rich man.)

"Party goes well," said Panggul, and he flashed his brightest smile. "Many get drunk now!"

And then I saw Ingan. He was sitting at the far side of the room and he was wrapped up in his own house of loneliness.

The Dyaks had given Ingan the social immunity that a man in mourning deserves, but he did appear pathetically deserted. Then he smiled warmly and his eyes brightened suddenly. "I come for you!" he yelled across the room, and his voice had nearly acted without his volition. "Today we lose one Dyak Katingan. But tonight we get one Dyak Katingan!"

It was important to Ingan that he attend this or any celebration that ever happened. He and all other Dyaks scrounged every day of their lives, digging to live, and it left them without amusement of any kind. They needed and hungered for the fun that a ritual and its trimmings would give them. Ceremonies were the brightest spot in the career of any tribe. Nothing could keep the people from them.

One of the pleasures in the ceremonies was found in story-telling. This happened about midway through the evening because it was the best time for the most credibility: most of the Dyaks were drunk.

The legends were told by talented men who planted a tiny seedling of a thought in the minds of the people and then allowed it to sprout by itself. The people listened while the storyteller told his great tale, and through their listening they became great too. The Dyaks peopled their brains from the legends with gods and goddesses, golden snakes and mythical dragons and let them grow and move about until they became real.

One of the finest storytellers in the area was Ingan. "I tell of legend of the crocodile," he whispered. He spoke in rhymes and sometimes in little rhythms but always in words that were meaningful. The effect left the people nodding to each other.

"Long ago, a man-god lived in form of beautiful white crocodile," and the people nodded for they were certain they had all seen a white crocodile at some time in their lives.

"He lived in the waters of the Bulan River. One day there

9. A child's sleeping hammock.

10. Doll used at witch doctor's child-healing ceremony.

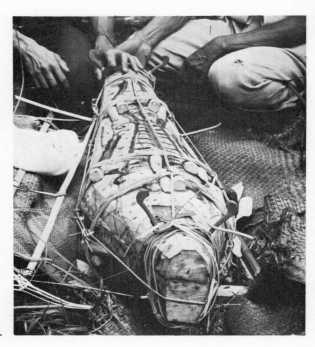

11. A child's casket.

12. Ingan, chief of
   Bawan, and me.

13. Jmy with Nangi.

14. Tewah, Panggul's mother, and me.

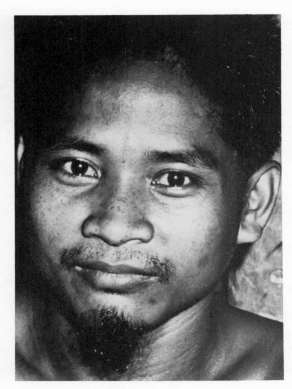

15. Panggul.

16. Sjam.

came a beautiful maiden to river and the white crocodile fall in love. He ask maiden to marry him."

The people listened and were quiet.

"The maiden believe he is only ugly crocodile. She say no, not marry him. This make great heaven-gods angry with maiden. Gods change maiden into big Kajuan Bulan [Moon Tree]."

The people nodded.

"Now maiden grow on banks of Bulan River, forever. She shade unhappy crocodile with her branches. You see crocodile today spinning circles there in waters, in front of tree."

Ingan did not cut or trim the legend into a tightly confined shape because it would ruin a story to finish it up. But all the Dyaks understood from the story that they must forever love and respect wood and water.

Panggul arose suddenly, straightened his good shoulders, and the mood of the ritual changed its face. "Please! You come now," he said.

Jmy and I were marched into the arena's center, where a hassling discussion was going on as to the exact location of the sunrise. When its dubious direction was finally determined, we were seated on brass gongs to face it. The Dyaks believe that Sang Hyang walked on the sun's rays to earth each morning, and they wanted to be sure that the god would notice us on his trip down.

Panggul puckered his brow in deep thinking, rubbed the tips of his fingers together, and wondered what to do next. The belian jerked his head and snapped his fingers. The jerk and snap put Panggul in motion. "Before you Dyak woman, you must agree to laws of Dyaks!"

Panggul droned out his long memorized list of tribal laws that dealt with property, marriage, and inheritance. "One more! If stranger come to village and disturb tribe, stranger get highest punishment. You must kill stranger!"

Somewhere behind me a gong sounded and Panggul wrapped a wild-pig-bone necklace around my neck. It went around three times and it was terribly heavy. One of the

bones dropped down and stuck itself inside my shirt collar
and Panggul took the stretching of my neck to dislodge the
bone as a nod of approval.

The belian descended upon us now, shuffling as he came
because he was armed with amulets and fetishes, heavy as
well as plentiful. He stood before us and searched through
the pile until he came upon two five-inch wooden gods
(Tormorang) and he placed them at our feet.

Instantly two Dyak men wheeled up from the crowd and
stood before them. They bowed in the direction of the belian
and bowed to the gods, and then they pulled out their
mandaus and cut their fingers open! They held their bleeding fingers over the gods, soaking their wooden skin with
their bright red blood. One of the men had taken a noteworthy slice off the top of his index finger which would
probably bring regrets for his enthusiasm later. When the
images were blood-covered, the men retired to the side
lines where they were commended by their friends for their
achievement.

The wooden gods were considered naked until clothed
in human blood. The raiment was urgent because these gods
were to be used as witnesses to the ritual and to glorify
those who performed it.

Suddenly, the amulets and fetishes began to slip out from
the belian's arms. They tumbled onto the floor and spread
themselves out in all directions. A moment of hysteria resulted which left the bewildered belian momentarily robbed
of his self-control. He beat his arms rather helplessly against
his hips and rolled his eyes to the heavens. Then he pinched
his brows together and with a repaired determination he
scraped the magic charms into one heap with his foot.

He looked around as though uncertain as to what to do
next. He was plainly out of practice.

He worked his mouth from side to side as he thought,
and when an idea finally arrived, he ran to a corner of the
room and returned with a small tree, which he shoved
into my right hand. A side sprig from the *saba belum* tree

had been tied to the tree. I was told to point my index finger skyward, against the trunk but beneath the sprig, because this gesture would beckon the attention of the gods. It was no time at all before my finger felt more painful than had it been amputated.

All kinds of notions began to tunnel into the belian's head now, and he acted as though he knew what he was doing. He went about the business nearly feverishly, placing his fetishes here and his amulets there, half running about the task before he was finished.

He stood back and admired his work. He had built a highly complicated and formal arrangement of Dyak junk over, around, and under his two ornaments of the celebration, Jmy and me.

Our feet straddled a large and sharply jagged "sacred" rock. A heavy fish net that smelled of yesterday's catch was wrapped around our waists, and betel nuts, combined with the burning of a strong-smelling wood thought to be incense, burned beneath our noses. On top of all this were the amulets and fetishes.

We were uncomfortable but we were ready.

The room was quiet now. The newcomers were sitting cross-legged on the floor with their hands folded in their laps, and the Dyaks sat with their legs drawn up against their chests. Most of the Dyaks had stretched their arms out to hang over their knees so that their hands dangled loosely and were ready for action. Shining eyes stared at the belian, eyes afraid of missing a movement, gesture, or expression.

The belian looked fearsome. His eyes shot out their own little yellow splinters of fire, and a clever smile was playing upon his lips. There was nothing reassuring about that smile.

The tree proved to be very little protection against the belian's glare. Jmy and I hovered beneath the now quaking leaves and smiled weakly at one another to keep up the other's courage.

The belian gave us a final stare, leaped to the side, and

trotted around the room in a circle. He repeated the circle, and then, midway, he turned, accelerated his speed, and arrived directly in front of us at nearly a dead run. His breath came heavily and he spat to clear his throat and then he threw back his head and howled. "God of Rice! Bring life to inner soul of woman and child!"

The air vibrated. I could hear the belian's breath whistling in his nostrils. He was directly above me but I was afraid to look at him.

And then, without warning, he lunged in through the tree and nearly knocked it over. I felt his hands touch my head and shoulders and throat, and all the time he was muttering little magic spells and humming to himself. His fingers were rough and violent as he rubbed a reddish-brown mud of some kind on my neck and chin. The wet, runny stuff seeped down through my shirt and then ran over my shoulders and arms. Even today I do not like to think about the odor of that "mud."

The belian separated the branches of the tree and stooped in to inspect his work, belched out a few more little magics, and then stood up and splashed tuak over my head and body without restraint of any kind. He repeated the mud and tuak routines, and when he was finished I noted that he had elaborated on both of the procedures.

The belian pitched his voice to a new, high sweetness, allowed an impressive rigidity to sweep over his posture, and then dripped a black oil called *undus* on my head. This oil is not unlike petroleum and serves as a repellent to evil spirits, so it was said. I felt the dark, oily slime travel over my scalp and onto my body, plugging up my ears as it went. The belian rolled his eyes up and chanted as he dribbled the oil on Jmy. When he was through, it was a certainty that no evil spirit would have dared to come near either of us.

A gray-brown haze hung in the room and my vision was becoming unreliable, but I was sure that the pot installed in front of us was filled to the rim with blood. It was black blood, clumped together. The odor that arose from it was sickening and thickly sweet.

The Dyaks stirred a bit and whispered between themselves. Their minds were turning over with curiosity because none of them knew what the belian was up to. Some of the Dyaks sniffed the blood from where they sat, flaring their nostrils at the smell of it.

The belian's eyes had retreated into the red-rimmed hollows of his head. He snatched up a woven palm leaf (*ketupat*) and made a few tentative drills into the lumpy blood. When he was satisfied that enough blood had clung to the leaf he looked up and grinned. He stood up, the blood dripping from the leaf, spat, and started to chant. The chant began as a moan but changed into a scream. In the middle of the second chorus I felt the palm leaf touch my forehead and leave a little clot of blood there. The belian punched the leaf back into the pot, scooped up more globs, and then dribbled blood on my eyes and nose, all the while screaming with energy and color in an effort to bless my life and soul.

He stopped to lick his lips. Then he began his chant again and the blood touched my body here, there, and everywhere, and I thought surely there would be no end to it until I realized that the chant had stopped and the blood bath was over. The red ooze trickled underneath my shirt and jeans, each trickle making its own little river path. When the clots moved, they tickled and some of the clots moved faster than others and still other clots mashed themselves between my clothes and skin.

One glance from Jmy told me that I looked more baneful and villainous than any headhunter who ever lived.

Now the belian was tying *mali mali* leaves on the feet of an anggang with small lengths of rattan. The bird was squawking in violent protest because his fingers were impolite and commanding. When the feet were secured, the belian put the bird on the floor and unsheathed his mandau, gently fondling the blade with his fingers. He let his thumb run the full length to test the sharpness of the edge and then laid it on the floor near the bird.

The belian grabbed the bird by its tied feet, swung it up into the air and held it over my head. Something wet and blue dripped out of the bird's mouth and fell on my hair. The bird and I looked at one another and I'm not sure which of us was scared the most.

Then the belian sputtered out the endless words of the *bakart haringan,* the Dyak magic formula that would make me a member of their Iban and Katingan tribes. The song had only four notes, but it was filled with a variety of vocal inflections and innumerable intervals. And all the while the belian was waving the tied anggang back and forth, to and fro, over my head. Only once did he stop chanting, more from a feeling of loneliness in the long song and to look at others in the room than to catch his breath.

There was a dark secrecy building up in his eyes, a secrecy that leaked through into his voice, then the chant became intimate: *"Mahpasku njiwa, njiwa semanja burung iang dawai, mahpasku ngatau, ngatau huesnu tuah ukui, mahpasku kalowa, lowa smeni burung iang dawai, mahpasku keatau, keatau semanja teung beta, supaja hidup majamn djandji iu!"*

"Spirits, spirits who make mountains tremble, spirits who make rivers flood, I wave live blood to the right, I wave live blood to the left, I hold live blood before you, white woman, obligating you to me, forever!"

I was wondering what "obligating you to me, forever," was meant to entail, but before I could give it much attention the belian was off, sputtering another verse. His words came weakly now, falling off at the ends, and soon the chant became nearly beyond hearing. He coughed, attempted a fresh start, but his voice was gone for good.

I was happy the chant was over. The blood, the singing, and the swinging bird had all presented the light vagueness of a terrible nightmare. When I looked at the little woven grass mat under the belian's feet, a clump of blood fell from my forehead and splashed on my hand and then the crisscrossed design in the mat jumped before my eyes.

The leaves on the little tree rustled, and Panggul thrust his face in and said, grinning, "You almost Dyak woman, now!"

Suddenly the anggang screamed shrilly. The belian had wrapped his fingers firmly around the struggling bird's neck and he had stapled its head to the floor with one hand. The bird's beak was open and a drip of dark fluid dribbled out of its mouth and wet the dirt floor. Its eyes bulged as it tried to turn its head from side to side in an effort to free itself. All the while its wings batted and flapped around on the floor.

The belian picked up his great mandau, jerked it skyward, and then let it fall upon the bird, and with one heavy blow the bird's head flew into the air and the anggang lay dead.

The belian looked with detachment upon the bright red blood that shot in little spurts from the hole in the neck. He put his mandau on the floor and positioned the bird over a coconut shell that had a little rice in the bottom. The belian held the shell as though it was some kind of beautiful jewel. He let the blood run into it until it was nearly half full. Then he stuck his index finger to the bottom of the bowl and stirred the rice and blood together. When they were well mixed, he formed rice balls on the side of the shell with his fingers.

The belian raised his fingers to his head, searching for a patch of unusually long and bristly black hairs, and when he found them, he smiled and all worry seemed to go from his face. He pulled fingerfuls of hairs out of his head and stuck them in the center of each rice ball. The blood in the balls oozed a bit from the movement of the belian's fingers and settled over the hairs, nearly covering them from sight.

And then, with red-crusted fingers, the belian shoveled up a bloody clump, aimed with a fine accuracy, and popped the blood ball into my mouth! I swallowed. The blood passed down easily enough. But the hair seemed to stick.

It was over. I felt flattered. But tousled and faint. The room began to spin and Jmy became concerned over my fading appearance. He poked me softly with his elbow. "Gee, Mom!" he whispered. "Don't you want to be a head-hunter?"

Chapter Eleven

The Flying Dead

Panggul had stalled around as long as he dared. There are limits to everything, and if we didn't leave soon, he knew our suspicions would be raised to an even higher peak.

The two canoes were ready to go. We had packed them with foodstuffs and other supplies the minute the morning sun shoved its uppermost edge over the jungle horizon. Now all of us were sitting on the riverbank wondering why we hadn't departed.

The chief of Sungai Hanja had sent his swiftest messenger to invite our group to a village event that was scheduled to begin in three days. Panggul described that event as "something quite special" and refused to talk about it anymore. And then he became moody. Last night found him rarely speaking, and this morning he was taciturn and silent.

He stood on the bank far above us and heaped up little mountains of dirt with the side of his foot or inquired about the condition of the earth with his fingers. His eyes were clear from sleep but not calm. It was as though Panggul was carrying a little cloud of fear about with him, filled with the foreboding of some coming misfortune. There was a little terror in him and it wrestled with his duty to take us to Sungai Hanja.

The little fear cloud folded itself over his heart and pinched, and when it did Panggul pulled his neck between his shoulders and looked around for something that could divert his attention. He examined his hands, cleaned his fingernails with the tip of his mandau, and when they were as clean as he could get them, he hid his hands behind his back as though to keep them out of trouble.

His hands were jerked back into action when a wave of itching touched his foot, and he doubled over to scratch between his dry toes.

And then his fingers picked up a twig, and he drew his ideas on the ground in front of him. Impatiently he broke the stick in two pieces and put his face in the palms of his hands. He pulled his thumbs down over his closed eyes and slowly shook his head from side to side.

When he lowered his hands, he twisted his neck around to steal a glance at us and he blinked and heaved a deep sigh. Panggul stood up. He straightened his shoulders, pressed his lips together in a tight, fine line, and started off toward the river. At the bank he stooped to pick up a flat, round stone, which he skipped across the water.

He stood at the top of the embankment a long time, legs spread and pulling at his knuckles before he crawled down the ladder and out into the river. He cupped his hands under the water and threw water on his face, hair, and over his back. He rubbed his hands together, dropped back a little, shook his hands, and then, balancing on the balls of his feet, he climbed the bank and approached us warily.

He looked with inquiring eyes at our group, and as he searched our faces for some answer that he needed, he rubbed a little handful of dirt between his palms and then let it drift through his fingers.

Panggul elapsed into a protective smile and spoke. His voice was delicate and shy. "We go see flying dead, now."

Dyak canoes are mathematically constructed to provide a guaranteed discomfort to the passenger. They are made from ironwood, a wood harder than nails, and for the most part they are crudely whittled and left splintery.

Two small canoes can be made from a single tree trunk, sliced down the middle and scooped clean. A canoe large enough to seat seven people is made from two pieces of lumber, held together in the center seam with natural asphalt, and the interior is sharply pointed at the bottom. There are no seats of any kind, but a raft of bamboo splits is sometimes thrown across the base upon which the Dyak sits cross-legged to paddle.

When one sits cross-legged in a canoe, he may depend never to uncross his legs for the rest of the day. He is hemmed in by the fellow sitting in front. One whole day traveling on the river can be an unforgettable and painful experience.

A canoe traveler may expect, sooner or later, to fall into the river at least once while living in the jungle. This morning it was my turn. In the excitement of things, I inadvertently stepped on an untied log, spun around, and fell into the water. Apart from a momentary loss of dignity, one suffers the discomfort of sitting in wet clothes for a while because no one changes clothes in Borneo simply because they are wet.

And at the same time I was trying to learn how to wear a mandau. The weapon, along with a sumpitan, had been given me at the initiation ritual. Sjam, seated directly behind me in the canoe, received the news that I was wearing it when the knife struck her a deadening blow on the leg.

The river hurried our canoes along with its own excitement. The water chattered happily as it splashed over the stones in its path and little ripples whispered at the sides of the mudbanks.

Puffy popcorn clouds sailed around in a sky turned blue with late morning, and gay, pleasant smells stole secretly up from an earth that was nearly choked with green grass and bushes. The trees leaned against each other for support and then joined branches at the top to spread an umbrella ceiling of foliage over the tangled undergrowth among the trunks.

There are not many flowers in the Borneo jungle, but the *lilis* was in bloom and its dazzling whiteness seemed to burn the air around it.

Anggangs, in cliques of three and four, coasted overhead, flapping their huge wings and stretching their necks around to get a better view of the land. They honked at each other, and when they saw our canoe they honked at us.

A crocodile navigated grandly about our canoe and left us with a feeling of dismay at its closeness. The reptile rose high on the surface of the water, stared about with its slitted yellow eyes, and sniffed the air once before it sank into the river, leaving rings that widened on the water until they were lost.

An enormous brownish-red *depang*, sister snake to the python, slipped from a warm trunk where it had been dozing and slid magnificently into the water. It floated out to the canoe, reared up its periscope head to look at us, and then wiggled away.

The day bugs, flies and winged beetles, flew around us in little clouds, humming monotonously in the hot air. They veered toward the canoe and struck us with their soft bluntness before they turned and droned on down the river.

The members of the expedition were in high spirits. The soldier and policeman, although both of them were duty bound, seemed to be enjoying the adventure. Abdul had resumed his habit of rolling a little stick between his lips and throughout the day he picked his teeth with it. Sjam's face was bright, enthusiastic, and encouraging again, and Jmy could scarcely wait to get wherever we were going.

The only restive heart lay in Panggul's breast, and none of us knew why. His eyes were wrinkled in rays around the corners more from frowning than squinting. He had thrust forward his forceful chin and had set his jaws tight.

In the late afternoon, an overhead cloud burst open and fat raindrops plummeted downwards and splashed loudly on the river. In a few minutes the cloud moved on and another shadow slid over the earth. We looked up and saw a tingang wheeling itself through a sky colored with the edge of evening. The tingang is as large as an American eagle with black, shiny feathers and a single horizontal white stripe across its tail. The stripe was pinched shut in flight.

"Is Bird of Paradise," whispered Panggul, and his words were edged with pain.

The tingang is intimately connected with the Kaharinjang religion. The bird was chosen by the Dyaks to fly the souls of the deceased into the Seventh Heaven, Paradise. The bird is placed on top of a pole (*pantar*) after a human being has been skewered on the opposite end and buried, hopefully, still alive.

"The Flying Dead" ceremony is called Tewah (also the name of Panggul's mother), and it was this event that we were to see in Sungai Hanja.

The Westerner recognizes the separation between God and Napoleon when he distinguishes between the spiritual and the physical, but no such thing is possible for the Dyak. In the Kaharinjang religion all forms of life are viewed as one, and gods are united to man, heavens to earth, and truth to fiction.

This school of thought allowed the Dyak to take human immortality for granted, and he believes that when a man dies his soul remains unchanged forever.

Souls in Borneo have their own hierarchy, and the order was established for several reasons. The Dyaks wanted the souls of their earthly chiefs to consort with those of other chiefs, and maybe with kings, upon their deaths. And, if a chief had maintained common sense on earth, then it seemed reasonable to believe he would be reliable in heaven. The Dyaks wanted someone there with a degree of importance to whom they could supplicate for their welfare.

Earthly Dyak babies, upon death, are still babies in heaven, crying and wetting, and the old people are still old, ornamentally decorating the heavens as they had on earth.

The Dyaks are not concerned about hell because they have not thought of it. All souls, regardless of sin, age, or society, went to a heaven, joined their ancestors there, met some of the gods, and associated with the souls of long-lost Dyak friends.

Since there was no hell to worry about, the Dyaks devoted their total energies to building the framework of seven different heavens. When they were finished, some of the heavens were complicated and all of them perplexing.

The heavens were gained by souls in the order of one through seven, and this writer found that no two Dyaks ever fully agreed on any one method to enter a particular heaven, but it was a certainty, sooner or later, that every soul could reach at least one of the heavens through manipulations performed by its earthly relatives. How fast the soul traveled and the number of heavens through which it journeyed depended entirely upon those manipulated accomplishments. A truly resourceful human family could jump a soul from the First Heaven into the Seventh in a single ceremony.

When a man died in Borneo, his soul stayed within his body until it was made available to travel. The Dyaks prepared the soul for its trip with dances, fire play, a sacrifice (human or otherwise), and a coffin. Then they alerted the gods that the soul was ready to go and off it went.

The more elegant the coffin, the better the chance to enter a higher scaled heaven, and every effort was made to bring about the most elaborate coffin possible.

There are fifteen different kinds of woods used to make coffins in Borneo, and one of them is found in the *runi*, which is a square coffin, constructed from six pieces of lumber, and tied together with rattan strappings. Although it is crude, the *runi* ensures the soul it carries a straight passage into the First Heaven.

The *raung* coffin is made from a tree trunk, round and hollow, and the body is pushed into it, feet first. When the ends are sealed with monkey skin, the Dyaks believe that the coffin is capable of taking a soul past the First Heaven and directly into the Second.

The Third Heaven is reached through the use of a *kariring* coffin, which is shaped like a water trough with a flat lid.

But there is no more powerful coffin in all of Borneo than the *kakurung*. It is made of *sappu* wood, in box form, and it holds the body in such a position that the feet rest upon the head. The Dyaks believe that the soul is found in the head and that the feet can walk the soul into the Fourth Heaven. It is every Dyak's dream to be buried in a kakurung.

Dyak babies are entombed in a balsa wood coffin made in two pieces and called a *tambali rang*. Although it is regarded as canoe-shaped by the Dyaks, it looks more like an Egyptian mummy casket. Balsa wood in Borneo is cheap, easily obtainable, and plentiful, and the freshly innocent infant's soul is spirited into the Fifth Heaven without much fanfare because the Dyaks rarely miss using the correct wood and coffin shape for their children.

A rectangular coffin (*rahaung*) is used for those Dyaks killed by another's action. The coffin is bound up tightly with rattan and then covered with asphalt. Although the result is a very heavy box, it prevents the soul from escaping. It is thought that the murdered man's soul will revenge the killer, and every effort is made to maintain tribal peace by boosting the unfortunate's soul into the Seventh Heaven at the earliest possible opportunity.

A canoe-shaped coffin (*riung*), large enough to hold an adult (similar to the coffin we had seen in Sapiri), could supposedly sail itself to the gates of the Third Heaven. The Sapiri Dyaks were certain, however, that with the addition of Bukung dancers and a belian on the spot, the coffin would arrive at the Fourth Heaven for sure.

Whatever the type of coffin, combined with a ritual embellished with fire, dance, and blood, the soul was guaranteed an arrival in one of the heavens, where it remained until such time that it could be dealt with further by its earthly relatives.

The coffin was placed in a grave lined with *tambak* wood, and plans were then made for the Njurat, a ceremony that would elevate the soul at least one full heaven, and hopefully two, regardless of its current position.

The most important thing to remember about a Njurat is that it takes thought and, therefore, time. The Dyak must inventory his possessions or potentials and then pledge a gift within his grasp to the deceased's soul. Since a Dyak doesn't have much and receives far less, the promise to give a gift of value is difficult.

Several years may pass before a Dyak is confident that he can offer any kind of gift. When the gift becomes a certainty, a pole is erected in front of the dead man's house, provided it is still standing, and the beating of drums and gongs summon all the Dyaks from their shacks to make their promises public.

The men line up in front of the pole, and one by one they cut notches in the pole for every chicken, pig, weapon, or human head they vow to deliver to the deceased's soul, and when they are finished they seal their promises with an x carved at the bottom of the list. Then the Dyaks can relax a little because the gifts are not due for collection until the Tewah, the final ceremony.

The Dyaks are aware that once the soul has reached the Seventh Heaven it is automatically liberated and, now free to travel around, it sometimes comes back to the village to take vengeance upon those Dyaks who were stingy at its Njurat. This knowledge encourages the Dyaks into sometimes absurd generosities and occasionally a man will lose all reason and offer the soul one thousand human heads in a single utterance.

Those souls in modest coffins, left in Heavens One through Four, can be pushed into the Fifth Heaven through an elaborate Njurat. In the Fifth Heaven all souls start off on equal footing.

The doors to the Sixth Heaven are opened when the Dyaks stage a cockfight in honor of the deceased. It is not a sport. It is a contest between the Light Forces and the Dark Forces, and the basic structure symbolizes the struggle of life and the conquest over evil. The cocks are not cocks at all, but wild roosters that have been caught running at random through the jungle. When two of them are captured, the contest ensues, provided the Njurat has already been accomplished.

The ideal fighting team should register a white cock and a black cock, but they are very difficult to find. The Dyaks usually correct whatever the situation by dusting the winning cock with white chalk. The dead cock is given to the family of the deceased and the winning cock is killed and eaten by its finder.

And now the soul (*salapuk liau*) is ready for the Tewah, the flight into Paradise.

It was not unusual that we were on our way to one funeral when we encountered another. There are more funerals in the Mentaja than anything else.

The Dyaks are thrilled to have you attend, since they believe that your very presence honors the dead, and they'll promise you almost anything, including things they don't have, if you'll simply come. One such fiesta was taking place in Sepajang.

It was our second day on the river and the afternoon was aging toward evening. The sun had descended behind some tattered little fragments of clouds on fire from its glow. The hot red hues swept through the village of Sepajang and settled around the straggling huts in the narrow bottom of the jungle. There were eight or nine shacks and all of them stood well apart from each other.

We disembarked and climbed the log ladder into the village.

"Dyak Duhoi," whispered Panggul.

There were about one hundred Duhois in the village, and some of them shared shacks with Katingan Dyaks although they did not share the same religious beliefs. Their differences were slight. All of them were Kaharinjang, but when the Duhois practiced their religion, they practiced it Duhoi style.

Most of their ideas were secret and therefore illusive, and while some of their practices were original and dramatic, the others were the same vicious and murderous practices of their Katingan brothers. All of their ideas were valuable to them and surely they would be a duller people without them.

The Duhois described their spiritual architecture in whole patterns of thinking and feeling, and although it appeared distorted and wreathed in nonsense to the Katingans, it was what the Duhois wanted and hoped for.

In the first place, death for the Duhoi was the best time of his life. A man, whether villainous or virtuous in life, became saintly in character upon the stroke of his death. He was immediately thought of as a war hero, and the failure to have participated in battle during his lifetime had nothing to do with it. After death he was regarded as one who had been irreproachably Solonian in village affairs and a loving, forgiving individual to all those who had trespassed against him during his lifetime. To his mother, he instantly became her favorite child, and if he was married, his widow promised to mourn him forevermore. To all the other rewards of death was added that of a trip to heaven at the expense of his earthly relatives. A Duhoi could hardly wait to die.

The spiritual cosmos in which the Duhoi soul found itself was within the same framework of the seven heavens and seven gods peculiar to the Kaharinjang religion. Man was, again, immortal, and in the minds of the Duhois this powerful and psychiatric thought gave safety to the dead and peace and contentment to the living. It was a pragmatic piece of reasoning.

Unlike their Kaharinjang brothers, the Duhois believed that the soul of the deceased passed through *all* of the heavens, and they did not hold to the thought that an elegant coffin could jump a soul over certain heavens and into another. Therefore, they did not use coffins at all.

A dead man was buried in the ground without a casket of any kind and without a grave marker. His body was promptly forgotten, so much so that a Dyak might find himself building a house on the site the following week without knowing it.

Prior to its burial a swatch of hair and a few fingernail clippings were cut from the body, and these items were placed in a wooden chest (*tjupuk*) no larger than a cigar box. This act automatically placed the soul in the First Heaven.

The Second Heaven was gained through a ceremony that offered goods and blood to the gods. These gifts were arranged on plates held by the family of the deceased until they could hold them no longer, and then the belian relieved them by burning the contents in a fire outdoors.

A fire play and blood play elevated the soul to the Third Heaven, and the Fourth Heaven was entered when the tjupuk was placed inside a hole in a nearby tree.

A Njurat, with emphasis on the giving of mandaus (provided there were no beneficiaries), enabled the soul to continue its journey into the Fifth Heaven, and the Sixth Heaven was reached by means of an earthly cockfight.

The Tewah is the final ceremony, and at that time the tjupuk is withdrawn from its hole in the tree, placed in a small ironwood house (*djiwab*), and half buried in the ground. These little houses are scattered around everywhere and they soon become a real nuisance. The houses are not easily seen, and when one is walking through the jungle they are stumbled over and cause serious accidents to the Duhois who forgot they had put them there.

We had arrived in time to see the aftermath of the Njurat. The ritual had been in progress for four days and the people

were tired of it. The Duhois had promised all that they were
going to promise, and the belian, they felt, had chanted
and prayed long enough. They threw him out and then the
roof came off.

The result was volcanic pandemonium. Men, women, and
children paraded out into the village's center path and began to screech and scream and holler, and then they
grabbed at each other and tore one another's clothing and
kept at it until most of the denizens of Sepajang stood
naked.

Dancing broke out and tuak flooded every corner of the
village. The Dyaks drank to the excess with which a Westerner might be familiar, and even the children, brave or
lucky, were included in the drinking.

But whatever the purpose of it all, the people were generally having a good time of it. And they were still having
a good time when we left the village at three o'clock in the
morning.

It was early afternoon, about four o'clock, when we
reached Sungai Hanja. We had heard the Dyaks of the
village long before they issued into view. Their screams
echoed through the jungle for miles around, and little spas-
modic earthquakes were sent up from the pounding of their
running feet.

When we docked, I aimed the camera in the direction of
a group of Katingan and Kahajan Dyaks clumped together
on the high bank. Through the lens I saw a great mass of
something hurtling itself toward us. It did not separate, or
fall apart, but it changed shapes as it came, from circular to
oval and back to circular again. And then it hit the camera,
slopped over onto my face, and fell to the ground, still in
one piece. Blood.

Panggul, sitting in front of me, yelled at the Dyaks, but
his voice was wasted in the screaming from above, and
then another clot fired over the top of the bank and still an-

other, and in no time at all Panggul and I were covered from head to toe with blood.

Panggul threw back his head and roared.

"Is *hadjamuk*," he said. "Dyaks play with blood pies."

Somehow it made sense. In America kids make mud pies, bake them in the sun, and in response to a dare will pretend to eat them. In slapstick comedy, cream pies are often thrown at the luckless individual with the straight man's role. And in Borneo, the Dyaks mix blood with mud and throw the blood pies at each other in pure fun!

When the barrage of flying blood let up a little, we climbed the ladder into the village. An enormous water buffalo lay dead in the center path, decapitated and disemboweled, and on the nearby head flies sat in circles around the animal's still open eyes. The buffalo had been bartered for in Sampit and had spent more than six weeks traveling the Mentaja River on a bamboo raft to Sungai Hanja for its execution. The Dyaks were nearly reduced to madness with the joy of having it there.

The men and the women of the village spent the night before dancing around the animal (*ngandjan*) prior to its slaughter at midnight. Its soul was meant to accompany the deceased's soul to the Seventh Heaven, where it would provide food, supposedly forever.

The village belian, a small man with sloping shoulders and a wisp of black hair sprouting from his chin, was "reading" the Njurat promises on the pole in front of the deceased's house. He fixed them in his mind and then dashed in and out of the shacks to collect the mandaus, plates, food, and animals from those who had promised them.

The coffin was dug up at six o'clock in the evening. The jungle had reclaimed the grave site with crawling tentacles of green vines, but the Dyaks had no difficulty in locating the area. The soil had sunk a little and had left a jagged crack around its mound.

A pair of young Dyak men stepped up to the grave and swung their parangs at the vines. The women pulled at the arms of their children to keep them away from the cutting knives, and a few of the older men hacked their throats clear of mucus in approval.

The crowd fell silent when the knives scraped the lid of the coffin. The eyes of the people dwindled on the dark ground and the men stirred their feet about restively and the children squidged their toes in the dirt. The coffin was buried not more than one foot deep.

The crowd studied the great box as it was lifted from its pit, a raung coffin, and some of the men hurried to give a helping hand even though it wasn't necessary.

The lid was loose, popped up and warped by the heat and rain of the jungle climate. A young Dyak boy with strong hands and slender arms placed the tip of his parang under the lid and the cover fell off to one side and thudded loudly on the ground.

In reflecting back on that moment, the absence of an odor of any kind was a greater shock than the appearance of the corpse. Lying in the bottom of the coffin was a woman, clothed in a now rotted sarong. Her long black hair had come loose from her skull. Her skeleton was covered with a black, filmy substance. There were two little piles of black bones where her feet should have been, and the long bones of her arms lay disjointed at her sides.

Panggul said that the woman had died more than four years ago at the age of twenty. The cause of her death was unknown, but the large jagged hole in the cranium indicated that her death had been other than natural.

The husband of the dead girl stepped forward and scooped up the bones and sarong and put them in a *buia,* a large clay-lined wooden box.

An elderly Dyak woman, perhaps the girl's mother, handed the husband a lighted torch and the strong was set on fire. The woman then turned the hard bones over and over with the point of a parang and the black film sputtered and burned away under the hot flames. When the skeleton was cleanly white the husband transferred the bones to a small clay pot and then carried the vessel to the center path of the village.

The belian jerked forward, chanting as he came, and he threw blood and rice on the clay pot, the ground and on the people standing near him. This offering advised the gods that the bones were in the clay pot, in case they had been inattentive and had not seen the husband put them there.

Two Dyaks stumbled down the path toward us, dragging a large statue (*sapundu*) between them. The sculpture represented something for the onlooker to remember the dead person by, and it pleased the dead's soul as well as secured it favor.

The life-sized figure portrayed a Dutch soldier in uniform. The Dyaks of Sungai Hanja had neither the time nor the inclination to carve up a wooden image of the dead woman, and they had simply stolen an old sapundu from a neighboring village. Dutch soldier sapundus were no longer in style and it would probably not be missed anyway.

The head of an orangutan monkey had been carved beneath the soldier's feet. Monkeys warn man of the approaching enemy and are therefore regarded as friendly. It was always a good idea to have a few monkeys around, whether on earth or in heaven.

The early sapundus were called *sandarans* and they were herculean affairs. Sometimes the Dyaks carved a series of statues (*ambatan*), all friends of the deceased, and placed the group near the sapundu. The sculptor was not concerned with the aesthetic satisfaction of the creation, nor was he motivated by any aesthetic pleasure that other Dyaks felt in looking at the object. He was interested in the *idea* of his subject and to represent its meaning. If a pregnant woman died, for example, it was likely that a statue, pregnant in appearance, would be found in front of her spirit house.

The belian transferred the Njurat promises to the sapundu with his parang and then shook his finger at the dead woman's husband. The waggle put the man in motion, and he picked up the little clay pot of bones and started off toward the jungle. The villagers fell in behind him.

At the end of the march was a newly built *sandun* (spirit house). These houses are built on two, four, and sometimes six pillars, and supposedly there are many human heads buried beneath them. The sandun merges the visible with the invisible by its existence as a shrine. It is meant to hold the bones of the dead and serves as the residence for the soul whenever the soul returns to earth.

The sandun meant even more to the Dyak. Like the sapundu, it gave him the opportunity to display his artwork. Nothing could have been more meaningful than something tied into the Kaharinjang religion, and it was with sap and vitality that the Dyak applied his taste and skill to sculpture on the sanduns. Most of the sculptor's work was found in masks, carved to fill the utilitarian purpose of the soul that lived within the structure. The masks represent a good spirit with greater power than an evil one. It is noteworthy that few masks in Borneo are carved with the intent to evoke fear and awe.

The Dyaks love birds and they carve out flocks of them at a time to perch about on the roofs of the sanduns although they have no magic or religious powers, they are ornamental and musical to the residing soul.

There are no doors in a sandun. The roof lifts off, the clay pot is placed inside the spirit house, and wooden nails close the structure forever.

The belian cast blood and rice around the sandun to alert the gods that this step had been completed.

And then Panggul disappeared. Fear seized my heart.

Borneo is a land where personal security, for one reason or another, cannot always be taken for granted. One does not deny that the people themselves are essentially headhunters, either practiced or practicing. If the Sungai Hanja Dyaks were products of their tradition, then this Tewah would require human heads to fulfill its measure, and the procurement of those heads was an absolute necessity.

Sungai Hanja, without Panggul, suddenly became an uncompromisingly bitter place to be.

We walked back to the village. The women began to disappear into their shacks, taking their children with them.

The men gathered wood and built a fire near the sapundu in the center path, and then they squatted in a circle on their hams. The firelight fell on the men and it lighted glittering eyes. The men began whispering among themselves, and then one of the Dyaks shouted something and the voices of the others rose in furious agreement.

Three of the men left the group and when they returned they were carrying a large urn filled to overflowing with tuak. And then the men drank. And drank and drank.

Sjam and I were the only women present and Jmy the only child. The soldier and policeman became enfeebled at the sight of blood and bones and Abdul had become deathly ill from it. They were all in the canoe and most likely asleep.

It was true that things would get worse before they could get better. The Dyaks still had to place the sapundu and a human head in front of the sandun, and then, of course, the final step, the catching of a man or woman and skewering that individual on the end of the *pantar* (pole) from which the tingang was meant to fly.

Some of the Dyaks were pitifully drunk now, staring uncomprehendingly around them, half awake and wondering. Others had lost consciousness altogether. But a few Dyaks were bright and the brightest of them had tightened their relaxed faces and sharpened their eyes.

A very dark-skinned Dyak, whose bushy eyebrows were kept in a high arch because they nearly covered his eyes, stood up and backed off a little from the group so that all the men would notice him. He was unsteady on his feet, bolstered as well as shaken by tuak. His eyes flamed with excitement. His whole face was alive with a heated passion.

The humming of voices stopped altogether as the men lifted their heads and looked toward this man. When the Dyak spoke, his voice was edged with brassy threats and challenges of some kind. Some of the Dyaks laughed. The man was hurt as he turned and crept off into the jungle.

In a few moments he returned and jumped with quick steps into the circle of men. From beneath his arm he withdrew a bloody round object. A Dyak with a nose crushed flat against his face grabbed the object and filled it with tuak and then, one by one, the men drank from the thing.

An older Dyak with a jaw that sagged sideways snatched the bloody phenomenon, held it close to his stomach, and then, with his arms wrapped around it, bolted into the jungle.

He returned at a tired trot, breathing heavily, the perspiration standing out on his face and body. He did not have the affair with him anymore.

Through the jungle came a cry and in the distance was a faint scraping of earth. The men rose and two of them picked up and shouldered the sapundu. The bushy-browed Dyak pulled a torch out of the fire, and all of the men followed him into the jungle.

A posthole had been dug in front of the sandun and the ground around it appeared darkly wet. The sapundu was dragged toward the sandun and all of the Dyaks rushed to push the statue into the hole. They quickly packed the ground with their feet.

My own feet were wet. In the dim light from the torch I looked down at the dark ground. I was standing in blood.

When we returned to the center path, one of the younger Dyaks in the group noticed the blood on my feet and he motioned to the other men. They did not find it amusing.

Neither did I. Without Panggul the blood had stimulated me into a new height of despair. Violence had apparently waited for darkness but not for Panggul's return.

Abruptly Sjam and Jmy and I became very important people to the Dyaks of the village. They mentally elevated our positions in a matter of seconds from weak unimportance to uncalculated risks, and they were afraid we would respond. Somehow we had become a problem to them, heavy to all and unbearable to some. Their emotions began to churn and boil up and suddenly violence had a meaningful direction.

Sjam asked permission for us to leave the ceremony, and although the Dyaks were reluctant, they let us go. In the canoe we spent the night wondering where Panggul had gone.

In the morning Panggul was squatted beside the canoe. A quiet calmness had returned to his eyes.

Panggul swung his arm in an arc and pointed to the pantar that rose in the jungle above Sungai Hanja. The wood-carved tingang was perched on the end of the pole. "Put *pantar* up at night," Panggul said. "Tewah over. All O.K."

Panggul received permission from the chief of Sungai Hanja for us to leave, and we pushed the two canoes out into the river's current and headed toward the village of Lubuk Kawan.

In part, Panggul's reasons for disappearing at the Tewah remain a mystery to this day. But he did tell us that a human sacrifice for the pantar is important only if that person's life is of value to other people.

And he wanted to be certain that the Sungai Hanja Dyaks agreed with him as to who was or was not important.

Chapter Twelve

"Ada Obat?"

There was a rock pile in the middle of the river and we disembarked to walk around it. The water crashed loudly against the rigid, unmoving stones and the spume rose far into the air.

Panggul tried to convince me that the rocks were children and grasshoppers.

The rocks were strangely oval, one stacked on top of the other, and all of the stones were more or less the same size. The pile spiraled into the sky, looking very much like a miniature pyramid. The heavy, wide base had nearly closed off the river.

An archaeologist would have had no difficulty in untangling the origin of the rocks, but it would be unuseful. The Dyaks knew how they got there and why.

A century ago, a Tewah had been held on the riverbank nearby. The visiting children, bored with the ceremony, set off to find their own fun and in their venturing came across a nest of black grasshoppers. A few of the rascals in the group picked and poked the insects until they had aroused their indignation as well as their anger and the infuriated insects then declared war upon one another. The grasshop-

pers divided themselves into troops and a bloody battle en-
sued.

The children were caught by their parents, severely crit-
icized and reminded of the seriousness of the Tewah and
their purpose for being there.

The naughty children, undaunted, scooped up all the
grasshoppers they could hold in their hands and moved a
little farther down the river to a new battlefield, where
they encouraged the massacre, out of the sight of the in-
terfering parents and in peace.

There were many gods attending the Tewah, and as they
journeyed through the jungle, either on their way to or returning from the ritual, a few of them caught wind of the
disobedient kids and they lowered a punishing judgment
upon them on the spot.

They changed the youngsters, as well as the grasshoppers, into rocks of granite and stacked them up in the
middle of the river. Today a child in Borneo will go to all
kinds of trouble to stay clear of a grasshopper.

The land had taken on an orange blush when we arrived
in Lubuk Kawan. The river, decreased in speed and depth,
was bluer and the bordering village sucked in the blue
from the water and the orange from the day and glowed
resplendently in both colors.

A little committee of snakes met us at the dock. They were
circling lazily around each other until the nose of the canoe
thudded softly into the mudbank, and then they circled our
canoe. A few of the snakes lifted their periscope heads,
caught the scent of humans in their nostrils, and quickly
dropped back into the water where they collided with the
other snakes and frightened them in their race to reach
the middle current.

Several days ago Panggul had received notice through
the talking drum of a witch doctor's "healing ceremony for
children" to be held in the village of Lubuk Kawan.

While we waited in the canoe for Panggul to obtain the

necessary tribal permission to attend the ceremony, a slender Dyak man, dark of face and with sharp, strong features, swung down the leaning ladder on the embankment and plunged into the water. He surveyed our group with mild interest, his small, restless eyes darting here and there, and then he abruptly turned his back to us, squatted and defecated.

He was joined by another Dyak, one with a shapeless face except for a bony nose, dragging his feet a little as he descended the log ladder. The man arrived at the river's edge and crouched beside his busy friend, down current. He curled the fingers of his hands into little cups and, holding them together, filled his hands with water, raised them to his mouth and drank thirstily.

Some of the villagers circulated at the top of the embankment, and when they saw us, a soft, tired conversation arose from the group.

Behind them the chief of the village and Panggul came into view chatting noisily. The chief had a large nose, narrow at the point but thick at the sides, and beneath it crawled a black mustache, not unlike a caterpillar in appearance. The chief straightened his head in nervous jerks from time to time, the better to hear Panggul.

We were invited into the village, and the people, in their hurry to make room for us at the ladder's top, sent dirt clods slipping and rolling from beneath their feet into the river. As we approached the villagers, the hum of voices fell silent. Some of the people inspected us at close range and then hurried off to their own business.

The Dyaks of Lubuk Kawan were, as a rule, kind, hospitable, and remarkably open with guests and strangers, but now they did not have time for any of it. The "healing ceremony" had been in progress for four days, and although the people were tired, there was still much work to be done. Most of their duties had to do with the scraping together of enough food to make up a meal, a difficult thing to do because the village was overcrowded. Those Dyaks who lived

in the outskirting villages had gone to all sorts of trouble
to get their sick children to Lubuk Kawan. In the exodus
they had trampled their friends, their relatives, and even
strangers in an effort to arrive at all, and then they deposited
their charges in the ceremonial shack and, with hearts that
were hopeful, left the shack to commit the usual excesses
known to accompany such ceremonies.

The chief welcomed us to his village in a thin, cracked
voice and hurried us down the center path to the ceremonial shack. There had been great drinking affairs throughout the four day party-ritual, and many of the men and a
few of their women now lay drunk or passed out along the
sides of the path.

To the right of the path, set back a few feet from the line
of foot traffic, rose a bamboo arch, a gateway for the
gods, and behind the structure was the ceremonial shack.
It was badly pushed out of shape. The walls bulged out in
every direction from the people inside leaning against them,
and the floor sagged beneath the weight of them.

In the doorway of the shack stood Kumbang, the witch
doctor. Lubuk Kawan was not the village of his birth. He
had spent five days traveling to reach the function on time,
and the journey had left him ill-tempered and impatient.

He was a big man, one of mighty frame and stature, and
his strength was unabated, so it was said. The most prominent feature on his dark face was a nose with nostrils
blocked shut with black hairs which curled down and lay
across the upper lip of his full, wide mouth. His eyes regarded our group with malevolence.

He was wearing a costume that had required considera-
tion to assemble and some practice to hold in place. A
frayed sarong was wrapped about the man's waist, and the
shredded streamers around the bottom of it were black with
dirt. Bracelets (*sunbang sawit*) of seed pods and animal
teeth jangled around his wrists whenever he moved his
hands, and they jingled around his feet whenever he took
a step.

His headgear was an arrangement that was nearly beyond description. Tiny crocheted balls blossomed off the ends of a knotted white fringe that worked its way into a lacy band running around his head. The balls hung with abandon over the man's eyes and wobbled about on his nose. The five middle strings in the group had been dyed red, and they not only added a certain grotesqueness to the witch doctor, they made him look as though he had suffered a recent nosebleed.

A red headband held the crocheted piece in place and jungle grass sprouted from it, both crushed and wilted. Bird feathers were stuck at strange angles into the matted grass, and from their sharp points long yellow reeds were tied and they cascaded down the man's naked shoulders to a point well below the waistline.

The headgear (*laung*) was in keeping with the ritual, with the exception of the crocheted works, which had been stolen from the Dutch. The theft gave timbre and profundity to the occasion and a position of majesty to the witch doctor.

He stood with his hands on his hips in the doorway of the shack and poked outward his elbows to take up as much room as he could, or dared. He was indeed the witch doctor but he didn't believe much in himself.

It was his misfortune that he had chosen the profession of witchcraft, done through either his own stupidity or that of others, and now he was stuck with it. It had made him unhappy, for he longed to do the things that others do, and he was in a constant state of turmoil with himself, both physically and mentally.

And he was a vain individual. Vanity had made him a smart man, but it did not make him a kind one and there was no goodness in his nature.

He stomped about in the doorway, scraped his bare feet on the ironwood floor, and poked his elbows tightly against the doorjambs in protest to our being there. He was afraid that the parents of his sick child-patients might court our ideas or medical suggestions, and he wanted to get rid of us as soon as possible.

He hopped down on the ground in front of the shack and began to dance excitedly about in the dust. He lifted his head and shouted at the chief of the village, bellowing his apprehensions in a harsh authoritative and frightening voice.

The chief read the man's temper on his face, a thin temper and plainly written, and he tried to imitate it in his reply. We listened to the chief with admiring but slightly skeptical ears as he attempted to placate the witch doctor and tell him that we were harmless.

Panggul finally spoke up and whatever he said was so strongly worded that it nearly singed the witch doctor's eyebrows beneath his crocheted balls.

The great man backed off a bit, lifted the crocheted fringe with his fingertips, and scrutinized our group more closely. Then he balanced himself daintily on the balls of his feet, turned his back to us and retreated up the ladder and into the shack.

We approached the shack, unaware of the damage that was forthcoming to our eyes, ears, nose, throat, stomachs, and nerves, not to mention our hearts. We passed through the doorway and the despair we felt at the sight within the room was incalculable.

The floor was covered with children, a solid half block of sick children, head to shoulder, and shoulder to stomach. Sometimes one child lay across the other for lack of space. A sickening odor of sweet decay and rotting flesh rose from the carpet along with the smell of urine, four days of urine.

We stared at the group with wide, unbelieving eyes. The policeman whistled softly under his breath to emphasize the quality of his disbelief.

The children on the whole had no identity, no personality, and they all looked alike. There were a few of them that were badly misshapen, almost gnomelike, and their arms

waved jerkily in the air in front of faces that were con-
torted with the disfigurement.

The children lay huddled together in positions that indicated the nature of their illnesses. A few of them hunched
their shoulders and drew down their necks against the fevers
that scampered through their tiny bodies. Snores came from
some of the children, snores born from bronchitis or pneumonia or some other dreadful sickness that closed their
little lungs and throats shut. And some lay on their stomachs
and looked about with eyes that were full of sleep, not yet
awake and not able to awaken ever again.

Many of the children had the wide eyes of sleepwalkers,
and it was terrifying to look upon them. They were gaunt,
skeleton people with long, knobby legs, crowded tightly together like members of a giant bone yard.

One little child sang softly to himself just to be sure that
he was still there and still alive. A young boy sat next to him
with glazed eyes, glassy and unseeing, leading his own little
parade of hurts and so caught in their cruel grasp that he
was unaware of his surroundings.

The children seemed such tiny targets for so much sickness. There were malaria cases in the dozens, anemia, worms
of all kinds, whooping cough, tuberculosis, different forms
of pneumonia, typhoid and paratyphoid, cholera, dysentery,
influenza, and plague, and they did not require more than
a mother's trained eye for diagnosis.

There were horrifying skin diseases and fungus growths
on the flesh of newborn babies and on the youthful skin of
a few unfinished children, those babes born without arms
or legs.

Some of the children were gray with pain and others were
red from it. Not one of them escaped the flush that ac-
companies raging fevers or the chills that tremble the body
when those fevers chase over damp skin. And there was not
a clear eye in the crowd of children.

One little fellow's mouth suddenly flew open and a jet of
blood spurted down his cheek and on down his thin neck.

Several of the children appeared broken and torn. One of them looked as though he had been crushed, perhaps by a falling tree, and he whimpered in his sleep and kicked his foot from time to time.

There were long, wet worms slipping out of the nostrils of the child lying next to him. The boy's face was pinched with the pains he felt in his stomach, pains that were so intense that the wiggling worms tumbled from his nose without his awareness.

One child beat his forehead on the wood floor until the blood from his head ran down over his eyes. His face was puffed and blue and his right cheek was torn. The blood was already dried black around the wound and the edges had gathered together tightly.

The children were afraid to be awake, afraid to be asleep, afraid to be alone, afraid of the confusion in the hot, crowded room, and their fear had reduced those of them who still clung to consciousness to tears.

The situation was overwhelming with hopelessness, and we felt a sorrow that weeping could not take care of, a sorrow so profound that it toppled all joys. Certainly it would be a bonanza for the witch doctor if he succeeded in keeping just one of the still-living children alive.

No one had the time to remove the dead children from the shack, and there was no room in the shack to set them aside. The witch doctor had tied rattan strings around their necks to prevent from escaping whatever evil spirit lived within them and they lay where they had died, the little strings tightening themselves with the humidity in the air and gathering the skin on the necks into little puckers.

A baby girl, her naked body rigid and her mouth partly open, appeared as though she had died only after a long struggle. In her clinging to the poor spark of life while still conscious, death had left her eyes staring wide open.

Below the children crawled the giant jungle ants, scavenging bits of rice, blood, urine, and whatever else, dead or alive, that could be found. The children lay in the midst of the moving army, scratching at the ants, picking them off their bodies and sometimes squeezing an ant between a thumb and index finger before it was shoved into their tiny hungry mouths.

Above the children buzzed the flies, flies larger than beetles. They smashed themselves against the walls and against each other and fell on their backs and twitched their legs in the air, trying to turn over until they were squashed when the children rolled over them.

On the opposite wall, the wall facing the doorway, rose a structure (*pelangkai*) regarded as a house for the gods. It stood nearly six feet tall and was divided into seven levels, one for each god. The compartments held offerings of food and "medicine." The uppermost level contained a plate of blood, a gift of highest value for Sang Hyang.

A newborn chick, yellow and wet, strutted about on top of the affair. The bird represented Djata, the benevolent river god who could do no wrong. The Dyaks felt that since Djata lived in the river outside their front door he should be invited inside to attend their ceremony.

There were geometric scribblings on the sides of the pelangkai, but most of them were covered up with "magic" leaves found in the jungle by the witch doctor in a moment of inspiration.

The structure was leaning heavily to one side. A wild boar had been sacrificed and its head hung from the top level. Blood dripped from the animal's neck down over the lower levels and gathered in a pool at the base of the tower on the floor. It was a very decorative arrangement.

To the onlooker all this craziness might have appeared hopeless, but to the Dyak the very fact that the witch doctor was present with the pelangkai to perform a "healing" ritual perhaps was an indication of the remote possibility.

In the first place, the people have been brainwashed by witchcraft for so many centuries that it reaches deep into their consciousness and in serious proportions. The dreams of the Dyaks are built on powerful and prominent memories

of a witch doctor's success, a success they have either wit-
nessed themselves or, at least, heard of. His methods are
unique and a mystery to them, and this matter of wonder
has placed the Dyaks in servitude to both need and igno-
rance. Apart from this, witchcraft has feeling for the Dyaks
and it is of a texture that they can understand.

The witch doctor always wins, never loses, no matter
what he does, and the people praise him for it despite the
fact that at times he is hurtful and sometimes murderous.

It is this writer's conviction that most of the witchcraft in
Central Borneo is performed by "doctors" that are dirty,
tricky, and a few of them downright crooked. Some of
their screwball antics are charming and original, but for the
most part they are malign and dangerous and their dis-
honest pursuit for personal gain in material goods leaves
them even more undesirable.

The Dyaks are exposed to some kind of witchcraft daily,
and although many die a few endure. Their endurance must
be accredited to something inherent in their race which protects them from themselves, and that, in itself, is not only astonishing but a matter for complete amazement.

A Dyak boy sat in the corner of the ceremonial shack,
tiredly beating a gong with a wooden stick. He stopped for
a moment, put the stick on the floor and brushed his long
hair out of his eyes. The witch doctor looked at the boy,
stirred his bare feet about on the floor, and pointed his toe
at the gong and then the stick. The boy picked up the stick
and resumed beating the gong.

The village's elders moved in through the doorway. Since
no parents were allowed to be in the room, these old men
were "scouts," and they would report the transpiring events.
The men were nervous, old men with sharp black eyes that
moved constantly about. They settled themselves down beside the door and clasped their arms around their legs and
became quiet, their faces expressionless.

A pitifully young girl, heavy with pregnancy, shuffled

toward the witch doctor, giggling and squirming with admiration of the man. She held a black hen in the crook of her left arm and was throttling the bird about the neck with her right hand. She bowed her head a little as she offered the hen with outstretched hands to the witch doctor, a gift of gratitude for his "pregnancy miracle."

The witch doctor grasped the hen by its neck, tied its feet together with a length of rattan, and threw the bird roughly into a corner of the room. He turned then and tramped across the floor in the direction of the hen, stepping on a stray hand or two. The children with the damaged hands howled with pain.

The witch doctor stooped over a little girl whose face was streaked with dirt and hair matted with blood, and he prodded her arm with his finger to gain her attention. The girl turned her head from side to side restlessly, trying to speak, but muttering mostly until she finally choked. The witch doctor shrugged his shoulders, scratched the back of his hand with the nails of the other, blew his nose into his hand, and flicked his fingers.

He stood and began to sift his way through his sick child-patients, his great shoulders jerking as he walked. He knelt from time to time to touch a child with his exploring fingers, on the face or on the stomach, and when he did the child would strain to be free from him. The other children whimpered audibly as much from pain as from fear when he came near them.

The eyes of the old men glittered as they watched the witch doctor move about through the room. Sometimes they nodded in approval of his maneuvers and then they nudged one another with their elbows to be certain that the other had not missed seeing it.

In the center of the room was a swing hanging by rattan ropes from the rafters. It had a strong back to it, in addition to arms. The swing was the symbol of a fancy familiar to all children and it was the only thing the doctor could think of to use as his pulpit, an emotional platform from which he could relate to the children and be comfortable at the same time. It was from this swing that the witch doctor would call upon the gods to cure the sick children.

He arrived in front of the swing, pulled at one of the ropes, and tested the seat with the open palm of his hand. He lowered himself into the swing, and it bridled and bucked beneath his weight. The main rafter to which the ropes were tied groaned, creaked, sagged, and then snapped into two pieces. The witch doctor plummeted forward, fell out of the swing, and chaos followed.

Two tiny children lay pinned beneath the huge doctor, the swing hit one child on the head in passing to rest on another's stomach, the rattan ropes whipped other children with stinging lashes, and the old men in the doorway jumped up in a single movement and in doing so they knocked one another down again.

Two Dyaks were summoned from outside to repair and hang again the precious swing while the witch doctor tried to put his finger on the individual who had done something wrong, or at least something not right.

When the "pulpit" was restored to a working, swinging order again, the witch doctor grumbled himself into the seat, muttering to himself because whoever had been responsible for the fall had not been found. His mutterings were therefore edged with threats that not only confused the sick children in the room, but dismayed them as well.

In the interest of space for future tumbles, a few of the children were lifted away from the area directly in front of the swing and placed against the wall in a spot so small that they were nearly stacked up.

Five young Dyaks brought five ironwood drums into the room, placed them near the swing, sat down, and began their rhythmical beating. The gong player had lost his stick in the confusion and had to dig around a bit before he found another. He picked up the rhythm of the drummers and the room burst with pulsating beats.

The witch doctor pushed himself off with his toes and

the swing moved into action. Up and down, to and fro, back and forth. Although his movements seemed to be a result of just pure restlessness and some nervousness, the swinging had to do with the nature of his business. This high-powered movement caused his healing powers to become more active.

I tried to reduce this ceremony to something I was already used to, something that was familiar, something that was found in all Dyak ceremonies, but it was impossible. It was a mad, dreamlike sight and the whirling of it made the head a little vague so that impressions ran together and sometimes one impression blotted out another. It was like a fairy tale, a piece of imagery beyond acceptance to the mind. Everything seemed hazy, and I felt surely I would not be able to recall exactly what was happening without improvising a bit.

The witch doctor was gaining height now as well as speed, back and forth over children who covered the floor like some torn, bloody brown blanket. In the middle of a high pitch in a backwards swing, he pulled an anggang feather from his headband and twitched it about in the air. The Dyaks regard the feather as a hook and one that is able to snag the illnesses in the room out in the open for the gods to see.

The drums and gongs were beating frantically, the doctor appeared frenzied from his swing, and the breath in the man rose and fell heavily, whistling through the thick hairs in his nostrils. He closed his eyes, coughed, spat, and then coughed again, and when his throat was as clear as he could make it, he began his chant (*manawur*), a prayer that was meant to call upon the gods to prescribe medicine for the children. "Ahem, ahem . . . oh, gods as high as the sunshine at midday, ahem . . . ahem . . . gods who talk to blood . . . ahem, ahem . . ." The syllables dripped monotonously from his mouth.

He had begun his chant in a fawning tone, one that flattered and admired the gods, but soon he worked it into a tone that begged, pushed, forced, and at one time daringly disciplined. The man had nerve.

Once he peeked over the edge of his swing at the children below with the hope that while he swung and chanted some miracle was taking place on the floor beneath him.

To the outsider it appeared that the doctor was suffering from a very sore throat of his own. He spat and scraped his throat after every utterance, but this sputtering was merely a device he had thought of to ensure the proper and continuing attention from the gods.

Abruptly the witch doctor began throbbing with emotion. A big jolt of spirit was growing up within him, and because of it his chant was no longer clear. No one in the room could make out what he was saying. The tone had quickened and it rose and fell with each rise of the swing, but there were no words to it, only a furor of wailing cries.

At the peak of a forward pitch, the witch doctor fell out of his swing and landed on the clear spot on the floor. One of the elderly Dyaks bounced up from his station in the doorway and threw a *kalulung* (gold chain) around the man's head. A few of the children sucked in their breaths at the sight because the necklace confirmed that the gods had indeed entered the witch doctor's body and he was now prepared to disperse medicine to them. None of them were looking forward to it.

The witch doctor staggered into a standing position and then twisted and dodged himself through the children on his way to the pelangkai. He stood in front of it, hands on his hips, shaking his head from side to side to clear the dizziness as he surveyed the medicine within the seven cubbyholes. He took his time. There was no sense of hurry in him of any kind, and he rocked to and fro on his heels, studying the assortment with a practiced showmanship. And then he got to work.

He pushed his great hands into the levels and withdrew whatever medicines he touched. Roots, ground powders, leaves, bones, raw birds' hearts and their livers. He scooped up as many as he could and then squatted a little and dumped them into the lap of his sarong. He held the hem of his sarong in one hand and with the other pulled out more medicines, some of them quite oily and others bloody. He heaped them into his sarong and the juices seeped through the cloth and ran down his legs onto the floor.

Then he turned, looked over the children, and began his trip through them. He gave the children whatever medicine was handy on top of the pile in his sarong. Those children fast asleep were probed and poked by the doctor's foot until they stirred. Then the medicine was shoved down their throats, received with protests. If a child was unconscious and could not be aroused, then he was passed by.

Those children who had been sleeping were now awake and crying. Those who had been crying were now scream-ing, and those children who had been screaming were now hysterical. The noise was damaging to the ears and the sight was devastating to the heart.

The swinging, the chanting, and the administration of medicine to the children had taken place at the twilight hour, and this, the fourth day, was the final ritual. There would be no more.

The old men creaked themselves up, hacked their throats clear of betel nut juice, and struck up a chant of their own, one that informed the gods that the ceremony was over. They made their way to the pelangkai and the four of them lifted the heavy, leaning structure to their shoulders and carried it to the doorway. The witch doctor jumped a little ahead of the old men, the gong boy fell in beside him, and together they led the parade to the river's edge.

Some of the parents of the sick children heard the beating of the gong and their bare feet brought them scurrying to the ceremonial shack. They stood with eyes wide and won-dering, hearts hopeful, and with prayers on their lips as they watched the witch doctor and the old men carry the pelangkai to a waiting canoe on the river.

The witch doctor stood on the riverbank surveying the

canoe. He placed his hands on his headgear, pushed it a little farther down on his head, and then turned slowly and looked at our group. He mumbled to one of the old men standing near him and the man nodded and hurried off into the shack. When he returned he was carrying a small ironwood drum, a medicine drum that had been used in the ceremony. The witch doctor roughly took the drum in his big hands and walked toward us.

He held his head so high that the red-balled fringe scrambled over his nose. He wrapped both hands around the drum and then he stretched them toward me. It was an offering of peace, one of great honor.

The witch doctor turned, descended the bank, and climbed into the canoe. The four old men settled the pelangkai in the canoe and then settled themselves. They meant to paddle to the deepest place they could find and call for Rawing Tempun Telon, lesser god of the First Heaven, in a closing *malabuh balai* ceremony. When they were certain they had Rawing's attention, they would throw the pelangkai tower into the river and return to the village.

We watched the group paddle off down the river, the little Djata chick wobbling about high on the six-foot structure. We could see them for quite a long while, chanting, playing the gong, and calling their god, and then the river turned and the canoe slipped around the bend and was out of sight.

I felt a little tug at my shirttail. There, in the dusty center path of the village, were two little children who had not attended the healing ritual. They were small children, boys who were brothers, seven and eight years old. The younger had led his brother, led him to our group by the hand, because he could not see.

The blind one stood with his fingers curled tightly about the shoulder of the younger boy, thin fingers bony and knobby at the knuckles, and he cocked his head to one side, the better to hear. That was just in case his brother said something. He wanted him to say something, needed his brother to say something. But nothing came, so the child stood, waiting, wondering, wanting, needing.

The child had not always been blind. A few months ago he had been more or less like the other children his age, but that was before conjunctivitis spread across his eyes and the whole upper half of his face became thick and swollen, and then the skin stretched so tight that in places it had burst open. A thin black bubble crept across his face where his eyes should have been, and fat flies sat in a circle around the bubble with their tongues stuck into the white milk that seeped from beneath its edge. His skin had turned purple in some places and red in others, scarred and rivuleted, and the tissue around the bridge of his nose had rotted away so that there was just one big bubble instead of two.

Over the bubble and under it glistened the wet shininess of the pustules that rose and broke open and spilled sticky purulence over his cheeks and then waned to make room for new sores when the child dug into his hurts again.

Of course, the child's eyeballs were gone. He had dug and scratched and torn at the eyes beneath the bubble until they had finally eroded away.

His brother had been infected in the right eye. He wiped at the weeping, watery eye with the tail of his coarse sarong, to relieve a little of the itch and pain that lived there.

His left eye was a leaden eye, and there was a desperate kind of sadness that the child never expected to be free from. It was a deep eye, one that rested deep within his head, so deep that when he looked out of that eye it seemed to come only from a great distance. It would be difficult to forget that eye, once looked upon, an eye that was destined to never sparkle again.

When the softly spoken words finally came, *"Ada obat?"* ("Is there medicine?"), we heard them, but it was the eye that spoke, the eye that formed the words, uttered the syllables, and carried the message.

Our skins thickened when we heard it, and there was a salty taste in our mouths and hard knots in our stomachs.

What does a human being do when a little child reaches out for a hand that cannot be there?

And because it had nothing else to do, the eye watched us move away, move very slowly at first because our feet felt like they hardly touched the ground and because everything was unreal and unfair and terribly wrong.

The eye followed us as we climbed into our canoe and the eye saw our shoulders shake with choked sobs.

Chapter Thirteen

Nine out of Twelve

He was dead. His heart had stopped pumping and his lungs had taken in no air for several minutes, but the blood still spewed from his mouth. It came in little gushes, a tablespoon at a time, and there were moments in between before another jet spurted.

The mother of the dead Dyak baby was not young but she was not very old, either. Her long coarse black hair grew halfway down her forehead and framed a face that was almost girlish in its delicacy. She had large eyes with a soft, sad look, but they were dry of tears, and beside her left eye was a mole about the same color as the little brown veins that stood out on her temples.

Suddenly her face hardened and her eyes grew cold. She wanted to get on with it. She had to wash and dress the body, but there was nothing she could do until the blood stopped discharging from the child's mouth.

She sighed deeply, leaned forward and wiped the boy's mouth with the hem of her already bloodied sarong, and then pulled another worm from his nostril.

The flies buzzed from everywhere, huge blowflies, droning around the boy looking for the blood. The mother's patience had worn thin with them. It was all she could do to keep the boy's face clean of blood and the flies away at the same time. She picked up a branch of mali mali leaves and swatted angrily at the buzzing pests, cursing them under her breath.

It may be difficult to understand that we had seen so much suffering, illness, and death we had become hardened and nearly used to such a thing. But it had happened, and our eyes were dry, dry with a sorrow that tears could not symbolize anymore.

The Dyak mother pulled at the lower edge of her sarong and ripped off a strip of cloth from the hem. The baby's mouth was open and she tried to tie the jaws together but they were stiff and unyielding.

I helped to close the child's jaws with my hands as the mother tied the cloth strip tightly about his tiny head. When it was done, the mother lifted the baby to her breast and then boosted him onto her shoulder and started off toward the river.

In the jungle nearby, the boy's father was cutting a coffin, and we could hear him hacking away at it. He was a handsome Dyak, about forty years old, a very strong man with shoulders that were wide and muscular from a work that required pulling or lifting. His full mouth was jovial and completely at odds with the morning loss of his son. The expression on his mouth never changed, not even when he talked. It always looked friendly and happy.

A parang swung heavily from his waist as he pulled and tugged the length of balsa wood from its place in the jungle. The trunk was only two feet long, long enough for such a tiny body.

The hot sun whipped at the back of the man's neck as he stood the log on its end in a little clearing, pulled his parang from its sheath, and began whittling the bark clean from the trunk. He puckered his brow gloomily as he cast his eyes over the child's body for a measure. And then he began to shape the trunk, shape it in the form of his son. It would be a *tambali rang* when he was finished, a canoe-coffin to sail the boy to heaven.

The mother puffed up the riverbank with the dead child in her arms. When she reached the top, she lay the boy on the ground and then wiped the sweat from her brow with her forearm. The little body glistened in the sunshine, river-wet, clean of blood and dirt now. His puffed, swollen stomach seemed out of place beneath the thin, skeleton face, the skin stretched tight and shiny over high cheekbones. The cloth strip around his jaw was soaked, and the loose ends where the knot was tied were limp with water and flattened against the child's neck. The mother straightened the boy's limbs and placed his hands at his sides, the little palms hugging his thighs.

She looked up at her husband and when she caught his eye she nodded.

The man stuck his parang in the top of the trunk, turned and walked toward a chicken that had been staked to the ground nearby. He bent to loosen the rattan cord around the bird's feet, picked it up, held it straight out in front of him, and cut off its head with a mandau. At a walk that was nearly tired, he approached his son and dripped chicken blood over the child's still open eyes. The devils forever claim attention, even in death, and the blood would keep evil spirits from entering the boy's lifeless body.

His good shoulders shook a little as his breathing choked and tears came into his eyes. The tears caused him to become angry with himself. He threw the bird on the ground and at a half trot returned to carve on the coffin again.

With the back of her hand the boy's mother swept from her face a long strand of black hair that had loosened itself. She shook her head from side to side, sighed, and set to work. She held the child's eyelids down with the fingers of one hand and with the other withdrew two Dutch coins from beneath the blouse of her sarong and placed one on either eye. The content of the coins was mostly tin, pure silver would have been better, but there wasn't any, so tin would have to do. The sun jerked its shine over the coins and exploded the metal into hard, jabbing reflections in the hot air.

The woman wrapped her infant son's body with narrow lengths of white cloth, around and around, bound him up mummylike with his hands at his sides. The head was the last to be covered. The jaw was still tied tightly shut, and the silver eyes gave a final glint in the sunshine before they were covered.

And now she would wait. She would sit by the bandaged body and keep the flies off and wonder about the family she had left in the village. She would wait because the coffin would take time. Two days of time to carve.

A week ago, in Saca Dua, someone had told the family about a small abandoned plot of cleared jungle downstream. It occurred to them that if they could make a little rice grow on that plot they could have something to eat for the coming year. But one of their children was sick and it was not a good time to leave him. He spent most of his time between pain and crying and he vomited a good deal.

The father decided to take the sick boy with them, to keep an eye on him, and if he regained his strength, he could play in the new rice paddy while he and the mother worked. But over the week in the field, the baby worsened and worms strung out of his nose and he vomited blood. When death finally came, there was hardly any struggle at all.

The boy would have to be buried in the village; it was the rule. If the belian learned that he was entombed elsewhere, there would be a heavy fine to pay, gourds of tuak and a chicken, maybe, and the family did not have food to give away.

But before they could return to the village the coffin would have to be made. Two days to make a two-piece coffin. One piece would be for heaven, the top part, and the lower piece would be for earth. It would be shaped like a canoe, with four little sticks on the sides to represent locks used for tying.

After the carving, the coffin would be decorated. A picture of the sun would have to be painted on the casket to symbolize Sang Hyang and take the soul to heaven. The boy's face would be drawn on the coffin to tell everyone who lay inside, and there would be pictures of canoes on both sides to inform the gods that the boy could navigate.

There was so much to do. The child's personal effects would have to be placed inside the coffin, things to keep him happy on his journey to the Fifth Heaven; a gnarled knot from a *sawang* tree, a dried betel nut he had used for teething, and a round river stone, the one he had held in his hand when he died.

His mother would put a few grains of rice and a bamboo split of water inside the coffin before it was sealed with asphalt and trussed with rattan strappings.

And then a Dutch coin, one like those on his eyes, would be laid on top of the coffin to pay the boy's passage to heaven.

The parents were familiar with every part of the ritualistic procedure.

They were burying their ninth child. They had brought twelve children into the world and nine of them had died. Nine out of twelve.

When they heard the gong, the women in Saca Dua poked their heads out from their shack doorways and then withdrew them. The men lined the riverbank and some of them held their hands in front of them and squidged their fingers together, and others tapped their bare feet restlessly on the hard ground. None of them wanted to be there. But they stood and they waited because they owed the dead boy the duty of memory.

The coffin was in the canoe ahead of ours. The father paddled and the tired mother sat in the helm, in front of the coffin, beating a gong. It had been a hard journey, a full day traveling against the current to Saca Dua and a full day of listening to the gong. But the gong had to sound out. The gong told the boy where he was going and it told him how to make his own way after his burial.

We docked and a few of the villagers rushed to help lift the child's coffin out of the canoe. The gong beat as the Dyaks trudged single file through the jungle, behind the village, to a likely spot for burial, one that did not need too much effort to clear, and it beat as the father bunched together mali mali leaves against his mandau and outlined a small plot on the ground to give the boy the right to a grave, one that would be his forever.

The couple's three children, two girls and a little boy, clustered around their brother's coffin, and each gave it a pat and then they settled down into squats. Quiet children, they were, with bare feet and dirty faces.

The gong stopped beating for a moment while the mother swatted at the flies with her hand, and then it struck up again. It continued as the men dug the grave, dug it with handmade shovels, scoops tied to straight branches with rattan cords. The grave was dug in relays, and as the hole deepened and one man gave out, another jumped in and little spurts of dirt flew out of the hole and into the air again.

It was a little grave, four feet long and less than two feet wide, but it was deep. Only one Dyak at a time could descend into the pit to chop and dig out the dirt.

And when the grave was so deep that only the top of the head of the Dyak digging could be seen, then word was sent up to bring in logs to line the bottom of the grave, and six smooth logs were cut and sent down into the pit.

The men carried the coffin to the graveside and gently placed it on the ground. The father knelt and tore off a small ribbon of cloth that had been tied around the coffin, and threw it into the grave. It would be used by the boy as a flag in case he needed it.

The men stood back a little, wanting to get on with the work, hopping from foot to foot to emphasize their impatience.

But the father could not be hurried. He took his mandau

and gently laid its tip on the coffin, a little to the left of the boy's chin. With slow, soft jabs, he poked a little hole into the wood to allow the spirit to escape. A terrible odor escaped too, for the balsa wood had caved in like an eggshell.

A small-sized Dyak, one who had helped with the digging, leaped into the grave and received the casket as it was lowered. He spread his legs to reach either side of the pit and gently laid the coffin on the log bottom. When it was done, another Dyak helped him out of the hole with his hand.

They filled the child's grave with handfuls of dirt. They spat on each handful before it was thrown in because it was their duty. The Dyaks believe that their spittle will kill the evil spirit that caused the death.

When the pit was filled, the people smoothed out the dirt and packed it down with their feet until it was flat and without a mound of any kind.

And now their work being over, the people moved their eyes over the grave and then secretly up to the face of the father. His head was bowed, his eyes closed, and his fists were clenched tightly at his sides. He lifted his head, threw back his great shoulders, and slowly he nodded.

And when the father nodded, the gong finally stopped beating.

Borneo is climatically and topographically uniform from east to west, north to south, and this makes the island just one kind of land. But the people are of every kind, from many ethnic categories. They call themselves "Dyaks."

Today it is no longer a disgrace to be Dyak, and citizens from Bandjarmasin to Pontianak will boast of great-grandparents who were the fierce headhunters of Borneo, whether it is true or not.

It is unfortunate that to the Western twentieth-century mind Borneo evokes thoughts only of a distant jungle land, one that is currently ribboned with savage wild men. To those of us in the expedition who had successfully penetrated the Central Borneo jungles and subsequently identified its indigenous people, Borneo meant something much more.

It is a certainty that something has gone before in Central Borneo, something is there now, and something will follow. Much of it is impossible to trace, for Borneo's past is not known. Most of it never can be, for little or nothing has ever been recorded. The tribes had no use for any kind of alphabet or calendar, and therefore nothing was written or dated. It shut the door on the early history of Borneo, a mysterious riddle to be solved perhaps only through conjecture.

But the people are there, and one wonders where they came from, how they arrived, and how they can be accounted for. Again, the precise origin of the people is still unknown. It is possible that the first river of strangers came from Southern China and they came as early as 10,000 B.C. Perhaps they were joined or followed by the Mongoloids, flat-nosed wanderers from Central Asia and the Veddoids from African antecedents.

They came before the glaciers of the ice age, glaciers that separated vast land chunks from the continent, broke them into nearly three thousand islands, and then threw them into the Java Sea.

There is evidence that the Negritos roamed about Borneo for a while. They left their racial characteristics on some of the people in smallness of stature, curly hair, and fine features and they left some of their habits, too. Today, what few heirs are left live in the trees in Malaysia.

Archaeologists and anthropologists know that the Malay-type people, variously called Austronesians, invaded the area nearly five thousand years ago and to some extent transformed the nomad hunters they found into farmers, but they did not make much of an impression on the untamable wild men of Borneo.

Each invasion meant a new people who swept over the land and defeated and sometimes absorbed their victims.

The conquerors set about carving themselves a kingdom from the ruins and as they carved they left a little of their culture in it. One civilization brought the Bronze Age and left gongs and spear tips scattered from one end of Borneo to the other. Another troop arrived cargoed with porcelain, and their glazed urns show up in the interior of the island as well as on the coastline.

But the continual conquests of migrating warriors left the land unsettled and in a state of unrest. In this fluctuant, shifting environment the people who remained never learned to cultivate rice in irrigated paddy fields or raise animals for domestic use. Even as late as 1930, while Djakarta was graduating a scant two hundred students yearly from the high schools, the people in Central Borneo were just beginning to learn how to build a house.

In the beginning the Dyaks were the majority group and their main interest was simply to survive in a world that was not necessarily friendly to them. Their strange, hostile wilderness was a country without a name, and they were people who roamed large sections of unmapped territory in places they did not have names for.

The geography of the land forecast every probability that sooner or later the large number of people on the island would separate themselves into tribes. It was a perfectly natural direction that each tribe develop and maintain its own social, religious, and political identity, and once this was done the tribes never shared a common view of life, customs, or even language.

The Ngadju tribe of Central Borneo took its clan names from the rivers where the people lived, Kapuas, Kahajan, Katingan, and Mentaja, and those rivers became their clan boundaries by instinct as well as by inner-clan agreement. They moved about their own regions collecting valuables from the land, sometimes gold, silver, and in rare instances diamonds.

The Dyaks never learned to gentle the land they lived

upon, to smooth it and make it habitable, not in a single area. They had little idea of permanency, and with the exception of the erection of an occasional tombstone there was never building of any kind. Their hearts and their roots were found in their traditions, and this fulfilled their need for security.

They were wild clans, clans who were travelers, energetic with restlessness. When disputes arose over their various directions, the clans split up and broke off into a variety of sects. It is a mystery that today the people consider themselves as one people, a "Dyak people," because it is contrary to their primitive intentions.

The little societies of clans and sects moved constantly about Borneo. Because they were predatory, they preyed upon one another. When one clan set itself against the people of another, it did so for its safety, its future, and for whatever profit it could get. Often the issue involved land, and the murderous results greatly diminished the numerical strength of the clans because of the total involvement of the Dyak population.

If an invaded clan survived the open intention of another clan to wipe it out, the survivors welded themselves more closely together, and spirited by their passion for life, they moved on and sometimes found themselves headed for extinction on land that was not only unpromising but was a land that welcomed them with diseases that eventually decimated the few that remained.

Prior to 1200 the four major clans of the Ngadju tribe lived in Central Borneo as a people that ethnically belonged together. They were marked not only by their pagan practices and techniques for living but by their stature, facial features, and even their way of walking.

The people of one clan all looked like each other. Perhaps it had something to do with their climate, food supply, or the work they did in the jungle. The Duhois, even today, are bowlegged, their heads are round, and their skin is quite dark. The Katingans are wide-shouldered, narrow-hipped, and their heads are long instead of round. There are a few Kahajans with almond-shaped eyes of the Oriental, although the slanted upper lid is much less pronounced. But all clans, nevertheless, share the common look of their ancestry; their small size, black hair and eyes, full lips, and, again, the way they walk.

It may or may not have been to Borneo's advantage that she was, for the most part, inaccessible to the Hindu invaders in A.D. 100. The island was fortressed by the Java Sea, unpredictable waters controlled by whimsical monsoons that blow in from India. The navigable risks closed the region to the world.

In 1200 Modjopahit established his Hindu kingdom in Southwestern Borneo. He brought with him Prime Minister Lambung Mangkurat and Princess Djungdjung Buih, and there is evidence that his empire reached as far north as Tjandi Angung (near Amuntai) in 1350.

A few of the clans and sects tried to get along with their invading guests. A very few. The Dyaks, who lived like the animals they killed, wild, savage, and free, resented having everything they owned taken away from them. They defended themselves and their land, sometimes at great costs to their own people, and those who were not killed or absorbed by the new culture scattered themselves north, east, and west where they could watch from a safe distance the dark-skinned Hindus take spices, timber, gold, and other things from their land and teach religion on the side.

What this writer learned about the tribal migrations of the Dyak people over the surface of Borneo was revealed by the Dyaks themselves. Their information was checked and rechecked by establishing the dates their present villages were founded, by talking to countless older people who remembered the birthplaces of their grandparents, and through the study of the monuments the people left along their migratory path.

The following presents an account of the Central Borneo Dyaks' own theory of how they got where they are today, and although their conjecture may not be true, it is, at least, credible.

In 1600 the Dutch East India Company moved in and around the southern harbor on the Borneo coast, and the activity caused the clan that called themselves the Kapuas to become nervous. Some of them stayed in the area, absorbed, but many of them did not. They picked up their mandaus and sumpitans and moved westward and unluckily found themselves in the middle of the Kahajan clan territory.

The Kahajans resented being moved in upon, and therefore the two clans did not live in peace. The Kahajans killed as many Kapuas as they could, and shifted themselves a westwardly geographical notch, where they fell in amid the Katingans.

The process of clan migration from east to west took a long and bloody time. It was a game of westward-moving musical chairs until the Katingans, aided by a few Kahajans, moved into Mentaja territory and found that the fierce Mentaja clan would not change their seats.

To their chagrin the Katingans and Kahajans had come up against the Duhois, Malahois, Sabaungs, and Sahieis, sects of the Mentaja clan already known for their ferocity, and the rivers ran red for more than half a century.

Although many were killed and the Malahois nearly obliterated, a few friendships were established between the Katingans, Kahajans, and the Mentaja sects, and their first major joint effort was the erection of a few tombstone sculptures (sapundus) in present-day Sampit in 1670.

For the most part the Kapuas clan tired of running first. In 1800 the Dutch moved onto the already Moslem southwestern coastline and gradually began to soak up what Kapua sects were still living there. When they founded Bandjarmasin (officially the capital city a century later) they allowed the Kapuas people to call themselves "Banjar Dyaks" provided they behaved themselves and got lost in the crowd. Many of them did. They became Moslem, Catholic, or Protestant, married adventurous Indonesians from Java or Bugis from the Celebes, and later, with Indonesian Moslem missionaries, migrated into the central southern coast to establish a little town called Samuda.

When the "Banjar" people arrived in Samuda, Sampit was not far away. In 1770 the Katingans, Kahajans, and Mentajas picked up their things, left their monuments, and founded Tangar, a place four or five days north by canoe and seemingly quite a distance to them. The river was deep and fish-full and the jungles abundant with game and wild berries. It was a good life. The Dyaks planted their monuments and felt "safe" for nearly thirty years.

(It should be noted that the Dyaks did not build houses, they had no use for them. When they "founded" a village it was done with ancestral burials and tombstone sculptures, and this made the land theirs.)

And then something dreadful happened. The Banjars and Indonesian missionaries filtered into Sampit, and the Dyaks discovered that Tangar was not as geographically remote as they had believed.

They started to run. A few Katingans stopped to settle Santilik, Tangarubah, Pemantang, Kuala Kuajan, and Djeriangau (Batu Hurui), and the Mentajas and Kahajans fled all the way north to build the villages of Gagu and Ngahan on the Kalang River, later abandoned for lack of food.

Other Katingans lost their heads completely and pushed into the Kuajan River, heading west, where they, with the help of a few Duhois, founded the villages of Sapia and Keminting in 1820. It was a grave mistake. The area was unhospitable; there was no game in the jungle and few if any fish in the narrow river. Hunger and ultimately starvation thinned the ranks of this once great clan.

What happened to the Dyak came slowly, quietly from many directions. In 1890 an Indonesian missionary poked his head above the jungle surface and peeked into the Mentaja area and Tumbang Manja, Old Kalang, Pahilep, and Sungai Hanja were hastily settled by the Dyaks to accept the fleeing clans as they abandoned Kuala Kuajan, Santilik and Djeriangau (Batu Hurui).

In 1910 the Dutch, their feet planted firmly in Sampit soil, sent "Banjars" and the Indonesian missionary into Kuala Kuajan to "civilize the place" for their own selfish motives. It would provide them with a greater security as they extracted the wealth of the land for their pockets. Today the resources are, with few exceptions, still there. More resources may be there, for much of the area has never been explored.

The Dutch had greater safety than they realized. Rambang Sawit's summit meeting with the tribal chieftains of the area had already adjourned.

The clans, who were now calling themselves "tribes," a psychological ego-building therapy for their numbered few, had finally come to the end of the line. They had run out of river in the north as well as in the west, and therefore they had run out of land. Surely the Dyak suffered an overpowering disillusionment when his country closed in on him and he found that the land did not stretch to infinity after all.

The Dyaks had practiced tribalism but they had never learned the lessons of nationhood, and it left them vulnerable to the newcomers. They were pitifully reduced to handfuls now, through pestilence, plague, wars, and disease. Without leadership, without a government of their own, and without strength in health and numbers, they were to become a people who had lost their way.

A few Katingans made crazy circles in the jungle and finally came to rest below Kuala Kuajan, where they built the village of Sapiri and watched the newcomers from there. They saw wobbly little houses erected on high stilts with an air of propriety about them.

The Dyaks decided to build houses too, believing that the structures would give them title to the land. But it didn't.

The invading newcomers, in time, simply burned them

out and scraped them off and moved themselves in. Mang-kup, Tukung Langit, and Ramei were the first to go.

The Dyaks were surrounded. But the worst was yet to come.

Although the Dyaks remember the Indonesian Moslem missionary having come to the area, none of them remember his having left. He must have been a very brave man.

Some of the Dyaks weathered the good intentions of the man and many did not. Few Dyaks ever abandoned their own Kaharinjang religion to embrace the Moslem gospel because it simply did not make sense to them. But some of the Dyaks learned a better way of life when they watched the missionary plant and cultivate rice in a clear patch in the jungle. They also stole his seeds.

The missionary was successful in building a mosque in Kuala Kuajan for the Moslem newcomers to utilize and for those "heathen" Banjars newly converted.

An Indonesian Christian came in 1939 from the same source as his colonial Moslem brother, but his success in Kuala Kuajan was much less. He built his tiny church as far removed from the mosque as possible, and those Banjars who had not been taken into the bosom of Islam were converted to Christianity in Kuala Kuajan. A few Dyaks did become Christians, perhaps a whole handful, and they were capable of slipping back and forth between Christianity and Kaharinjang as easily as between one culture and another.

But for the most part the Christian doctrine fell flat in the Mentaja area. The doctrine was too foreign and antithetical to the Dyaks' traditional beliefs and too difficult to swallow. And besides, the Christian man did not bring along any rice seeds.

In 1942 the Dyaks were frantically scraping enough lumber together to build houses and enough food to fill stomachs when a new disaster struck. The Japanese invaded the island in World War II and marched into the Mentaja. During their four-year occupation the Japanese took over the Dyaks' houses, their land, and sometimes their women. And they took over something else, too. The Japanese eliminated the Dyaks' permanent food supply of deer and black bear. Japanese tropical medicine is based on bear hearts and deer horns, and the lower region of the jungle in the Mentaja was cleaned out within a year.

And then they began to eliminate the men. The Japanese reached the northernmost village of Pahilep on the Kalang River and the westernmost village of Sapia on the Kuajan. They caught the healthiest Dyak men, those who did not hide in the jungle, and shipped them off to Pangkalang Embun, west of Sampit, to build their airfield. Most of them never returned. The Dyaks suffered great losses at the hands of the Japanese, losses in population that were never replaced.

When Indonesia was liberated, the Japanese left Borneo, and the Indonesian revolution for independence sprang up in 1945. During this time the Dyaks not only had a "breather," they received a few rewards as well. Mandaus and sumpitans stole out from their hiding places and heads flew in all directions. No one paid much attention whether they were Dutch heads or Banjar.

In 1966 a new government was set up in Sampit. It was called the "Indonesian government" and it was neither stable, responsible, trustworthy nor respected, and it invariably functioned with motives that were muddied and vague. The power was weak, balky to handle, and incredibly difficult to exercise. The bupati had real power, but the people were never certain where the authority lay or how it worked.

The Banjars in Kuala Kuajan wanted "government" too. In January 1969 a few of them traveled to Sampit and talked with the bupati. They were converted into a half-obedient military and they returned to Kuala Kuajan as heroes. Then they tried to enforce "Indonesian laws" upon everyone in sight.

The military found the Dyaks difficult to communicate with, difficult to deal with, and difficult to understand. They feared the Dyaks' fierce reputation as headhunters and the Dyaks feared punitive punishment for their past "crimes."

Kuala Kuajan learned that it could not enforce laws upon a people that were beyond its reach. The military regarded the Dyaks as stupid, dangerous animals and as savages incapable of learning; they were, therefore, worth ignoring.

A few months prior to the establishment of the military in Kuala Kuajan, our expedition had discovered nearly three thousand Dyaks living in a jungle populated with more than fifteen thousand newcomers.

We found that the love for survival felt by the Dyaks was the leading distress for the newcomers.

It was merely a question of time before the Wild Men of Borneo would be snuffed out entirely.

It was time to say good-by. Time to say good-by to Panggul. We were standing in the river water by his canoe in Sampit, the same canoe we had slept in, lived in, eaten in for the most part of our journey into the Mentaja jungle. There were little half-moon marks on the right side of it where my fingernails had dug into the wood during a malaria seizure, there were Abdul's bloodstains on the inside and bottom, and there were tears and perspiration in the canoe, although they did not show.

The canoe was not tied. Panggul held one end of it in his hand and we watched it make a wide arc in the gentle current.

Panggul rubbed the side of the canoe with his thumb and then raised his eyes. His face was grave and serious. "I wait," he said, and the words were barely above a whisper. "I wait for you here. You have seen my people. You have seen the cost of their standard of living and you have seen what few have managed to survive.

"I hide nothing from you. You have seen the Dyak man sit on a little piece of land with no food, no medicine, and no hope, a Dyak man with no purpose to fulfill and no reason for life, anymore.

"I show you all this to make friendship with you. Now, I ask you, do you take me to be your friend?

"If we are friends and if there is truth in God's eyes, then we will meet again.

"So, I wait for you, here. I wait."

He climbed into his canoe, turned it toward the center current, and paddled up the river. Back into the jungle to return to his people. And I was alone. Left with his tears running down my hand.

Chapter Fourteen

The Letter

Of all the things that can happen to man, to be caught up in the backwash of a cultural shock is at once humorous and at the same time painful. It happened to Abdul, Sjam, Jmy, and me.

We were a people who had suddenly changed directions. Under the dark cover of night, the police boat brought us from a terra incognita, a savagely primitive black jungle land, and tossed us into the hustling, zany "modern" town that called itself Bandjarmasin.

The town, founded by foreigners, Hindus, Dutch, and such, grew up helter-skelter, without much plan and with dubious purpose, out of which came a mixture of habits, customs, races, religions, and laws that were left unenforced.

For us Bandjarmasin was a city suspended in time, hanging in a white, blinding light, stinking from its gutters, and bustling with noise.

Apart from the affairs of Bandjarmasin, the schools, the hospitals, fire department, and police station and the protocol that goes with it, there were a thousand details that might escape the ordinary traveler but that directly involved the four of us, as a people returning to "civilization."

A common reaction to this kind of shock is invariably lethargy, and Sjam, the quietest of us all, was the most badly hurt. She stood staring at the city, her mouth open, breathing very lightly and high, trying to get the feeling of the place. She could not relate to the sudden dissonance, it was too much for her, and she reeled abruptly under the strain of such intense concentration.

To recall, reorganize, and reassemble so many thoughts and patterns on a moment's notice, you get nothing. The mind is simply unaccustomed to this kind of shabby trick. It is made worse by the loneliness of the situation. It is difficult to talk to anyone because of the impossibility to sustain a sensible thought or idea for more than a few seconds.

The picture before us was a whirling furor of ill-defined images, lost in meaning or nearly forgotten, a picture that seemed to be some kind of lethal trap.

In front of us was an overturned rowboat and a little boy was hiding beneath it, lying on his stomach, peeking out from under its silver rim. Behind the boy were buildings, buildings with four walls and a roof and glass in the windows. The door on the front wall swung on metal hinges, and when it closed, the doorway was completely covered and there was a clicking sound as the latch fell into place and the door could not be opened again until the door handle was turned.

And in the buildings were clothes and food, and some of the food was fresh and some was in cans. There were small radios that operated on batteries and leather caps and pieces of machinery, and there was a motorcycle in the window of one of the buildings. There were pork chops and tobacco in another building, and next door was a store with fishing equipment.

There was a building with furniture in it and the furniture had shiny metal arms and legs. The furniture was covered with colorful plastic and all of it was for sale. On a table in the window were lily bulbs from China and long strings of firecrackers, too. There were pots and pans of all sizes and glass and crockery in all shapes, and there was even a pincushion in one of the windows.

In these buildings was nearly everything that a person wanted or needed to make him happy, and seeing them in such abundance made us feel ashamed.

An Indonesian man came out of his doorway, yawned, stretched, and scratched his stomach. He was wearing a shirt, a pair of trousers, and there were no holes in them.

A sea gull came flapping through the air to sit on the corrugated roof of one of the buildings, a building that had a sidewalk in front of it.

A sidewalk made of cement and a road in front of that, a real road with asphalt on top of it. A car with round rubber wheels came sputtering down that road, and there was a man inside of the car wearing a straw hat and he was smoking a cigarette.

The man ran over a pipe that had water coming out of it. Water was coming out of a pipe.

From somewhere a whistle screamed and the street filled up suddenly. Men and women scrambled out of the buildings and ran in every direction, racing to their work. The people moved about with a rush, hurrying themselves in a mangled craziness, a frantic, trussed-up people, trapped and somehow ruled.

The town sucked up the people and the scenes, the trees, buildings, and threw them into a warped pattern, one that seemed suspended and spinning somewhere between the earth and the sky.

A bicycle careened by us, an honest-to-goodness bicycle, and there was a boy riding it. He wore clothes and shoes.

We walked through the middle of a dogfight in the street without even the knowledge of having done it. We passed a white cat that was sleeping on a pile of mangoes, stacked up in the shade of a tree that had red flowers on its limbs.

On the corner were women who wore dresses that had sleeves and a yoke and a collar, and one of the women had a belt around her waist. They brushed the street with grass brooms, sweeping the bits and pieces of paper and other debris into little piles. An older woman smiled at us with teeth that weren't black. Her skin was smooth and bronze, free from sores and fungus, and her hair was neatly combed into place and caught at the nape of her neck with a three-colored ribbon, red, green, and yellow. And there was a string of little pearls around her neck, not a seed pod. Not a gnarled knot from some sacred tree.

Everyone in town was wearing clothes and there were shoes on everyone's feet. Some of the children ran and walked and their shoes were noisy on the sidewalk.

The street rumbled and groaned with people, it boomed and barked and creaked and rattled and squeaked with people, people who rushed about carrying things wrapped in paper sacks and bound up with strings.

And there was music, a jukebox with a record spinning around inside on its turntable. A voice was singing on that record and behind the voice were a saxophone and a piano and the jukebox never stopped playing.

All of this puts a little humming in the head. And it casts the mind about searching for answers, arranging memories and exhibits into known, familiar categories. It's time to plan, to choose, to judge where to go, what to do next.

He was a kind man, whoever he was, the man who had taken us by the hand and therefore by the heart and led us into the Ki Damang Guest House.

We had slept in beds with mattresses and sheets on top of the beds, and no one had spat or hacked his throat clear of betel nut juice during the whole night.

The following morning we discovered a white toilet in the next room with a lever on the side of it. When the lever was pushed, it caused the water to swirl and rumble and finally cough. The noise was deafening and the motion left one feeling seasick.

The door handle to the bedroom door came off in my

hand, and from it fell little screws that bounced up and down on the tile floor and scurried off to find a hiding place beneath the bed.

I wrapped myself in a sheet because I couldn't find my jeans. My underwear had, long ago, rotted and fallen away in the jungle, and I was left with nothing to wear.

Between us Jmy and I had one complete pair of shoes. Jmy's feet were sore and badly infected between his toes. It was decided that he should wear the shoes, but when he pulled them on, the shoestrings broke, the leather separated at the seams, and they fell to the floor in pieces.

I poked my head out of the doorway into the guesthouse lobby and nearly fell over a wooden crate that stood in the hallway, a crate stuffed with Dyak blowguns, funeral masks, mandaus, and the like. The sheet fell to half mast as two astonished Indonesian guests rounded the corner. They undoubtedly experienced a cultural shock of their own. They politely turned their backs while I clutched my sheet and skidded to safety behind a low lamp with a large shade.

A woolly brown dog sauntered into the parlor and wet on the floor. He was followed into the room by an Indonesian houseboy who was carrying my jeans and shirt, tattered and torn, but clean and pressed.

Breakfast was learning to sit in a chair at a table, not on the floor, to eat. It was getting used to plates again and using a spoon and even a fork. Breakfast was learning to put a napkin in your lap and having a whole bowl of rice placed before you, a bowl just for you. And you could eat all of it if you wanted. It was a time to recall the names of the fruits on the table; bananas, pineapples, *rabutans,* and to look at the beautiful crystals of white sugar in a porcelain container and the salt and pepper too. And breakfast was coffee. Hot, black, strong, sweet-smelling coffee, and you could drink as much as you could hold.

It was a day for "good-bys." Good-by to the governor's representative, to the commander in chief of police, to the newspapermen and the radio men and to everyone, except to Abdul.

Abdul was sick and had sent his farewell message through a friend without telling us too much about the nature of his illness, and it put me to pondering. I was not feeling well, and Jmy looked worse than he had when we were in the jungle. Was it possible that, in returning to civilization, we had brought the jungle out with us?

At noon, we climbed into the same old car that we had used months ago, driven by the same old driver and still suffering from the same old tire-punishing. The engine turned over, caught, faltered, and then caught again, and the driver advanced the gas pedal. We jumped ahead, out onto the asphalt, and jiggled and clattered over the hole-filled road to the airfield and an airplane that would take us to Djakarta.

The building at the airport had mahogany walls, about thirty feet long and fifteen feet wide, a tar-paper roof, and a few square windows, none of which had glass in them.

Behind the building was the airstrip, and on both sides were the trash and litter of man; tin cans, glass, bailing wire, buckets, a rubber boot, paper cups, chunks of concrete, pieces of splintered wood, all gathered and scattered everywhere. Permanent litter. Nature's litter usually disappears with the passing of a little time, but not man's.

Money had been unuseful to us for so long a time that we had forgotten how to make it work for us. Sjam groped among the bits and pieces of her mind, tried to frame up a request for air tickets to Djakarta and figure their costs at the same time. The responsibility required thought and it stirred her to uneasiness and some anxiety.

She stepped up to the ticket counter. First was the necessity of being heard, and her voice was soft, trembling and laced with emotions. The ticket seller stopped listening in the middle of her story, stood back, and looked off through the window as though she weren't there and hadn't said a thing.

She was stunned. She had laid out everything she had, finished it up. There was no response.

Indonesian ire flamed up within her. She gritted her teeth and a few well-chosen, if not hot, words burst out. They fired the man into action as three air tickets slid across the counter in exchange for the rupiahs she was holding in her hand.

A Constellation bounced down the runway and skidded to a stop at the end of the airstrip. We were herded into the interior and told to fasten our seat belts. All three of us closed our eyes during the entire flight.

Jmy was seriously sick. His face was as yellow as the blond roots that stuck out sharply from beneath his dyed black hair. The house doctor at the Hotel Indonesia in Djakarta informed us that he was suffering from hepatitis and influenza. We would not be able to fly home until he was strong enough to stand the trip.

Outside the hotel's windows, the newsboys bellowed the headlines of the morning papers. "Woman and child enter Central Borneo jungles. Courageous American woman and son risk lives to live with headhunters."

The newsmen, television crews, and radio announcers had met our plane at Kebayoran airfield and got their story. It was disastrous.

Nothing was mentioned about the Dyak people and their urgent need for food and medicine. No notice of their desperate plea for help.

That night I borrowed a typewriter from the hotel's front desk. The following day the newspapers carried a different kind of story:

> "My son and I have just returned from a journey to the back-side of the world; from an unknown people struggling to exist in an unknown land. These are 'little' people, the forgotton people of Central Borneo, the Dyaks.
>
> ". . . . . . . Almost extinct now, the fiercely proud

Dyaks of Central Borneo . . . . are lost and dying, left behind and forgotten in this new world of revolutionary progress.

"The death rate is staggering . . . . . alarming for the greatest cause is malaria. Why are the Dyaks dying from malaria in Borneo when the only quinine factory in all Asia is located in Bandung?

"I appeal to the people of the Republic of Indonesia to save these 'little people' from the sickness and disease to which they are surrendering. Save their bodies with your quinine and antibiotics and their minds and intelligence with books and educational materials.

"I beg you—let these proud and beautiful Dyak people live. They are waiting for you, these 'little people' . . . the forgotten people of Borneo."

The roof fell in. The newspapers, the TV and radio media not only picked up the story, they overdid it. They rapped the government, its officials, its methods, and they attacked the ministerial head of the Department of Internal Affairs with a dry viciousness.

There was going to be trouble. The situation might be compared to a visiting Frenchman's discovery of an unknown tribe of Indians, starving to death in Northern California, and shouting the notice of them from the Pentagon's pinnacle in Washington, D.C.

It was embarrassing. When the invitation to visit with the Minister of the Department of Internal Affairs arrived, I could not expect the Indonesians in the department to bend over backwards in gratitude at the sight of me.

The official greeters at the department were hospitable, with a marked absence of hostility of any kind.

The minister general was an extremely kind man and one of great brilliance. "We are concerned with the problem you have brought us from Central Borneo, Miss Sargent," he said, "and we thank you for expressing your kind interest in our Indonesian people.

"It has been my pleasure to ask you to come into the Department of Internal Affairs so that I might explain to you what we, as officials of the Indonesian Government, are up against. It is my sincerest hope that you will be left with a better understanding of our present situation.

"Our Government, you see, is quite cumbersome and struggling. We did not inherit a smoothly running administration, but we are trying to create something workable out of it.

"We have been pestered with revolutions and more revolutions. Our country is run by the braid on a man's shoulders and not by the brains in his head. We have too many generals and not enough lawyers, but then, we have too few graduates to have reached that degree. What administrative skill we have is in short supply, and most don't delegate authority because their subordinates lack education, experience or misuse the authority for their own gain. And, of course, there are some ministers who prefer to keep all the power to themselves. This is Indonesia.

"Our black market, as you know, is a thriving profession, particularly in foreign currency and luxury goods. We have more corruption from it than is good for anyone, and inflation has consumed us in terrifying proportions. The rupiah is worthless, you know. Take a fistful of notes, a whole fistful, and they are still worthless and you have nothing. We can't even mint a coin! Who wants a coin that runs hundreds to an American penny?

"It is difficult and painful for us to hear that the Dyaks are hungry and dying in Central Borneo, when we know that Indonesia ranks as the third richest country in the world in terms of natural resources. This is very hard to take.

"The lack of development of those resources is our fault, and we know it. It has to do with the leisurely pace at which our lives go along. We have the unfortunate attitude that what is not done today can be done tomorrow or the next day, and in fact, it's perfectly all right if it's never done at all.

"And so, what do we do, Miss Sargent? How do we explain ourselves to other people and to other countries?

"The words we use to explain ourselves are revolutionary turmoil, corruption, nepotism, personal and political animosities, casualness, lack of honesty, equipment, efficiency, and most of all, lack of funds.

"These words explain us. Perhaps, the Indonesian picture is clearer to you, now."

Aboard Japan Air Lines DC-8's connecting flight to Pan Am's Round The World, Jmy and I received a final glimpse of the green islands, strung together like a necklace of fine emeralds.

The southern coast rim of Borneo issued into view below the right wing tip, and my heart saddened at the sight of it. Somewhere down there was Panggul. Panggul and his little people and Panggul waiting. . . .

No help from Indonesia, Panggul. No help for your people. We must accept it with good will, Panggul, and with patience and good humor. We must be understanding that Indonesia is in no position to assist any headhunters right now, Panggul. Chin up, Panggul. Chin up.

I am certain that a few members of the American press found my story incredible and were nearly convinced I was a liar. But no one ever said so.

They took their interviews and their findings with tongue in cheek and wrote about an "American woman's great courage," and one who had lived with the "savage headhunters" in the Central Borneo jungles.

Most of the reporters got the point. They reported a lost, dying people living on the back side of the world, a people who desperately needed help if they were to survive the rigors of an encroaching civilization.

I wrote a few articles myself but soon lost whatever enthusiasm I had for the writing of them. My heart just wasn't in it. I was persecuted by the thoughts of a people who were waiting for a help that would never come.

I yearned to help the Dyak people and that yearning soon became an obsession. It was uncanny and sometimes it was frightening to me because the yearning was gigantic.

But what could I do? I wanted to help but I simply did not know how to get started.

Another kind of thought occurred to me; if the human mind could send a man to the moon, then why couldn't the human heart send love to mankind? It would mean the giving of medicines and materials from one people to another and organizing a help program of some kind.

I did not believe I was capable of putting together such an organization, one that would gather together the materials for the landscape the Dyaks needed and wanted. The more I thought about it the more I realized that I had no talent for such a thing. I faced my limitations and shared them with others and still went through the torments of self-doubt. But I had to at least try.

I accepted the challenge and committed myself to the responsibility of doing whatever I could for the Dyak tribes of Central Borneo. I asked a dear friend of mine to put me in touch with someone, anyone, who had influence in a pharmaceutical laboratory somewhere, anywhere, in the United States.

Fortunately, "Indonesia" was a magic word that year. It aroused the interest of those prospective investors moving in the foreign markets, and many of those investors were in the pharmaceutical business.

I flew to New York City and was given the opportunity to talk with interested individuals. I began by apologizing for my lack of professionalism and then told my story as it was.

The following day, seven of the leading pharmaceutical laboratories in the United States pledged their support to the program of helping the Dyaks. Their pledges came in promised tons of medicine.

Now I had an overwhelming problem. Those drugs offered were of a highly sophisticated nature and would require a licensed physician to administer them. Left alone, the Dyaks would kill themselves using the wonder drugs.

On December 18, 1968, I sent the following telegram to Regent Rachmat in Sampit and copies to President Suharto and Ambassador Greene:

> "SARGENT ARRANGING FOR AMERICAN PHARMACEUTICAL LABORATORIES TO SUPPLY FREE MEDICINE FOR MENTAJA HULU DISTRICT FOR ONE YEAR. URGENT YOU CABLE ME IMMEDIATELY SAMPIT DOCTOR'S RECOMMENDATION FOR SPECIFIC DRUGS AND QUANTITIES REQUIRED FOR DYAKS. VERIFY AVAILABLE PERSONNEL TO ADMINISTER DRUGS."

In the law offices of Dennis D. Hayden, Santa Ana, California, the Sargent-Dyak Fund was incorporated with the objectives to "contribute to the improvement of the health and welfare of the Dyak tribes in Central Borneo, Indonesia, by acquiring and distributing funds, medicines . . ."

I had no idea of the agonies involved in being a president of a charitable California corporation, but I was soon to find out. It wouldn't have mattered if I had known, anyhow.

I received a thank-you letter from the President of Indonesia but still no word from Borneo. I cabled again.

I knew it was useless. How could I expect tons of medicine to arrive in Borneo when two telegrams had so easily gone astray?

There was an alternate solution. I could deliver the medicines to the Dyaks and at the same time take an American doctor to administer them. I contacted the Direct Relief Foundation in Santa Barbara, California. Dennis Karzag, director, promised to secure a physician-surgeon for the corporation by September.

The pendulum, having swung in a positive direction, encouraged the corporation to extend itself into departments other than medical. We incorporated an Agricultural Department and made plans to collect seeds and farm tools, and perhaps a small tractor or jeep to clear the jungle. We planned to ask for a volunteer worker to serve as agriculturalist in Borneo, to teach the Dyaks how to use the materials on their land.

We envisioned an Education Department equipped with educational materials and a volunteer schoolteacher. And we developed an Animal Husbandry Department to take over the livestock we would ask for.

We had set for ourselves an impossible dream and we knew it. Furthermore, we imposed upon ourselves a one-year deadline for the accomplishment of these objectives.

The ideas came and with such lightning-like speed that we couldn't work fast enough to carry them out. There were not enough hours in the day for all the work that had to be done. What started out to be morning dimmed into evening before any of us noticed it had begun. Time lost its meaning and substance and there seemed to be fewer days in each month.

I wrote letters, thousands of letters, around the world to inform people of what the corporation wanted to do and to ask them for their advice if not for their assistance. Letters were sent to Ambassador Francis J. Galbraith at the American Embassy in Djakarta; to Ambassador Sudjatmoko at the Indonesian Embassy in Washington; to Edward E. Masters, Country Director for Indonesian Affairs in the Department of State, Washington, D.C.; to Secretary of State William Rogers and I even wrote President Richard Nixon.

As a result the corporation was made aware of the application procedures for securing a license to import relief goods, duty free, and it was warned of a procedure that was "lengthy and complicated."

The Dyaks were dying and we didn't have time to wait.

We needed someone to work a miracle, someone who could pass the men and materials into Borneo with a nod of the head and waive the red tape of customs, duties, immigration, and the "lengthy and complicated" procedures.

On a long shot, I asked a person whom I had never met to

be the "Honorary Recipient" of those gifts offered by the American people to the people of Borneo. It was requested on a woman-to-woman basis. That woman was Madame Suharto, wife of the Indonesian President. She accepted.

The corporation inched forward, sometimes with the sideways movement of the crab.

There were moments when the future for the program looked black and formless. It seemed impossible to move ahead, to go anywhere in the tight, frozen structure into which it had settled.

But never, at any time, did I experience depression. I simply didn't have time.

There was a certain ruggedness to the path of asking someone to give you something free. The members of the corporation board had to learn to fight their way in, and when they did they donned armored skin for protection. All of us worked under the twin pressures of maximum speed and minimum of waste, and the combination left us extremely aggressive if not obnoxious. Some people met us with curiosity, others with remarkable kindness, but it was hard to find a man or woman who did not want to help if it was possible.

The Sargent-Dyak Fund was a people-to-people operation. Although the effort was loyally supported with "best wishes for success" by the United States State Department officials, they kept their noses and their fingers out of it.

We chose as our field of action for fund raising the many clubs and private organizations in the country. They were immediate and accessible victims. And they responded. Kiwanis, Rotary, Lions, Charity Leagues, Ebells and Junior Ebells of this county and that, and the Garden Grove Community Church, of which I am a member.

My son's school, Harbour View, dreamed up and sold tickets to a "Headhunter's Ball," and the funds purchased new books for the corporation's proposed sister school in Central Borneo, River View.

The kids down the street gave up their lunch money so that a Dyak child could eat. The ladies in the community of Huntington Beach staged a Flea Market and sold things they had taken out of their garages to raise money for the effort.

After working hours, a few of the more daring women raided houses under construction and picked up dropped nails to be used in the corporation's proposed jungle hospital.

We asked everyone for everything we could think of. Sometimes we were turned away and sometimes we received things we had not even asked for: black lace brassieres and lawn edgers showed up. Although the gifts were useless, they were, at least, thoughtful.

When we needed generators, clothing, tools, toys, lanterns, stoves, and the like, we found the Yellow Pages to be a rewarding resource. We asked the Direct Relief Foundation in Santa Barbara to donate hospital furniture, and then we approached an oil company for a flat-bottomed boat to serve as a river-ambulance to bring sick Dyaks into the jungle hospital. We asked the Philippines to provide us with tons of Indica IR-8 rice seeds, and we asked for garden produce seeds from companies in the United States.

We never stopped asking. Nine months of asking.

On one occasion I naïvely flew to Detroit because I understood that they manufactured automobiles in that city. I elbowed my way into the offices of a leading automotive concern and asked for a jeep-type vehicle, one equipped with an electric winch capable of pulling down jungle trees, and I got it!

As the materials began to arrive in California my garage filled up and I could no longer park my car inside. I approached Bekins Van & Storage and asked them for free space. They not only gave us storage in a local warehouse, they assisted us in the transportation of the materials later.

We committed many errors, some of them unforgivable mistakes, but they did not keep us from pushing forever forward. Heifer Projects, Inc., for example, gave us five hundred pregnant rabbits before we learned that the animals were prohibited in Indonesia, and then we had to give them back.

The "woman with a cause" is invariably a pushy, "gutsy" individual, and from time to time an observing person would candidly remark about my "courage," out of kindness for a better word.

I deserved it. Especially when I placed telephone calls directly to a busy president of some company. "Yes, this is Wyn Sargent, President of the Sargent-Dyak Fund, Inc. May I speak to Bob, please?"

"President of the what?"

"Sargent-Dyak Company."

"Sargent-*Diet* Company?"

"No, no. *Dyak*. It means 'headhunter.' "

It was amazing how quickly the man would come to the telephone.

And the conversation would begin.

"Say, Bob, this is Wyn and I lived with the headhunters last summer. . . ."

In reflecting back on those days, it is astonishing that someone didn't have me strait-jacketed and locked up.

Then the word "humanitarian" did not exist in the Indonesian language. Sjam voluntarily took on the job of introducing that word to the Indonesian people, and by doing so she paved the road for the Sargent-Dyak Fund to enter the country.

It is impossible to see how she could have worked so hard and covered so much ground in so little time. Her effectiveness was remarkable. It is hard to overestimate the importance of her achievements.

Her work was, by far, more complicated than mine. If I made copies in duplicate, her country required eight and ten copies of everything that passed through her hands. When she received invoices from the corporation, she was imposed upon to trot the streets of Djakarta to collect the necessary seals and stamps to validate the documents.

I was able to place telephone calls to people on a decision-making level directly from my office, but Sjam was required to visit the various government departments and ministers in person. And there were many. She traveled by *betjak* and when she ran out of money she traveled on foot to the Departments of Health, Labor, Internal Affairs, Immigration, Customs, Public Works, Education, Agriculture, Information Service, Industry, and Social Affairs, and sometimes she visited the departments more than once.

I don't know where her great energies came from, but she was indefatigable. Surely there must have been times when her hours were as lonely as mine, but she never said so. The letters that flew over the Pacific between us, thousands of them, were always filled with excitement and hope and positive faith.

There was magic to the girl, real magic. When she asked her own country to support and donate to the corporation, they did.

And when she was finished asking, she had singlehandedly accumulated more than eight tons of materials and livestock for the Dyak people in less than four months. Now, that's a woman for you. Her contribution toward the introduction of the word "humanitarian" personified Sjam herself, and it made her the greatest humanitarian Indonesia may ever produce.

It takes a very special kind of person to fill the position of volunteer worker for a humanitarian cause.

That person should have a twinkle in his eyes, love in his heart and possess a nature that is relaxed, easygoing, and peppered with an abundant sense of humor. He should be tolerant, patient, adaptable, self-reliant and have title to a natural love for people. He should be able to act tactfully and respectfully toward the people with whom he is working as well as toward the people he is helping. He should realize that he might be thrown into a position of great responsibility, more properly the province of someone twice his age and experience, and accept that position with considerate good manners and comradeship.

That was the person I was looking for to fill the positions of schoolteacher, agriculturalist, doctor or animal husbandryman to live with the Dyaks and to teach them how to live on their land.

Facing the reality of the situation, I knew that no volunteer but a nincompoop would accept such a position with a salary of nothing.

At the end of the interviews, we narrowed the selection of the many young men who applied for the positions to six people who were a mixture of idealism, apprehension, and excitement.

A few of them were successful in fulfilling their parts of the operation. A few were not. One volunteer saw himself as a noble and highly superior creature, a dedicated servant of the underprivileged, and found himself thrown in with pagans and then suffered miserably when he tried a spot of evangelizing on the side without success. One of the boys became an "instant humanitarian" to escape his local draft board and the parental control that was strangling him at home. In a less informed moment, another felt he had stepped into the hypocrisy of considering himself holier than those who accepted huge salaries for giving aid to the less fortunate.

But for the most part those young volunteers, sturdy, stubborn American boys, learned a sharp lesson in humanitarianism by beginning a program in Central Borneo, establishing it, and then returning to America knowing that they had made a substantial contribution to the longevity of the Dyak people.

There were unusual but humorous moments for the corporation. Dr. Leo L. Martello had reprinted, with my permission, an article I had written for *Scholastics* in his new handbook on witchcraft. The book somehow fell into the hands of a Mr. U. S. Charles in London, England, and I received the following letter:

"Dear Sir: My life is burdened with opposition for over five years. None of my plans are coming true; worst of all is a woman I supported for six years, leave me, on advice of her friends. I know some of their names. Among them is one name I do not know. She assaulted me with a broken bottle to fight. I have seen her only once. The lemon ritual may help me to work on her. Please advise me how to construct it, on vacation, in a small room. I am living privately. I want a small wand and the witch requirements for individual ritual. Would you get me a little do it yourself book."

The letter was one of many received in my newly acquired but dubious position as an "authority on witchcraft."

In May 1969, the corporation attacked the problem of transportation to Borneo for the cargo, livestock, and personnel.

Chet Huntley was instrumental in getting an interview on the *Today Show* in New York, and Priscilla Buckley spirited some interesting happenings through her publications in the *National Review*. One of them arrived in the form of a telegram from a leading aircraft manufacturing corporation. They offered to fly us across the Pacific in a C-130, provided the Sargent-Dyak Fund paid for the jet fuel.

We got the necessary JP-4 military jet fuel from an oil company that made it, only to find that the aircraft company, pinched in the closing crack of delinquent tax payments, was compelled, suddenly, to limit its offer to that of volunteering American pilots to fly a C-130 that had, long ago, been purchased by Indonesia and was presently stored in a hangar somewhere in Djakarta.

I found myself in the uncomfortable position of asking an ambassador to allow me to borrow his airplane.

I cabled the State Department to let them know what I was up to and flew to Washington, where I met and talked with Ambassador Sudjatmoko concerning the loan of Indonesia's C-130. The ambassador enthusiastically agreed and promised that indeed, if we supplied the fuel, his country would supply the plane.

We fixed our departure date. There would be plenty of time to meet Madame Suharto for the gift presentation on the prearranged deadline.

It is the nature of the pendulum to swing, and while we were busy arranging for the necessary ground support for the C-130 at the Los Angeles International Airport, we received the bad news. There would be no airplane. The Indonesian C-130 existed. It simply did not operate anymore. The maintenance of the plane had suffered drastically during the financial distress of the country and rust had set in its wings and gears.

I sent Sjam the following telegram: "ARRIVE BY BOAT NOVEMBER."

The letter from Sjam was lying in the bottom of the mailbox. It was not a long letter. Just one page, typewritten, simple and direct.

Sjam said she had been informed that Panggul would not be waiting for me when I returned to the jungle. Not waiting as he had promised.

Panggul had kept another kind of appointment. The journey he had led to save the lives of his people had cost him his own. Panggul had died of malaria just shortly after I had returned to America.

The Sargent-Dyak Fund, Inc., boarded the freighter U.S.S. *President Madison* in San Pedro, California, with nearly twenty tons of materials, personnel, and livestock to begin the first leg of the journey to Central Borneo.

As the ship pulled out of the harbor, I looked over the rail at America and at the Americans who had made this impossible dream come true.

And I wondered how one says thank you. Thank you to people who believed in you, followed and strengthened you before they really had the time or opportunity to test your skills and sincerity. How does one say thank you, to people like that?

Chapter Fifteen

Saja Sjahsam

How strange it was to return to the jungle without Panggul.
He belonged to the jungle and the jungle belonged to him,
and you couldn't separate them.

I couldn't think of Panggul as being dead. The evidence
of Panggul's life had been his effect on the Dyak people
and his effect on my life. And those things still lived.
While there remained even a plaintive memory of him,
Panggul could not be dead.

Panggul was a barely five-foot-tall giant with hair cut
short, hair about the same color as his face. He dressed in
"white man's" clothes that never seemed to fit quite right.
Panggul was a man whose life had been caught up in an effort to make men brave and dignified at a time when they
were frightened, starving, and dying from the ugly forces
that had worked against them.

Panggul was an uneducated man and therefore illiterate.
When he spoke, it was without being ornate, for he was also
a simple man. But his visions made him a complex man and
those visions were beyond the shattering by anyone.

Although he had been a headhunter, Panggul was against
tribal warfare. He was naïve enough to believe that peace
would be good for his people and his world.

The cosmopolitan character of his ambitions lay in the dreams he designed for his people, dreams that would enable them to develop their own initiative and resources.

The first time I saw Sjahsam was in Sampit. He was walking along the riverbank, headed in the direction of the Kabupaten, wearing ordinary clothes, green wash trousers and a cream-colored shirt that was open at the collar. He was barefoot and without a hat of any kind.

I don't know what there was about the man that caught my attention. I didn't really even see his face.

The second time I remember seeing him was one evening at the bupati's house. He was standing outside the house, on the porch, and he looked through the window with yearning. Our eyes met briefly and then he lowered his head and stepped quickly away. That was all.

And then I saw him again near the spot where Panggul and I had said good-by. He was sitting high on the riverbank, his legs brought up to his chin, like Panggul used to sit, and his thin arms were wrapped tightly around his knees. His face was younger than Panggul's and thinner, much thinner. It was a face with fine features, indescribably fine with a full-lipped mouth which was badly burned by the sun. All of him, every exposed part of him, was burned by the sun. I supposed he had that type of skin that left him hardly a time during the year when some part was not burned raw or peeling. His sleeves were rolled up and the soft inside of his arm was nearly white. This was surprising because the man looked to be Dyak.

He stood suddenly and his hands went to gripping at his sides because it seemed to him to be the most comfortable thing to do. He wore *maniks*, Dyak jade bead bracelets, on his left arm, and around his right was fastened a Japanese wrist watch. It was unusual for a Dyak to wear a watch.

And then he turned suddenly, lowered his arms, and walked toward me on legs as slender as grass blades. His head was cocked to one side, the better to hear if something was said.

When we were face to face, he spoke with words that were filled with affection and pride. "*Saja Sjahsam*," (I am Sjahsam) "I would be happy to take you to my people. I would be guide for you. I ask nothing, only to be guide for you."

I suppose Sjahsam could be called a half-breed if such a thing is possible in Borneo. His Sampit father had been sent, years ago, to Kuala Kuajan to civilize the place, and he had extended his field of influence by marrying a Dyak Katingan from the village.

Sjahsam was the first-born and the beloved of the family. He was a strong-headed boy and he possessed his father's balance and his mother's good humor.

Whenever Sjahsam could fit it in, he turned loose his infectious laughter. I never knew until much later that he cried for the Dyak people.

And so, Sjahsam picked up Panggul's fallen banner.

It seemed strange, too, to be in the jungle without Jmy, without Abdul, and without a police-military escort. Abdul was sick in Bandjarmasin, and Jmy, home in America, was studying in school.

For administrative convenience, the corporation set up its operation in Kuala Kuajan. The village was located midway in the Mentaja district. The river was deep enough to allow the transport and delivery of the cargo, personnel, and livestock.

While plans were put into action for the construction of the jungle hospital, a school, the rice-farming demonstration project, and a livestock training center, Sjam, Sjahsam, and I tackled the job of informing the village chiefs about the program. We visited each village on the Mentaja, Kuajan, Mentubar, and Kalang rivers, and while visiting them we were able to complete the first census in Central Borneo history. We registered ten "new" villages into the program, in addition to the known forty, an effort that consumed nearly six weeks in the doing.

When we entered a village, the chief ordered the Dyaks to attend the meeting and to listen to what we had to say. They could have come and listened anyhow, but commanding them somehow gave the chief a feeling of management.

The Dyaks crouched around us, wide-eyed and staring, and hung onto every word. They had to remember everything that was said, because none of them could read or write.

We asked them to discuss with us every kind of problem they could think of. The Dyaks, to get things going, offered us betel nuts, and then as they chewed they unfolded their troubles. Food and medicine were high on the list. The Dyaks in some of the villages had found gold nearby, and they knew it was worth something if they could get it out of the ground. Could we help them? Still other villages wanted to learn something about extracting rubber from the trees on their land because the Chinese had offered them money for it.

And a few confused Dyaks interjected their own domestic problems, too. One man complained that his wife had left him and another complained that his wife wouldn't leave him. One tiny, shrunken old woman confessed that her husband drank too much tuak the night before and had disturbed her all night long.

We tried to diagnose the problems of each village and prescribe a policy that would promote the cures.

Sjahsam presented the program as only he knew how. He walked through the villages with the people, picked up the soil in his hands, and crumbled it in his fingers, and he talked with the Dyaks about the crops they could have in their villages. He planned with the Dyaks the raising of animals for their domestic use, and he dreamed with the Dyaks that their children would someday read and write.

The Dyaks liked Sjahsam. They considered him one of

them, and because they recognized a man of common sense and structure, they were happy he had come with us.

Sjahsam explained the basic rudiments of the program; come to Kuala Kuajan, see the materials and learn how to use them, and then take them home to your village. That simple.

The Dyaks were smart enough to realize that the acquisition of the knowledge and materials would have a decisive effect upon them, and they were restless with enthusiasm to participate. When they learned that the materials and instructions were free, many could scarcely force themselves to remain at the meeting until after we had left the scene. It was easy for the Dyaks to understand and accept the principle of free aid. They had been helping themselves to another's possessions for years.

So the Dyaks streamed into Kuala Kuajan. The sick became well and the well became owners of rice seeds and many learned to read and write because they wanted to. Others became the owners of the animals, badges of superiority, held with pride and honor, a symbol of wealth.

Later, the Dyaks learned that the animals were a kind of living currency, and they used them and rice as a medium of exchange.

They were a people determined to make the most of whatever was offered. Something, finally, had raised the corners of the Dyaks' mouths.

Tumbang Hirin is in the northern part of the Katingan Hulu District, and although it meant fourteen extra days of travel to arrive in the village, it would be worth it. I wanted to see Panggul's grave.

The chief of the village led us to the grave site himself. He was a small man who, in his youth, had broken his left leg. The bones had set themselves at random and had left their jagged ends sticking sharply out through the skin in a wound that never healed. The poor fellow jerked as he walked, moving along at a painful pace and suffering terribly from the unfortunate healing of his leg.

The chief led us to a place behind the village where a path had been cut beneath the jungle trees. Tall grasses grew on either side of the path and it was wide enough for only one person to travel upon at a time. We followed him for more than two hundred yards, and then, abruptly, the chief stopped and pointed straight ahead at the thing that was in front of him.

It was some kind of an open glade. The area was nearly circular, perhaps a hundred feet in diameter, with no grasses growing on it except in the middle. The glade was flat, smooth, covered with deep brown soil, and bordered with tall reddish trees that stood as straight as soldiers and as close together.

The trees looked nearly human. Their trunks resembled torsos with bones inside of them, and they stretched out their muscular limbs, embraced the next nearest tree, and twisted upward over the opening to form an umbrella covering over the glade.

The brown soil around the base of the trees spread out to the center of the glade where a low green grass covered three graves.

Panggul lay in the center. The grave on the right held Tewah's body. After one hundred seventeen years of living she finally gave up the struggle and had died quietly in her sleep. The other grave was smaller. It was the same distance across but it was shorter. It held the body of Panggul's son, Nangi. Nangi had died from malaria at about the same time as his father.

I knelt at the foot of Panggul's grave and reached out to touch the grasses that grew there. I wanted to remember every detail in that place. I wanted to remember the human-torso trees, the dirt where no grasses grew, and the glade where the graves, all three of them, lay side by side. I wanted to remember that place, because I would be needing the sweet strength of that place.

Chapter Sixteen

Three Hairs and a Fingernail

It took about twenty years for the pitiful handful of Mentaja and Kahajan Dyaks who had settled the village of Tumbang Gagu in 1800 to come to the conclusion that they couldn't make a go of things.

Gagu rested in an area more than 3,500 feet above sea level. The dribbling river was fishless and the dense jungle surrounding the village held no game. The Dyaks were plainly starving to death.

The living buried their dead, planted a few monuments and in one grand swoop abandoned their village for better parts. The Kahajans drifted downstream to join their friends in other Kahajan villages, and the Mentajas walked west into the jungle, and to this day they have never come out. They lost themselves in the jungle and by doing so they lost their identity. Today they are called the "Nomad Dyaks," the most baneful Dyaks that ever lived.

Despite the failings of the first settlers, several Dyaks Katingan, along with a few Duhois and Sahieis, followed a Katingan chief named Singa Djaja Antang* to old Tumbang Gagu to build a new Tumbang Gagu.

The Great Lion believed that so ill-endowed a village

* The Great Lion, unusual for there were no lions in Borneo.

deserved at least one possession of notable grandeur. He decided to build a "long house."

It took the Dyaks nearly seven years to construct the phenomenon, and when they were finished, they had a structure that rose seven meters off the ground at its lowest point. It was long enough, nearly fifty meters, to accommodate every inhabitant of the village, all sixty of them.

The Dyaks erected a fort on stilts in front of the long house to protect their mighty prize from jealous invaders. They took turns guarding themselves with blowguns in the tower day and night.

The newcomers were aware of the long house, and although they were curious to see it, they were afraid of its strength and uncertain as to the intent of its owners. They kept their distance.

Today the building lies smoldering with neglect and nearly hidden from view with the wild overgrowth of the jungle. There still prevails, however, the same sternness and ferocity in the structure as well as those who live within its walls.

The unusual mixture of Katingan, Duhoi, and Sahiei produced a curious breed of Dyaks. They furthered that curiosity with strange habits. The originals, a standoffish lot, denied themselves the privilege of marrying anyone outside their long house. The marriages and intermarriages eventually led to a new but slightly crazy generation. One of the products was a woman called Gangan.

Gangan was born with a head much too large for her body and one that she held at a slight tilt when she walked, the weight of it being too much for her thin neck to support. Her physical deformities were accompanied by a mental derangement which left her gibbering the nonsense of the insane to herself and to others when she could get them to listen.

Whatever spirited Gangan into pulling out her hair, she had responded to it and had succeeded in doing a first-class job. She began at the temples, pulling a few strands at a time and worked upwards and backwards until she was hairless to a point well behind both ears. One patch of long black hair grew from the back of her head only because the spot was safely out of reach from her frantic hands. Gangan was breech-birthed and could not raise her elbows above her waist.

Gangan had learned of our arrival in the village and she sent word that she wanted to relate to us her latest discouragement. She was sane enough to be self-conscious and she itched with shyness and perhaps shame when anyone looked at her bald head. She hid her face with both hands and asked the chief to speak on her behalf.

Bodud, chief of Tumbang Gagu, listened to Gangan's babbling prattle, and when he thought he had all of it, he related her story.

Gangan, it seemed, had contracted malaria. To produce a cure, she had been visited by a seventy-five-year-old female witch doctor who lived in Penda' Tangaring, a village on the opposite side of the jungle.

When one remembered that the jungle belonged to the Nomad Dyaks and was a jungle few dared to enter, it was difficult to believe that a seventy-five-year-old woman had crossed through it. As the story unfolded, however, it appeared that the female doctor had walked its path not only once but on several occasions.

How the doctor was alerted that a sick woman lay in Tumbang Gagu was uncertain. Perhaps the message was sent with drums or by spirits. But the news was received and the witch doctor hobbled through the jungle and found Gangan.

The doctor brought a certain ferocity to her work by convincing Gangan to surrender to her a fingernail clipping and three long black hairs from her nearly bald head. The three hairs were yanked from the small selection of those remaining near the nape of Gangan's neck and a half-moon paring cut from her right thumbnail.

The witch doctor curled her hand around the items and

trudged back to her village to perform magic and produce a cure by remote control.

With the passing of a few days and no noticeable improvement in health, Gangan's frame of mind took on a new picture. Bizarre and weird thoughts invaded her head, and she imagined that it was the witch doctor's intent to do her harm rather than the promised good.

A second message was fired across the treetops, a message that demanded the immediate return of the three hairs and fingernail paring.

The witch doctor labored through the dense jungle bearing the hair and fingernail in a small *sirih* leaf that had been pulled together at the top to form a bag. She held them in front of Gangan, who begged, pleaded, whined, and cried for their return. The witch doctor begrudgingly gave up the items, leaf bag and all, and hastily returned to Penda' Tangaring.

Gangan untied the leaf and surveyed the contents. To her sudden, unhappy dismay she discovered that one hair was missing and half of the fingernail.

Another message was sent to the witch doctor to surrender the missing parts. The old woman answered the appeal by saying that she would never set foot in Tumbang Gagu again.

Chief Bodud was a worried man. He watched Gangan's family polish up their mandaus and blowguns and dip the points of arrows into freshly secured *ipuh*. The family was filled with a wrath so vehement that they were willing to instigate open warfare between the two villages.

Bodud fluttered about the long house like a confused butterfly. He did not really know what to do. He went from family to family asking for help, but there wasn't a soul in the village who wanted to walk through the jungle into Penda' Tangaring to demand the return of the half fingernail and hair.

Chief Bodud presented the problem, and at the same

time the solution, to Sjahsam. He begged Sjahsam to encourage the Great White Fish to retrieve the stolen effects.

The danger in the jungle between Gagu and Penda' Tangaring was correctly ascribed to the Nomad Dyaks, to whom
the jungle belonged.

Although Sjahsam had never had an encounter with the
Nomads, he was aware of some of their customs and a few
of their habits. He felt that if we secured their permission to
enter the jungle, we could pass through their territory with
some element of safety.

Sjahsam assembled a "gift offering" in a round rattan
basket, and when he was finished the basket held a mandau,
a few shells, a cup of rice, and a little salt. He picked up the
basket, stuck his parang in his belt, and headed off toward
the jungle, alone.

In less than an hour he returned, unharmed, and he
looked quite pleased with himself. He said that he had
seen the *dondon,* a three-poled bamboo structure flanked
with a poisonous spear, considered the entrance gate to the
Nomads' domain. He had placed the gifts at the gate and
beside them he compiled a message of little sticks pointing
toward the village of Penda' Tangaring. Supposedly the
sticks asked permission for our safe passage there.

The following afternoon Sjahsam returned to the jungle
spot and found the basket gone. In its place were little arrows stuck in the ground, their ends pointing skyward. This
was an arms-at-rest position and supposedly ensured a safe
journey for us. If the points had been placed in the ground,
the message spelled death.

We decided to walk the jungle at daybreak, a decision
which had the full support and enthusiasm of the village
chief.

No jungle is ever walked at night regardless of its owners.
As far as anyone knew, this particular chunk of jungle
yielded no living thing except Nomads and a few snakes.

But the jungle is filled with whispers at night. The Dyaks are able to take care of themselves in any kind of wilderness, but they are naïve and helpless against a whisper.

Penda' Tangaring lay dead ahead, a straight line to the west. Sjahsam was certain it could be reached in one day's walking. He felt he knew how to get there, and I believed that he did. He reminded us that his Dyak instincts would apprise him of exactly where we were at all times and how much farther we needed to travel and in which direction.

It is impossible to reduce into a few simple terms the mystic powers that are felt by the Dyak people. The feelings are simply there and they are lived by because they are there. Questioning the feelings was useless.

Apart from Dyak eyes and a Dyak heart, Sjahsam possessed a fine pair of Dyak feet. He was as sure-footed as a pack burro. It may have been my own blank belief that those feet were indeed capable of walking through the jungle without stumble.

Or it could have been that I had finally learned that, when a Dyak spits on the ground and mumbles a spell to himself, then everything else becomes automatic.

When morning finally turned the sky to pale blue, Sjam and I packed a few provisions in rattan baskets and slung them over our shoulders and followed Sjahsam into the jungle.

The sun shone hotly on the trees and broke up into strips, sending columns of light that slanted through the heavy branches and spreading sunshine on the ground. Although the sun breaks through in spots and dries part of the jungle, most of it is wet. The leaves fall from the trees and carpet the ground and the undergrowth and ferment in the dampness. There are no breezes and nothing moves on the wet leaves.

We walked beneath the trees as long as we could. Each step of the way had to be chiseled out, and Sjahsam's parang never stopped swinging. The cutting was done with great care that wood did not strike wood. That sound was the Nomad signal for war.

When the vines knit themselves so tightly that we could not chop our way through, we climbed up the vines and walked on top of them, like traveling on a shaky trampoline. There were places where the vines raced up the treetops, and then we walked above the jungle and could see for miles around.

At one point we descended and crossed over a slender stream that twisted its way back and forth on a shallow bed of black sand. The trees on the sides of the stream thrust their roots deeply into the black mud and sucked up the water, leaving the ground behind them as hard as iron. The water was filled with larvae tumbling end over end on the surface. Around the base of the trees were more leeches than anyone would want to think about.

Tarzan may have swung on vines in his jungle. We were never able to find a vine that was long enough or free enough. Most of the large ones, those that would support our weight, were covered with smaller vines and were well buried in the tangle and bramble that make up all jungles.

The afternoon was advancing rapidly and we were tired, but we never stopped walking. Not even to eat. Sjahsam handed us back a fistful of cold rice and we munched as we walked, trying to make each bite last as long as possible to pass the time away.

The sun had grown into a richer tone with the coming of late afternoon, and it threw in threads of gold through the trees.

Suddenly a thunderhead throttled the sun and the light was gone. Lightning shattered the air and fat drops of water plummeted down through the trees. The drops grew until they ran together and then the rain came down in columns, columns that bored holes through the trees and drummed upon us until we were as wet as we could get.

When the rain trailed off a little, the sun sent in its dusty yellow shine, and the jungle dripped noisily before it left off dripping entirely.

Sjam and I blinked at one another through lashes filled with water, and then we noticed Sjahsam. He was crouched down on one knee, unmoving, and his head was cocked slightly to one side as though he was listening to some small sound that was charged with danger. A column of water fell abruptly between us and Sjahsam's nostrils flared at an odor that displeased him.

We looked up into the trees and there, frozen to resemble a limb, was an enormous python. The snake was lying on top of the limb. It was not twisted or coiled around the branch and it was quiet and still, perhaps sleeping. The snake had not seen us.

The center part of the python was looped loosely downwards, and the loop hung about a foot below the limb. The snake was as large at one end as it was at the other, and it was difficult to tell which end was the head. The body was as big around as a dinner plate and it stretched from the tree trunk to the outermost end of the branch, a distance of fourteen or fifteen feet.

The snake's skin glistened from the recent rain, sleek and glassy, except where a stiff ridge of scales stood up on its back.

Out of the corner of my eye I saw Sjam move away. She side-stepped backwards and I tried to follow her, but a fine stable of fears had developed within me and left my body heavy and earth-bound and it wouldn't move.

The loop grew suddenly, sagging downwards, and it dropped nearly a foot before it stopped moving. And then it dropped again, becoming larger and larger until more of the snake was in the loop than on the limb.

Then we saw the head. We were standing directly beneath it. The snake, aroused by the movement of its sagging loop, had raised its head in an effort to swing its dropping coil back up on the branch. The loop kept coming down, picked up speed, and dropped again. And then the snake lost its grip on what little was left of the limb beneath it.

A cold horror ripped through us as the great python spun over the limb like some human whip and lashed out through the jungle, cracking its tail as it went.

The snake crashed to the ground, landing more on its back than any other part. It began rising and falling in the vines, whirling around dizzily in mid-air, twisting its coils in circles to turn itself over onto its belly. It swept the jungle in a moving, circling, whipping arc that covered the ground. There was no place left to run from it.

The head of the snake was very near and my heart began to pound, flicking a little at each beat. One of its eyes was bubbled outwards, as big as a half dollar, and it seemed that down deep in the pupil I could see my own face reflected.

On the other side of the python, Sjahsam crawled his way toward the snake's head, groveling and tunneling himself through the twisting, turning coils. The snake jerked a loop toward him abruptly, and the coil struck Sjahsam's knife. The python swung its huge head toward its injury and when it did saw Sjahsam.

The snake laid a coil down on top of him and pressed hard against the ground. I heard the air whoosh from the snake's mouth as Sjahsam buried his knife into the trapping coil.

Sjahsam scrambled out from beneath the imposing weight and clawed his way forward, closer to the snake's head. As he reached the head, another huge coil rose up behind him, towering like some gray monster. He did not see the coil, he was watching for the snake's mouth to move, for the jaws to unhinge and drop open.

The mouth opened. The jaws unlocked from seemingly halfway down its body and the mouth spread open in a wide yawn. And then, suddenly, the huge head with its open mouth shot upwards and Sjahsam's knife crashed down through the snake's thick head.

The body rotated around the severed, bloody head, thrashing and twisting violently, and the jungle boiled beneath it. I was switched across the face with the lashing vines, and then the middle part of one coil turned, fell forward, and pressed against me. I put up my arms to protect my face and felt my stomach pushed up against my chest. I remember rolling over and over in the jungle and I remember the smell of the crushed jungle grass beneath me and the dank odor of the dampness on the ground. I remember a shadow falling on me when Sjahsam placed himself between me and the expiring snake.

I looked at Sjahsam's blood-soaked hands and at his tired eyes. A stillness fell on the jungle; a sweet, peaceful, beautiful stillness.

When we reached Penda' Tangaring, the hard bright stars were out, millions of them, penetrating the hot night with their sharpness.

There was a skittering among the natives in the village when we came into view. They had never seen a white person and none of them expected us. The people were Ot Danum Dyaks. Some of them looked tame and a few of them appeared prosperous. The chief welcomed us without knowing who we were or what we wanted.

On the edge of the village Sjahsam conferred with the chief, a conference that took nearly an hour to complete. Sjam recognized a few words that passed between the two men, and reported that the body of the conversation had to do with talk of birds and child care!

When Sjahsam felt it was safe to mention the point of our visit, the chief warned us that we would be dealing with a woman who, when angered, possessed an eye capable of flaying the skin off our bodies and who could eat up our souls at the same time. And she was in that state of anger presently. He suggested that we spend the night in his shack, promising that morning would bring finer results.

The houses in the village were well-constructed stilt

shacks, suitable for jungle life. The chief lived in a two-room house. One of those rooms was called a "parlor." A bench had been fixed to one wall, although nobody ever sat on it.

The natives, curious and intrigued, piled into the little parlor and sat on the floor, in front of the bench. They kept coming until they had filled up the room, and they never left. Most of them slept where they had sat down; a few slept against the persons next to them, having fallen over in their sleep. Sjam and I sat up all night because there was no room to lie down.

During the night the witch doctor crept into the shack, unobserved, and wedged herself into the opposite corner, as far away from us as she could get.

When morning sunshine filtered through the thin cracks in the walls, it revealed the woman to be sitting inside of a big sack.

The fabric looked like burlap, rather loosely woven and dark brown in color. The bag was open at the bottom and her feet were withdrawn into the interior. No single part of the woman showed outside to the viewer, and it was impossible to see through the material to detect either face or form.

The witch doctor appeared to be as tiny as a child and bent over somewhat in the back. The deformity projected her head forward and outwards, and it was difficult to tell exactly in which direction she was looking, whether up or down or sideways. It was disconcerting. If she had her angry eye fixed upon you, it would be valuable to be alerted.

She surprised everyone by announcing that she knew why we were in the village. The mystic powers and Dyak black magic had informed her, she said, that we were to be expected. She had already communicated with the spirits, and they had advised her to relinquish the hair and half fingernail in exchange for hairs and fingernails from the white woman.

Sjahsam loaned me his parang and I pared off the top of

my thumbnail and pulled a few hairs from my head. I walked the length of the room to confront the witch doctor, face to sack. Surely it must have been hot inside that sack. The fabric was thickly heavy and appeared to be wet around the top.

Abruptly the sack shook. The movement began at a point near the witch doctor's lap and then it tripped downwards until the doctor's hand popped out at the bottom of the sack. The hand was clenched up like a fist, the palm turned downwards. It was an old, aged hand and the skin was wrinkled and badly splotched with large brown spots. She slowly turned her fist over. Her nails had grown a half inch beyond the ends of her fingers, and she could not curl her fingertips into her palm.

She waited a moment and then she opened her hand. Lying on the aged palm was another hand. A tiny, shriveled monkey's paw. The fingers on the paw had been crushed and broken at the joints and were curled over the palm, and the thumb had been tucked inside. Covering the paw was a withered black skin that was twisted and tied at the wrist with a piece of rattan and with a diameter so small the bones must have been removed.

I stared at the monkey's paw and halfway expected it to open by itself. With the fingers of her hand, the witch doctor pried open and held back the fingers on the paw. In the little palm lay a piece of fingernail and one long black hair neatly wound to resemble a thin metal spring.

My own hand trembled a little as I reached into the monkey's paw to extract the cute little articles, and my fingertips scraped the bottom of the palm. The touch sent a shudder through my body and I quickly dropped my own nail and hair on the monkey's paw, and the witch doctor snapped it closed and pulled her hand into her sack.

In the discomfort of such an exchange, I had not heard the drums beating in the distance. Sjahsam's brows were puckered together and he frowned gloomily.

"Maybe," he said, "we too late. Drums from Gagu of family of Gangan. They send war message."

And then the drums in the village of Penda' Tangaring answered the challenge from Gagu and the low pitch of them quaked the jungle air with threatening vibrations.

We walked back through the jungle, nearly one full day of walking. When we arrived in Gagu, Gangan was sitting in the center path, waiting for us.

That night, I did a little bargaining of my own. The fingernail and hair were returned to Gangan after her family promised to commit her to the new hospital in Kuala Kuajan.

Chapter Seventeen

The Flower in the Circle of the Moon

The Dyaks in the village of Tumbang Kalang were rosy in the sunset. They stood in the doorways of their little shacks, exchanging whatever gossip they could think of, and if they had saved nothing to tell, then they tried to invent something.

The moon left its color on the faces of the Dyaks, and their eyes shone in its reflection. A little of the heat went out of the earth, and although it was not cool, the heat was less than it had ever been as far back as the Dyaks could remember. They took it as a good omen, a sign that the gods would help them accomplish their latest endeavor.

When Sjahsam and I decided to become blood brother and sister, the decision had the enthusiastic support of every Dyak in the Mentaja, but nobody knew how to perform the ceremony that would create such a union. The people were certain that the ritual existed. They simply didn't know how to do it. And because it had not had much call in the past, none of them had ever seen it.

The Dyaks put their heads together and talked things over until they were certain they had the solution. If anyone would know how to properly join the bloods of two people, it would be their chief, Maban. He was a man who knew everything simply because he was so old.

When the Dyaks arrived to settle Tumbang Kalang, they had found Maban sitting in the jungle, alone. He was a short, broad-shouldered man with a tremendous duster of black hair and with a face that had been squared by a bristling unkempt black beard. He was already very old and he appeared harmless, so no one interfered with him very much. No one bothered to ask Maban where he had come from or who he was, and as time passed, even Maban forgot about his own origin.

Maban had sat in the jungle and had watched the Dyaks build Tumbang Kalang from his tree across the river. He told the people where they could get rattan and other building materials for their shacks, and sometimes, when he had caught a wild boar in the jungle, he waded across the river and shared the meat with the people.

The Dyaks realized a good thing when they saw it. They made him chief of the village.

Maban was pleased with his acceptance by these people and flattered by the position they had given him, but he refused their efforts to install him in a house. He preferred living in the open jungle, sleeping in his own tree, and generally enjoying the life of a hermit. Maban's infatuation with solitude caused Tumbang Kalang to become the only village in the Mentaja whose chief lived alone on the opposite side of the river.

The Dyaks waded across the river to hand their problem over to Maban, and Sjahsam and I went with them. Maban welcomed us to his tree, and when we were comfortably seated, the Dyaks daintily unfolded their request.

The old man whistled between his teeth to indicate his interest and enthusiasm for the affair, and his eyes took on more twinkle than a man of his age should have had. He smiled broadly and his grizzled, bearded face blushed with emotion from having been asked to supervise an event of seemingly such staggering importance.

Maban's mind leaped to the problem with unbelievable energy. He bounced around his tree with the litheness of youth, and even his aged body seemed to take on the fresh firmness of a new weed.

And then the Dyaks were nearly sorry they had asked him, because none of them spent a private moment from then on. Maban asked every Dyak in Tumbang Kalang to work for him, and a few stray Dyaks from other villages were corralled and they worked too. He untapped energies from the Dyaks that they did not suspect they had. They worked day and night.

In their night excursions, the Dyaks waded back and forth across the river and held meetings with Maban. When they spoke, it was never above a whisper, because Maban had sworn the Dyaks to a secrecy with an oath so fearsome that it left them trembling.

Although Maban didn't realize it, he had set a style more rigid than it had ever been before. Ideas sprouted and spread into elaborate, extravagant happenings, and then the Dyaks even surprised themselves. The slightest deviation of Maban's orders brought forth a torrent of abuse from the others and engendered so much guilt on the part of the wrongdoer that the deviation was corrected before daylight.

Sjahsam and I followed some of the men about and tried to listen to their discussions, but when they saw us, they stopped both their work and their talk.

The preparations were shrouded in mystery and it was difficult to discover what was going on. One afternoon we waded across the river to visit Maban, but we might just as well have stayed home. He welcomed us to his tree, and when we sat down to talk there was one moment when Maban thought to tell us something about the ceremony. But a quick instinct stopped him and he put on his best face and told a joke instead.

A little information filtered out when the five rowdy chiefs representing the different tribes in the area showed up in the village. Their first effort was to cleanse the air of evil spirits by burning *gusar, kemenjan,* and *garu* wood in the center path of the village. The odor and smoke were extremely heavy, and by the end of the second day everyone in the village complained of burning eyes, clogged noses, and a few headaches. The chiefs decided that the village was clean enough and stopped burning the wood.

Sjahsam found it hard to make time with any of the chiefs. One of them finally confided that the ceremony was called Sawang Untung Kabeluman, but that was as far as he would go. Another chief volunteered that the blood exchange was called Hakinan Daha Hasapa Belum, and then refused to reveal how it was done.

After nearly a week of preparations, Maban finally decided that they were as ready as they were going to be, and he scheduled the ritual to begin before noon of the following day.

Sjahsam and I listened to the whisperings of the Dyaks as they made their last-minute night excursions across the river to confer with Maban. We looked forward to the coming of morning with sentimental wistfulness.

When dawn finally arrived and the sun was red through the window of the little shack that had been chosen for the happening, old Maban climbed down out of his tree, held up his sarong with his fingertips, and waded across the river to supervise the beginning of things.

The Dyaks met him on the riverbank. They were gloriously happy and together they buzzed over this and that and the other. When they were sure they understood everything that had to be done, they set off to work.

The materials that had been collected for the ritual were brought out from their hiding places and transported into the shack where one of the chiefs either accepted or refused their delivery. The materials were severely judged. Every bird's egg of questionable shape and each grain of imperfect rice was thrown out and replaced.

A large fishing net called a *djala* was brought into the

shack and spread out over the floor, and there wasn't a torn thread in any of it. The net symbolized the livelihood of the Dyaks, and its presence would give stability to the ceremony.

River stones were scattered over the net as symbols of solidity and strength, and above them the Dyaks balanced flat pieces of lumber, an effort to inform the gods that Sjahsam and I would be building a house together. It was an enterprise that we had not planned on.

Several Dutch coins appeared. Two of them were not good enough. The ill-shaped discs were discarded by one of the chiefs, and the rest were arranged in a circle on the "house" in payment to the gods for their participation in the ritual and to compensate for any inconvenience they may suffer during their attendance.

A chief placed a bundle of garu roots on the lumber house, dropped a hot coal in its center, and instantly the fire sighed up and a heavy odor breathed over the room.

Maban marched into the shack with a wild chicken beneath his arm and walked over to the fire. He held the chicken above the burning garu to cleanse the black feathers of evil spirits. One of its wings caught on fire. He slapped the chicken against his thigh in disgust, brushed the singed feathers with his hand, and threw the smoking bird into a corner of the shack.

A stumpy little Dyak with hands that hung nearly to his knees brought in a rattan basket filled with birds' eggs and placed them on one corner of the fishing net. The eggs were about the size of pigeon eggs and all of them were white except one, which was blue with tiny brown speckles on it. The eggs were believed to be the gifts from the gods. Because there was water within their soft shells, they were considered capable of imparting temperance to one's character.

Maban waited until the stumpy Dyak with the low-hanging hands deposited his charge, and then he turned and picked up a square wooden box from the far corner of the net. From the box he took handfuls of ashes and scattered them on the floor, covering the net and "house" with a fine film. In several places the ashes clumped together, and Maban took his mandau and stirred them about with the knife point to even things up. He took handfuls of dust from a small basket given to him by a chief and threw layers of the powder over the ashes. Rice, every grain now perfect, was sown over the floor in a hurry. Time was running out.

The ceremony had to be completed before noon if it was to be valid, and noon to the Dyaks of Tumbang Kalang was that time of day when the sun arrived over the coconut palm at the far end of the village.

Worry began to form in Maban's eyes and the worry had the taste of truth to it. It appeared as though the sun would top the palm in less than thirty minutes. Whatever was going to happen would have to come all at once.

I had been asked to wear a sarong for the occasion, a request that was a reminder of my continuing failure to keep such an outfit up. Despite whatever efforts, I was never able to master the slipknot wrapping required to hold the thing in place, and the slightest movement loosened the valuable knot and sent the dress on its way to the floor. There was nothing reassuring about donning the collapsing costume in a mixed crowd. But I would try.

I held the sarong with both hands as Maban escorted me to the center of the room. I was able to give it one more good hitch before Sjahsam and I were seated amid the fishing net, lumber, rice, dust, and ashes.

From somewhere outside the shack a gong sounded. It experimented a bit, feeling about for an appropriate rhythm, and then set off on its beating.

The gong brought the villagers piling into the shack, elbowing one another for a place to sit down. The women tucked their sarongs around their knees and sat with their feet drawn up. The men squashed in between each other, sat cross-legged and hacked their throats clear of betel nut juice, and then looked about for a hole in the floor to spit through. The children danced in, sat down by their mothers, and twisted and squirmed until they noticed that everybody was smiling and then they settled down and wondered what they could smile at too.

The gong broke into a feverish beating as still more people climbed into the shack and wedged themselves into its corners.

Maban, who had been nearly covered up with people, brushed away a few arms and legs and rose in the center of the room, his black hair standing straight up in little spikes.

And then the beating of the gong stopped and the hum of voices fell away and every eye in the room was automatically turned toward the old chief. Maban rubbed the sides of his mouth with his fingers and studied the two of us sitting on the floor. I boosted the sarong upwards another inch beneath his glare. He ran his eyes over the Dyaks, and when he thought he had the attention of everyone in the room, he explained the antiquity and symbolism of the ritual, none of which made much sense to anyone but to him. His eyes brushed over the array of material on the floor, and he wandered vaguely from one to the other and talked about each in turn, and his talk became so complicated and tiresome that when he was finished he appeared as though he had even bewildered himself. And then he turned toward the sun and began his opening chant:

"Ahem, ahem! Spirit of rice, I call upon you. Don't be surprised or lose consciousness or die because I call upon you to witness this ceremony!"

Maban was talking to the handful of rice he held in his hand. The Dyaks watched with enormous wonder and curiosity.

"Naturally you are rice [talking to the rice], from the drop of the flower that lives in the circle of the moon. I know that!"

Maban threw a few grains of rice around on the floor, out

the door, and then he turned and covered our heads with as many grains as he could get to stay there.

"Rice," he whispered to Sjahsam, "is main gift from gods and has the complete fertility circle."

The last words stirred an uneasiness. They sounded more like a marriage ceremony than a brother-sister ritual.

Maban reached across Sjahsam's knees for the rice flowers in a basket on the floor near the burning garu. His hand dropped into the basket and he withdrew the tiny flowers and daintily placed them on our heads. "This flower tell gods that we want you to be brother and sister."

A Dyak with a breathless enthusiasm for his part in the ceremony passed Maban a shell of tuak, nearly tipping over the beverage in its passing. Maban mumbled a strong spell over the tuak, and another over the clumsy Dyak, and then he gulped thirstily from its rim and handed the shell to us.

The old chief turned to look at the sun. Suddenly he could not move things along fast enough. He began firing materials at both of us, some of which I remember, and others went by so fast I was unaware that they had happened.

The chicken with the burned wing was killed and its blood was poured over our bodies. Although the kill was hasty, the pouring of the blood had no sense of hurry to it of any kind.

Wet earth was smeared on our throats, our shoulders were bathed in black oils, and the birds' eggs were cracked open on our heads, and the yolks and whites were left running down the backs of our necks.

And then the ritual came to a standstill.

As often happened the old chief simply forgot what to do next.

His eyes looked over the crowd in the room in pain and bewilderment, and the look drew a comment from one of the chiefs that was so fiercely worded that Maban, out of embarrassment, didn't listen.

Maban groped about in the dark corners of his unpracticed mind, and he groped until he thought he had found something that would satisfy everybody.

He started the ritual again by making up the rules as he needed them.

After a false start or two Maban began to chant. His voice rose and fell, swelled and paused, and at times he cracked his voice because he believed it gave timbre and profundity to the chant. "This time," he called, "we ask the flower in the circle of the moon to witness these two human beings as they swear brotherhood. If one is not loyal, faithful, and honest, but only pretending, then we ask the flower in the circle of the moon to cut off his breath, like a piece of broken rattan. If one is traitor to the other, then may his life blow away like the dust in the wind and be forgotten."

Maban coughed, drank his way through another shell of tuak, and asked for the knives to be brought in. Two mandaus with gold scrolls inset in their blades appeared and were placed in Maban's hands.

The knives raised my interest to a high point for no other reason than their size made them a force to be reckoned with. I felt a strong desire to interfere with the ritual, not to halt its proceedings, but to ask a few questions.

It seemed unbelievable that I was to be cut with a knife, especially a mandau, whose sole purpose was to disembowel or decapitate. The thoughts sent a choked feeling of illness through the stomach.

Sjahsam's manliness had melted away and left him clothed in the defenselessness of a child. His mouth hung open and his eyes bugged out. He looked as though he was going to his own execution, which left me with little hope for myself.

My imagination was on the verge of becoming outraged, when things suddenly restored themselves to a decent proportion. The Dyaks wouldn't hurt me, of course, they wouldn't. It would be quite an honor to be cut with a headhunter's knife. Not many people get that kind of opportunity in their lifetime.

Maban raised two fingers and the signal brought the

chiefs' wives running to his side. One of them was a nervous soul with a cold, deathly eye. I hoped I wouldn't get her.

The woman knelt in front of Maban, plucked the knife out of his hand, and struck Sjahsam across the breast with the blade. And her eyes narrowed and her lips moved and a crafty look stole over her face when she did it.

I leaned forward to see what damage she had done to Sjahsam, and I felt the blade of a knife cut across the flesh above my heart. It did not hurt until I saw the deep slash, watched it fill with blood and spill over to flow down the front of my sarong, and then it hurt a great deal.

I glanced over at Sjahsam to compare wounds. He got the worst of it. We smiled weakly at each other as the wives seized our hands suddenly, pinched up the finger pads on our ring fingers, and with sweeping movements sliced the tips open with their knives.

Maban came forward and bent down in front of us.

"Now, make hearts in unity," he whispered.

He took our fingers, sliced and bloody, and gently pushed them into the open wounds above the other's heart and left us bleeding into one another's body.

Several minutes passed before Maban decided that our bloods were well mixed. And then he asked us to swallow blood by sucking on the other's bleeding finger, which would not be as bad as from the bloody spot on the other's chest.

My finger had dried up a bit and Maban was disappointed with the blood flow. He deepened the wound with his mandau, and when the blood appeared worth while, he allowed me to put my finger in Sjahsam's mouth.

In the final step of the ceremony, Maban tied maniks around our cuts. The maniks touched and sanctified the bloody spots on our bodies and served as tourniquets as well. Maban had bound my finger so tightly that the circulation had stopped completely.

The ritual arrived at a happy and successful finish. Neither Sjahsam nor I had fainted, my sarong had stayed up, and no

one noticed that the sun had long since passed over the coconut palm.

The Dyaks rushed forward to congratulate Maban on his
performance and assured him that the blood brotherhood
would stick forever. And then they bent themselves toward
celebrating the event by committing every excess they could
think of.

Chapter Eighteen

Selamet Tinggal

By September 1970 there was no question that "Dyak country" was in the process of changing itself into a self-respecting territory with a new way of life and carrying its past culture along with it.

The sky had finally opened up to the Dyaks, and for the first time in history they had the means to rise into it.

The Sargent-Dyak Fund, Inc., introduced into the area a system that worked. Outsiders found it astonishing. Some of those outsiders included the Indonesian people themselves.

The reason it worked was a simple one. The Dyaks made it work. They were a desperate people, a "little people" lost and nearly forgotten. They were smart enough to recognize the fact that unless something was done they had little chance of survival.

Driven by the memory of hardship, poverty, and death, they took an active interest in whatever promised to be a change in their lives. The want for medicine and the need for food gave them a new purpose to fulfill and a new path to follow.

The Dyak chose the one way to be noticed when he entered into the corporation's agricultural, medical, educational, or animal-husbandry field. By extending himself he altered the direction of his own life and this alteration permitted him survival with his family as well as with his tribe.

In our own history we have had time to learn of ourselves and some of the things that have happened to us. We have learned that many American attempts to provide relief goods to foreign nations have backfired and sadly ended up with "Yank, go home!" Perhaps the reason is that we have tried to impose, along with the free goods, democracy and the principles of equality upon people who neither knew us nor understood us, and the attempts were clumsy and therefore unfruitful.

Surely there were campaigns over the past to push upon a foreign people our politics, our religions, and even our military authority, and those efforts left the people resentful, contemptuous, and entrenched in cores of rebellion.

On the crest of these feelings, the Sargent-Dyak Fund, Inc., was founded as a nonreligious, nonpolitical organization, one that was keyed to phase itself into the hands of the people for whom it was intended, given as an outright gift and without entangling alliances of any kind.

Embodied within the corporal structure were certain ideals that the Board of Directors felt were worthy of pursuit. One of them was the determination to leave unchanged the existing and traditional laws of the Dyaks, their religion and their culture.

The corporation had no desire to create a "little America" in the heart of the jungle. Although America might work well enough for us, it does not mean that it would necessarily work for the Dyaks.

Nor did we want to poison the Dyaks with "things." We felt that it would be an unkindness as well as an injustice to the Dyak civilization to trap and tangle these primitive people with "things." We believed we would be able to provide the Dyaks with "enough," enough to give him life but not enough to kill his incentive.

The Sargent-Dyak Fund, Inc., pursued this objective by

using a very simple, elementary formula. Purpose, growth, renewal.

Action invariably brings reaction. The activities of the American volunteers in Kuala Kuajan were splashed about in the headlines of the Djakarta newspapers, and the news aroused the interest and reaction of the Indonesians who read about them.

Seven young Indonesians from Djakarta ventured to Kuala Kuajan, and the American team handed over their work to the new humanitarians. The desire felt by these Indonesian volunteers to help their own people reflected great credit not only upon them as individuals but upon the nation they represented.

The Indonesian team speeded the corporation's advancement in each of the four fields of action. The agricultural department became newsworthy. The Dyaks had found a new source of food power in the Indica IR-8 rice seeds, and after the first harvest the reports were filed and sent away to Djakarta, where the newspapers published the figures of the largest rice crop ever produced in the history of Indonesia, raised by a handful of headhunters in the Central Borneo jungles.

The Dyaks cultivated more rice than they needed or could possibly use that year. They distributed much of it to the newcomers and to the Chinese merchants visiting the area in exchange for nearly whatever they wanted. One Dyak family ended up with a transistor radio, and his neighbor became the proud owner of a treadle sewing machine with promised lessons on how to use it.

Lettuce and tomatoes, cucumbers and melons, and other vegetables and fruit were planted in the gardens of fifty villages. The Dyaks had never learned moderation of any kind, and they flooded our jungle hospital during the fruit season with cases of uncontrollable diarrhea.

When large rice paddies, grown with the seeds harvested from the original Rice Demonstration Project, were cultivated in each village, leisure came to the farming Dyaks for the first time in their lives. They hardly knew what to do with it. Many naturally yearned for hand craftsmanship and found mat weaving and basketry to be rewarding efforts. They did not make new things because they did not know how, but they created the things of their ancestors, and sometimes they made them with new designs.

Before the large, roomy elementary-secondary school in Kuala Kuajan had received its last shingle, it was filled to the doorjambs with children as well as old people. It was here that the rules concerning life were taught to the Dyaks, the rules that would allow them to survive, to live together, and to increase.

Those rules incorporating health and hygiene were put into effect with maximum speed and efficiency. The rules which defined honesty, manners, and conduct were given more slowly. And because there was great interest, we taught the Dyaks how to make money off the newcomers. The Dyaks found the rules very much to their advantage. Because the rules worked, they were believed in and therefore they were obeyed.

When it was time to teach reading and writing, the Dyaks were eager to learn. They sent prospective "teachers" from their villages to the Kuala Kuajan school. Later these "schoolteachers" were installed in the one-classroom school the corporation built in each of the villages.

It was a very glamorous, dramatic event to see the building of a hospital in the heart of a jungle. The six-bed structure was a small one, but in the eyes of the Dyaks the building was enormous. The medical service offered within its walls was gratis, because you cannot charge someone something when he has nothing to give you.

The Dyaks readily accepted medical treatment because they were already aware of it. They had been treating themselves, or were treated by witch doctors, for centuries. But they were unprepared for the impact of modern drugs.

Conjunctivitis was cured and cholera was conquered.

Plague buckled under the medical whip and malaria turned into a minor nuisance. Sickness no longer caused panic.

When the death rate lowered and the birth rate increased, the population experienced an explosion. Once the main body of humans was bunched together at either one end or the other, with the babies who were dying off as fast as they were born or the old people who sat around cluttering up the villages, too tough to die. The middle generation was nearly missing. Today the young have extended into adolescence and the odds for their survival into adulthood are very great.

The Dyaks watched the modern medical conquest of child-killing disease in action and found it was keeping more children alive. They were grateful and they wanted to show their appreciation. They brought their newborn chicks, eggs, milk, or fresh vegetables to the hospital in return for the medicine. The hospital moved a tremendous inch toward becoming self-operating.

Animal-husbandry proved to be the slowest in starting but the most startling in the end, and in some areas the most comical.

When the animals arrived the majority of the older stock was pregnant and therefore nonlactating. The chicks were too young to lay eggs, and although the piglets were colorful, they were too tiny for pork chops. When the corrals and hutches and stalls were built, the animals were settled in their new homes and spent the first months eating and sleeping and resembling bumps on a log.

The Dyaks surveyed the menagerie from a more exciting viewpoint. The animals, they thought, would be excellent subjects for sacrifice at their religious festivals. A few of the Dyaks tried their hand at cattle rustling one night about midnight, but without much success. The Indonesian veterinarian scarcely shut his eye in a wink of sleep for months.

Production and reproduction came about at the same time, and the Dyak interest changed its course. Many streamed into the Animal-Husbandry Demonstration Project to learn about animal care and the raising of the stock domestically, and others came simply because it made good sense to co-ordinate a religious function with a fried chicken Sunday dinner.

The gaudiest achievement in the agricultural department was accomplished by a mischievous, joke-loving Dyak with a flare for the bizarre. He caught a wild jungle turkey, and with the help of the veterinarian the bird was bred to an American rooster. The result of his enterprise of desperation was a product resembling a Christmas goose. Surely it lives to this day, somewhere between honks, clucks, and gobbles, with its strange descendants waddling behind it.

Soon the program and its materials were primarily in the hands of the Dyaks, and the corporation was beginning to phase itself out. There remained only the supervision of the hospital and school and the need for an authority to settle whatever disputes might arise. Sjahsam was given that authority.

Sjahsam was a man to whom the Dyaks could talk and a man who understood what the Dyaks were saying. The people respected and admired him because he was a man who belonged to them. But they nearly wore him out with their requests for this or that or the other. They did not mean to abuse him; they simply gave him more work to do than was possible for any one single individual to do. In the end, Sjahsam appealed to the Indonesian government for someone to help him.

And how will the Indonesian government act and react to Sjahsam's plea and to the new set of circumstances that are present for the now remembered Dyak people?

We know from the past that Indonesia is currently suffering the perplexing problems of change. The country is running in all directions. Despite her busy running, there are whispers of using the Sargent-Dyak Fund, Inc., as a "pilot program" to develop other underpriviledged areas found within her islands. These whispers are by far much more than the country has ever done before.

The longest, darkest journey is yet to come. It will begin when Indonesia reaches into the dark jungle and takes the Dyak people by the hand and leads them to becoming a contributing force to their own growing nation. The journey, with this purpose, will come, although it may be unthinkable now.

At the time of this writing, my hopes and dreams for the Dyaks are compounded of some fear, but with great confidence. The people are no longer forgotten "little people" living on the back side of the world. They are no longer without food or medicine. The Dyaks are traveling into a livable future, alone and at their own speed. It is in this travel and in their refusal to become extinct that my confidence and hope lie.

Chapter Nineteen

West Irian

West Irian!

The words kept popping up like the lyrics to some irrepressible, haunting melody and with so much frequency that they seemed destined to become some kind of a downright fad.

"West Irian!" said President Suharto. "West Irian is the place you should go!"

And he was saying it to me.

The President sat stocking-footed in the Presidential Suite of the Disneyland Hotel in Anaheim, California, and the little muscles between his brows were pinched up because his feet hurt. He and Madame Suharto had just returned from walking the many miles required to see a reasonable balance of the excitements offered at Disneyland.

The President's eyes were a very dark brown, and sometimes little flecks of gold flashed about in them. A toasted almond shape, they turned up at the outer corners whenever he smiled. And he smiled all the time. Even when he was talking.

"You really should see West Irian. The people are very primitive there and they need help badly," he said, pulling at the knot of his tie until it came loose. He yanked the knot to one side of his white starched shirt and then pulled the collar button through the hole to give his neck some relief from the tightness of the band.

Brigadier General Sutikno, the presidential secretary, also mentioned his interest in my visiting the West Irian theater. It was obvious that together the two men envisioned another Sargent-Dyak Fund, Inc., loaded with free goods and supplies, on its way to another part of their world.

One of the most shattering and tearing experiences known to the human heart is the saying good-by to a friend, one whom you are certain you will never see again. That friend was Sjam. With Sjam, the knowing had been instant. And through the long months, that knowing got better.

Sjam had become a partner and the association was without competition of any kind. Her greatest contribution and quality of genius were found in her ability to make something out of nothing, and that ability was always on tap and ready for action.

Sjam knew how to have fun, real fun, when nobody else knew how to do it. She had more fun in discovering new people than nearly anyone else I have ever known. And she was distrustful and deeply suspicious of anyone who could not enjoy the same thing.

Her mind was always open because there were no doors to shut in on it, and therefore every challenge aroused enthusiasm in her. She met them head-on and won most of them, and it was usually done by stealing the bone from the other player when he wasn't looking and then running down the field to victory with it. And some of those victories were monumental.

When Sjam gave you something, whether a song, a thought, or a semiprecious stone, it was yours before she gave it to you because she made you feel that way. There was no indebtedness or obligation to return such a gift to Sjam. She simply lived in a creativeness of giving.

Now Sjam was dead broke, thanks to the two years of volunteer work she did for the Sargent-Dyak Fund, Inc., and she was without a job and with no immediate hope of finding one.

And this was the person to whom I had to say good-by. We stood at the airport in Djakarta and watched the other passengers for a while, and when they left to board the plane, we looked down at our feet and up at the ceiling to avoid looking into each other's eyes.

"Why not come back someday and go to West Irian, Wyn?" she said.

"Would you go with me as interpreter?" The words slipped out by themselves. I had raised a flag to see if she would salute it.

"Wouldn't let anybody else do it!" she said.

"Well, look. It'll take some time to write up the Dyak book. Maybe, after the book is finished, maybe . . ."

"I need to work and get back on my feet. Want to see my folks in Sumatra, too. Been a long time."

"Well," I said, "want to make a tentative reservation for West Irian for the year 1972?"

"Sure! Why not?" she said.

And so we assured each other that we'd meet again, smiled, and shook hands on it and then quickly looked away because neither of us really believed it very much and we were embarrassed the other might see it in the eyes. But talking about the proposed adventure made the parting easier. But not much.

I took a final look at her from the top platform before entering the airplane, a look that would have to last a long, long time and maybe forever.

She appeared so small and very lonely as she stood there, her sleeves pushed up to her elbows, seemingly very much out of place in a dress, after so many months in jungle trousers.

There were yards and yards of distance between us, but

I could still see the tears in her eyes, and I am certain she could see them in mine.

Throughout the writing of *The Headhunters* I was never without a reminder that somewhere in the world there was a West Irian.

Sometimes I involuntarily came across something to remind myself of the territory, and during lapses my friends reminded me. "Wyn! West Irian's on the television. Channel 4!" a friend rang in one evening. And without resistance of any kind I obediently turned on the television set.

Most of the programs were shorts from old missionary documentaries, but they were lively. The jungle on the screen invariably looked exactly like a good jungle should look. There were tall green trees interlaced with climbing vines and spread between high mountain peaks which swooped down into valleys that held low, watery swamps. In between were black, nearly naked men racing around with tubular gourds to assure their modesty and with kinky beehive hairdos that had been saturated with pig grease. Black soot had been rubbed on their faces and it made them look more fierce than they probably were. They wore all kinds of stately shell jewelry, and sometimes a man would run by with a white boar's tusk stuck through his nose, and it stirred the heart just to see it.

The women wore fiber skirts that were so low that they seemed to be held in place more by magic than anything else, and there were long nets hanging from their heads to cover their backs and buttocks, and those nets dropped well below the backs of their knees.

This highly decorative and colorful group of people lived in little thatched houses that were both round and small, and no two people ever seemed to enter any one of the houses at the same time.

Just about when the program had spiked up real interest, and men and women were running in swift circles with their heads down, screaming and yelling guttural, savage war cries and waving their weapons at each other, the program was over.

It left one with a disappointment nearly too deep for utterance.

I was in the middle of writing "Ada Obat?" when someone sent me a borrowed copy of the March 1945 issue of the *National Geographic* magazine. Within its covers were accounts of West Irian given by Richard Archbold, the leader of a scientific expedition sponsored by the American Museum of Natural History in New York. Richard Archbold is credited with having discovered the Baliem Valley in West Irian in 1938, and it was the Baliem Valley in which I was becoming more and more interested.

Another friend presented me with a secondhand copy of *Cannibal Valley*, the very title of which suggested that I'd do well to stay home. The book represented a "savage New Guinea with the most perilous frontier in the world." The inhabitants were supposed to be hostile, arrogant, tricky, and cruel cannibals whose cycle of existence was warfare and violence.

But it was an old book, published in 1962, and hopefully something had since moved into, or out of, the area to make it more hospitable.

Cheer entered my office one morning when the Los Angeles *Times* was placed on my desk. It carried an article about "civilizing West Irian" by something called "Operation Koteka," which would bring clothes to tribes that had no crime or poverty. There was a picture with the caption "Stone Age and Air Age," and it showed the back of an unclothed native standing in front of an airplane. He looked gentle enough, his right hand caught the elbow of his left arm behind his back. Just standing there. Naked. Not much wild action.

And Tom Sawyer began beating the drums of my heart again. By 1972, West Irian had become to me much more than just a name, place, or thing. It had become a sound, a color, a style, a manner, a mood, a melody, and a dream.

And it had become a curiosity of men and women and children and all of them were black in color and all of them were mighty.

That curiosity was one that could be satisfied only in the seeing and recording. I yearned to photograph and study the fragile threads that made up their cultural fabric. Theirs, from all appearances, was a culture that dated back to neolithic times, where farmer-warriors guarded their lives and their property against attack from enemy tribes in one of the least visited places in the world.

If it is possible to envy one's own working position, I am guilty. Nothing can be so stimulating and rewarding as to research the arts and customs, traditions and cultures of other people living in the world. That work provides me with the opportunity to understand new circumstances and civilizations and thus better to understand my own.

Therefore, it was no sudden development that Sjam and I entered the Baliem Valley in West Irian in October 1972 to begin what eventually was to become the strangest adventure of our lives.

It was in the Baliem Valley that I met Kelion. Kelion was a big, lumbering stumblebum of a chief who had never done anything right in his whole life.

He was a chief without a village. He had unwittingly burned down every shack in his own compound one day when he was playing around with some matches he'd found, and then he had to move in on his next-door neighbor, Walek, who resented every moment he was there.

Kelion was irresistibly lovable. He had come by his name as haphazardly as he had come by his life, a chief with no plan and with no ambition beyond eating and sleeping. And it was Kelion who was eventually to become my blood brother.

Kelion's neighbor, Walek, became one of my chiefs too. Only, as it turned out, neither of us was sure which one of us was the leader.

Walek was left-handed, but he didn't know that. He knew that, where ordinary men found strength in their right arms, his left arm was the stronger, and he came to the dubious conclusion that God had given him a supernatural power and had therefore appointed him to be a chief.

He was a slightly crazy, lisping chief who spoke a lofty Dani language without ever using the letter *s*. Walek's mind was sometimes hunkered down and choked up with uncatalogued memories of the enemies he had killed or of those he proposed killing, and there were times when he couldn't remember which was which. He had killed for things he had wanted, but he had also killed for things he had no use for whatsoever.

But Sjam and I loved him very much.

And it was in the Baliem Valley that I met a boy I called "Mi Hijo."

Mi Hijo was a young boy, sixteen or seventeen years old maybe, and proud of his beautiful pig-greased black hair that had white lights in it.

He became one of my Dani translators, although he found himself in constant turmoil, wrestling between his duty to me and his terror of others. His courage was continually trembling on the edge of abandonment, and he was ready to bolt every instant of the time. And often he did.

Mi Hijo was the kind of boy who smiled vaguely at everything and anything, and sometimes he smiled at nothing at all. He did it to cheer himself up. He wanted to forget that he was an orphan.

I adopted Mi Hijo as my son.

It was in the Baliem Valley that I met Kolo.

Kolo's real name was Umataok and he was chief of Analaga. He was a set-apart man, one whose heart was filled with angry little hates and envies of nearly every conceivable nature. Kolo thought dark, broody thoughts all the time because he liked to. They made him happy.

But when Kolo smiled, it was rich and warm and friendly and in the end, Kolo softened up and crumbled a little and asked me to become a member of his family.

And it was in the Baliem Valley that I met Wimbilu, Marok, Ilmunkuluk, Kaok, Wayacom, Niren, Wagaga, Talago, Lobok, old Dialec, and many, many others.

And, of course, it was in the Baliem Valley that I met Obaharok.

Chief Obaharok.

Obaharok wore a ring beard on a face that told the truth, and his eyes reflected great friendliness because he had a desperate desire to make everyone he knew happy. Behind that face and those eyes was a mind that was both cool and warm and one that was filled with honesty, wisdom, charity, courage, and heroism.

These were the qualities that earned Obaharok the devotion, admiration, and respect from the Dani people living in the Mulima-Siepkosi area of the Baliem Valley, who had placed him on the imaginary throne that rules over the valley kingdom.

Obaharok was a small man, but he was stalwart and very strong. He could kill any living thing, without scruples of any kind, if there was purpose in the killing. But he could not hurt someone's feelings, not even in anger.

Obaharok's heart was filled with kindness and humility and he possessed a valuable balance of self-knowledge and great understanding of others. When people brought their problems to Obaharok, usually the contents were just plain nonsense. But Obaharok listened patiently and unfailingly and then somehow changed whatever the nonsense into a remarkable kind of wisdom that always made sense.

Obaharok was capable of great generosity, for he gave away nearly everything he had.

He was interested in everything anyone had to tell or show him, and there was hardly anything he didn't like.

Obaharok dearly loved children. He exercised his special gift of being able to talk with children rather than to them, and he told them very profound things in such a way that they always understood what he was saying and, more important, what he was meaning.

And I believe Obaharok, in his own way, loved me.

I believe he loved me in the same way he loved Michael Rockefeller and if he did, then that would make me feel richly honored.

Michael Rockefeller, along with Robert Gardner, cinematographer, Peter Matthiessen, naturalist, and Karl Heider, anthropologist, was the sound recordist and photographer for the Harvard-Peabody New Guinea Expedition in 1961. The group lived in the valley for approximately six months, gathering information about the social and cultural structure of the Dani.

There was a certain quality of leadership in the young Rockefeller that attracted Obaharok's interest and his concern. In those days, now more than ten years ago, the youthful, unnoticed Obaharok was still embryonic, preparing for the chieftainship he holds today. It was a natural course for the apprenticing Obaharok to turn to Michael Rockefeller to better himself.

A strong affection evidently developed between the two men. Today, when Obaharok speaks of his "beloved friend Mike," it is with tears in his eyes. He remembers a friend, now gone and somehow lost.

After Michael Rockefeller and the others, with the exception of Karl Heider, left the valley, Obaharok gathered his forces and burned a path from Analaga across Siepkosi to Mulima, and it left a long, wide scar, one that he could call his own.

He was still at it in 1966 when he counterattacked Kurulu, the great but aging overlord of the northern valley. He had nearly defeated the thus far unchallenged champion when Kurulu blew the whistle on him and yelped for help from the government military.

To show the great might of the man, Obaharok, in July 1972, outraged at the torturous and sometimes murderous methods used on his people by the police and military officials, tried to put down the whole Indonesian government! He simply could no longer bear to see the physical sufferings of his people at the hands of those who were supposed to be "helping."

But Obaharok's bows and arrows were no match for government guns filled with live ammunition, and realism moved into the heart of a man who had wanted to fight to liberate his people from Indonesian terrorism.

When I appeared on the scene, Obaharok associated me, my white skin and men's clothes, and my work of photographing, writing, and recording with that of his previous friend, "Mike," and because of it he could never quite get used to the idea that I was a woman.

Despite these odds, in January 1973, Obaharok and I were married in a traditional but "symbolic wedding" in a ceremony intended to cease the hostilities and begin the era of friendship between the tribes of Kolo, Walek, Kelion, and Obaharok. The ceremony, dedicated only to tribal peace, inadvertently made world news.

The ritual took place in the village of Wiyagoba. Obaharok set his men about building a *pilai* or *pelamo* (chief and warrior house) for Sjam, Mi Hijo, and me to live in.

Sjam, Mi Hijo, and I lived in it for three days. Three whole days.

Kelion sighed deeply, tired because he knew that, unless he could think of some kind of an escape, he'd have to answer the many questions I had on my mind, and that meant he'd be stuck with me for the rest of the afternoon.

"The wedding ceremony is when you change your clothes," he said despairingly.

"What do you mean, 'change your clothes'? Aren't these good enough?" I said, smoothing the deep wrinkles in my fast-fading shirt and brushing at my trousers to make them appear more important and attractive.

Kelion's mouth dropped open and he stared at me in pure wonder. "When women put *yokal* on you, then you married woman! Yokal means you're married!" he said in a sweat of impatience because he thought I should have known it all along.

"This," he said, "is the *wedding ceremony!*"

"And that's it? You mean there's nothing more to do? Nobody makes any speeches or anything? That's all? I put on a yokal, a married woman's skirt?"

Kelion had stopped listening somewhere in the middle of the conversation. When he took up thinking again, it was with effort, but his answer gave no indication that there had been a lapse in his attention.

"Obaharok kills a pig. That is his part. Women put yokal on you. That is your part. Yokal is proof that you are married. Marriage ceremony for you ends when women tie last yokal knot. You belong to married women group and you are part of them."

So, the yokal was the *wedding ceremony* and the *marriage document!*

The yokal was a very important key to understanding the social and economic aspect of the Dani culture. There are no careers in the jungle valley for a single Dani girl. The day she sheds her *thali* grass skirt for the yokal, she finds herself not only suddenly useful, but prominent. The yokal gives her a ticket to enter and to belong to a valuable and esteemed group of women, and that membership presents a certain purpose, pride, and therefore beauty. It all comes in a single day.

I thought about the yokal and the yards and yards of threads that went into its making, threads woven from *buen* bark and then laced with red and yellow *urai* fibers.

The yokal, when finished, is a beautiful piece of craftsmanship. The Dani women who wear them are quite as modest, in their own way, as other women of the twentieth-century cultures.

"Kelion, it's a lot of work. Can't we just tell everybody I'm married without going to all that effort?"

Kelion had never worked his mind hard enough to ever cause it much strain, so his answer must be put down to magic. He was not known for his profundity of thought. "When pig is killed and you wear same clothes as before, people might think you cheated and made joke of Obaharok and not really marry at all."

"How long would I have to wear this dress?"

"This day and this day," Kelion said, and he pinched the tops of the little finger and ring finger of his left hand with his right thumb and index finger, indicating two days.

"Tonight," he said, "you sing in the kitchen with women. And this day," he pointed to his ring finger, "you sing with all people at Haratsilimo."

Haratsilimo is a site near the Aikhe River and one large enough to accommodate the thousands of warriors that made up the tribes of Kolo, Walek, Kelion, and Obaharok.

I had received more information from Kelion than I had ever hoped for, and then he volunteered an aspect that was astonishing.

"Since you are my sister," he said with sad, innocent eyes, "you must give me a piece of your old clothing. This is the custom. Girls give their thali skirts to their families when they are put in yokals. You can give me your shirt."

The reader should be alerted that Kelion's whole direction in life had, for the most part, been mostly unlawful (according to Western standards) and with the singular impulse to withhold the truth. It was a constant amazement to me that Kelion had somehow escaped the Wamena police blotter, because nearly everything he did was against the law. But it was *their* law, not his, nor was it the law of his people. His people not only admired him for his pursuits, they loved him. But it would take checking and rechecking to discover whether Kelion's latest campaign to acquire my shirt was truly a custom or not.

"Would you settle for my socks?" I tested.

"Yes. One pair."

It was probably a custom.

To accommodate my Western modesty, the yokal was re-modeled to improve its coverage. I was afraid the innovation would outrage the Dani eye, but I discovered with some surprise and a great deal of pleasure that the people didn't care and most of them didn't even notice. The fact that I wanted a skirt "high and long" and the Dani women wore theirs "low and short" meant nothing to them at all.

The added feature of wearing a Western brassiere caught the women's fancy, and it started a rash of bra-buying at the local Wamena market. The Dani women showed up in their villages with twin circles of red, pink, and blue splashed on their fronts, and sometimes the circles came in purple. The ladies were charmed by the colors of their new apparel as well as by their instant uplifted appearances.

The Dani women are not known for being brisk people. They had something against hurry. It took them nearly eight hours to wind the skirt on me. Each strand and fiber had to be placed just so, turned just the right way, and hardly any two of the four women who were working on it ever agreed on its correctness at the same time.

It was only after the finished yokal had been wound on me that I realized the necessity for the low cut of the Dani women's skirts. My skirt weighed more than seven pounds and stuck out at least three inches on each side. The grassy fibers, although beautiful, itched and scratched, and they were bound around my middle and legs with such ferocity that I thought my circulation had been cut off forever. I was trussed up into a stiffness and immobility known only to an Egyptian mummy and to the strait-jacketed insane. I could not raise or bend my knee in any fashion whatsoever, and to double over from the waist guaranteed the disaster of degutting myself on the spot.

The former owner of the *walimo* that had been tied around my neck wore a smaller size than I did, and therefore, whenever I swallowed, I had the feeling of acute strangulation.

To all the other rewards of this costume was added a gift of nets, long carrying nets that hung from the head and covered the back. They were donated by the charitable, loving wives of the various chiefs in the area, and because I was tall the nets were made heavier and longer than usual.

To marry a common man was one thing, but to marry into royalty was another, and the number of nets one wore made the difference. The difference was in the wearing of fifteen nets, at two pounds each.

From the very beginning a headache launched itself with both energy and vigor and with such strength that no aspirin was ever able to reach it. And then I worried about some passing if not permanent injury that was in the making on the top of my head.

Walking was done more in the nature of shuffling than anything else. I had to be steered by four women and Sjam's strong hand if I wanted to go anywhere. My total weight was a menace to anyone standing near, and to become suddenly unbalanced and fall on an innocent bystander assured a certain mutilation if not death by crushing.

Somehow I lived through the twenty-two hours in the wearing of the ensemble, and hopefully I was able to give it at least a part of the princely dignity and respect it rightfully deserved.

But I will always remember the outfit as being both torturous and merciless and, having lived through it, I guess I need never again fear anything in the whole wide world.

The "wedding ceremony" was officially over when the last yokal knot was tied around my waist and Obaharok had killed his pig. But the singing in the kitchen and at Harat-silimo heralded the "wedding celebration." It was a glorious event which continued for nearly one month.

During that month the tribes of Kolo, Kelion, Walek, and Obaharok streamed across the valley to attend the pig feasts which celebrated the wedding. Many of these previously hostile warriors became brothers, an accomplishment achieved through the Dani cultural laws.

Dani family structure is based on patrilineal descent as well as kinship. A brother kinship can be formed when the natives of one tribe agree to eat the pork offered by the natives of another. The kinship has great strength, greater than that of patrimony, and any violation of the bond is considered a crime against human feelings which is the highest crime in the Dani world.

But on February 7, 1973, that feasting came to an abrupt halt with the arrival of a letter from Indonesian Immigration. The letter ordered me to leave the country.

Sjam and I suspected that my letter writing to the government officials in the area had finally caught up with me. The letters were dangerous because they demanded human dignity and justice for the Dani people from a government that was supposed to be helping them.

When I learned of the brutality and maltreatment inflicted upon the native population by the government police, schoolteachers, and military, I was overwhelmed with a desire to help the Dani. The people had been beaten, burned, and sometimes broken, their pigs as well as their money stolen, their women raped, and many had been submitted to forced labor.

I wrote letters to the government officials requesting the return of stolen goods, a stop to the beatings of the people, and the granting to Dani the rights and liberties enjoyed by all other human beings.

As a result, Policeman Auri fired two gunshots over my village on February 3, 1973, to remind me of the strength of the police force. It was a chilling experience and I stopped writing the letters at once.

I knew that my letter writing could have provided the government with enough worry to terminate my stay in the valley. If the government had also learned that I had impulsively photographed the evidence of their torturous brutality, then this documentation would have undoubtedly stimulated the officials to new heights of worry.

Sjam and I flew to Djayapura the following day. There, for the first time, we read two-week-old newspaper stories which described me as a highly undesirable "anthropologist" supposedly performing a sexual survey on the primitive Stone Age tribes in the Baliam Valley!

The government had provided the press with the stories they wanted printed, and it was a matter of wonder to me that they possessed such lively imaginations.

After the first shock, I found the stories somewhat amusing. Then I learned that the world-wide wire services, without checking the source, had picked up the stories and it was probable that my young son was reading these reports back home. My amusement changed to grave concern. I wondered what it would be like for Jmy to read such dirty things said about his mother.

I needn't have worried. Jmy's great trust and belief came through a press interview. I read the account in Djakarta. No mother has ever felt as proud as I did when I read my son's words, "My Mom knows what she's doing."

I was amazed that the Indonesian press worked as well as it did, and surely even the Indonesian officials must have been astonished at their own effectiveness. I think they surprised themselves. Those who had wanted to plant only a "little story" were probably frightened when it hit worldwide coverage, and they must have been the most ashamed of all.

In Djakarta I learned a little bit about being "railroaded" out of a country. I also learned to keep my mouth shut, because the conductors on that railroad were policemen. They held the keys to the political prisons.

At Immigration I was never *asked* anything but I was *told* a great deal, and there was no sense or purpose in my questioning any of it. I was *told* my work was of a "scientific nature" and that my visa, although identical to the one issued me in 1968 for Borneo, did not permit such work without a letter of support from LIPI (Indonesian Institute for Scientific Research). I was *told* that it was "too late" to obtain such a letter and to leave the country in seventy-two hours.

Indonesian Intelligence *told* me not to talk to the press and to say nothing against the Indonesian government. Intelligence is an organization which is frightening in itself, but not half as frightening as the men who run it.

My outgoing mail was seized, the telephone was bugged, I was followed by the police everywhere I went, and then I learned that my film and manuscript were to be confiscated by Intelligence at Customs. The danger was absolute.

The morning I left Indonesia, I remembered all the things I can never forget.

I remembered the night I told the Dani people I had to leave their valley. Kolo, Kelion, Mi Hijo, Walek, and Obaharok and many others were sitting in a circle in my *pilai*, and all of us were crying. It was so hard for them to understand. They only knew that I was leaving and that probably I would not be able to return, but they couldn't understand why. The Dani are a noble people but unsophisticated politically because they are not a part of our world.

I remembered seeing Kelion's big shoulders shake in hysterical sobs, his eyes rimmed red with sorrow, and watching the hot tears roll down Walek's face, a face battered by grief, and hearing the soft cries from Kolo, who sat with eyes filled with tears of despair, and Mi Hijo's whimpers in the corner of the pilai, whimpers that sounded as though he was lost and somehow afraid. And I remembered Obaharok sitting motionless and quiet, staring down with wide, unbelieving eyes, and I recalled that usually the quiet man is the one who is the most hurt.

The following morning I remembered seeing the hundreds of cigarette butts that edged the fireplace and the thousands of teardrops that soaked the grass floor. I remembered walking stiffly out of the village like an artificial, mechanical person and listening to the sounds of the people crying.

And until I can go back again, I guess I will remember these things every day of my life.

Now I am writing a book about these people with this dedication:

> "This book is written for Kelion and Kolo
> For Walek and Obaharok.
> And for all the people who followed them.
> The people called themselves the Dani,
> A people whom I loved.
> And was forced to leave."

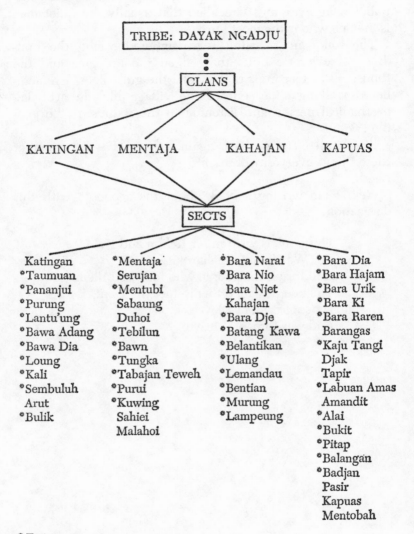

TRIBE: DAYAK NGADJU

CLANS

KATINGAN   MENTAJA   KAHAJAN   KAPUAS

SECTS

Katingan	*Mentaja	*Bara Narai	*Bara Dia
*Taumuan	Serujan	*Bara Nio	*Bara Hajam
*Pananjui	*Mentubi	Bara Njet	*Bara Urik
*Purung	Sabaung	Kahajan	*Bara Ki
*Lantu'ung	Duhoi	*Bara Dje	*Bara Raren
*Bawa Adang	*Tebilun	*Batang Kawa	Barangas
*Bawa Dia	*Bawn	*Belantikan	*Kaju Tangi
*Loung	*Tungka	*Ulang	Djak
*Kali	*Tabajan Teweh	*Lemandau	Tapir
*Sembuluh	*Purui	*Bentian	*Labuan Amas
Arut	*Kuwing	*Murung	Amandit
*Bulik	Sahiei	*Lampeung	*Alai
	Malahoi		*Bukit
			*Pitap
			*Balangan
			*Badjan
			Pasir
			Kapuas
			Mentobah

* Extinct sects.

GLOSSARY

Anggang: (Dyak) Long-necked blackbird, native to Central Borneo
Babung: (Dyak) Large oval-shaped drum
Balian: (Dyak) Stage of Dyak marriage ritual
Belian: (Dyak) High priest in Dyak religion
Betjak: (Indonesian) Tricycle used to carry passengers
Bracas: (Dyak) Small fish native to Central Borneo
Bukung Kahajang: (Dyak) Funeral dancers
Bukung Kambak: (Dyak) Funeral dancers
Bupati: (Indonesian) Head of district
Djimat: (Indonesian) Group of charms, fetishes, and amulets
Djipen: (Dyak) A fine imposed by priest for crime
Dukun: (Indonesian) Witch doctor, medicine man
Elang: (Indonesian) Eagle or hawk
Ipuh: (Indonesian) Poison from *tuba batang* tree roots
Kaharinjang: (Dyak) Religion for Dyak people
Karundeng: (Dyak) Flute
Kenjah: (Dyak) Dyak war dance
Lamiang: (Dyak) Dyak jade used as talisman
Londju: (Dyak) Eight-foot-long spear
Makan: (Indonesian) Eat, food
Mandau: (Dyak) Sacred decapitating headhunters' knife
Manik: (Dyak) Dyak jade bead considered a fetish
Njurat: (Dyak) Ceremony meant to elevate soul to higher heaven
Pantan: (Dyak) Sacred log used in membership rituals
Pantar: (Dyak) Pole used in Tewah ceremony
Parang: (Indonesian) Knife, sword
Pelangkai: (Dyak) God house used by witch doctor in healing rituals;
   Pelangki: (Indonesian) Palanquin
Pilai: (Dani) Warrior's house in West Irian
Salagi: (Dyak) Bamboo cross used as danger sign
Sandun: (Dyak) Spirit and bone house for deceased
Sang Hyang: (Dyak) Highest god in Karharinjang religion
Sangkoh: (Dyak) Blowgun spear point;
   Sangkur: (Indonesian) Bayonet
Sapundu: (Dyak) Sculptured statue of deceased
Selamat pagi: (Indonesian) Good morning
Selamat tinggal: (Indonesian) Farewell, good-by
Selekat: (Dyak) Bamboo musical instrument
Siren: (Dyak) Poison extracted from tree bark
Sumpitan: (Indonesian) Blowgun
Tambuni: (Dyak) Umbilical and placenta urn

Terbang: (Dyak) Talking drum;
  Terbang: (Indonesian) To fly
Teweh: (Dyak) Ceremony "to fly" dead souls to heaven
Tewah: (Dyak) Name of Panggul's mother
Thali: (Dani) Single girl's skirt, West Irian
Tidak apa apa: (Indonesian) It doesn't matter
Tingang: (Dyak) Blackbird thought to be sacred bird of paradise by
  Dyaks
Tuak: (Indonesian) Fermented coconut milk, palm wine
Totok Bakaka: (Dyak) Dyak communication
Tujang: (Dyak) Child's sleeping hammock
Walimo: (Dani) Shell necklace worn in West Irian
Yokal: (Dani) Married woman's skirt, West Irian